Working with young children in Europe

PROVISION AND STAFF TRAINING

Pamela Oberhuemer
and
Michaela Ulich

P·C·P
Paul Chapman
Publishing Ltd

This book is adapted from P. Oberhuemer and M. Ulich *Kinderbetreuung in Europa (IFP Handbuch)*, © 1997 Beltz Verlag, Weinheim and Basel.

Paul Chapman Publishing Ltd
144 Liverpool Road
London
N1 1LA

British Library Cataloguing in Publication Data

Oberhuemer, Pamela
Working with young children in Europe
1. Children – Services for – Europe 2. Child care – Europe
3. Education, Elementary – Europe
I. Title II. Ulich, Michaela
362.7'094

ISBN 1 85396 331 3

Typeset by Anneset Ltd
Printed and bound in Great Britain by Athenæum Press Ltd, Gateshead, Tyne & Wear

A B C D E F G H   9 8 7

Contents

Foreword

At a time when most of the countries in Europe are experiencing economic difficulties and the threat posed by global companies which seem to have no loyalty to any particular state looms over different groups of the population, it is important to draw attention to the ways in which we think about and treat future European citizens, our children. Pamela Oberhuemer and Michaela Ulich, with Monika Soltendieck, have conducted a much-needed and comprehensive survey of the provision and training of staff who work with the very youngest of those children in childcare and education services in fifteen Western European countries. Those of us in the field understand how difficult it is to make comparisons, because the varied histories, attitudes, education systems and other influences have resulted in differing levels, aims and types of provision for the children and differing expectations, roles and career routes for staff – sometimes even within one country.

The idea of job mobility and equivalence across the European Union is an exciting concept but in order to make such a project viable we must be able to understand the systems other colleagues have experienced as well as the qualifications they hold.

Throughout the European Union, work with young children tends to be feminised, though there are much higher proportions of men employed in Scandinavian nurseries in comparison with other member states. The gendered nature of the field tells us a great deal about the ways in which young children and their learning has been conceptualised. The attitude seems to have been firstly that women as mothers have innate capabilities for child-rearing, which does not require any training or cleverness, and that 'After all, they just play don't they?' In assuming that babies need only 'care' and that they can be treated rather like parcels, an ignorance of the potential of these tiny people is betrayed.

The more we are learning from research about the complexity of the development and learning of our youngest children, the more we must help policy-makers recognise the need for highly educated staff. Equally, colleagues in other sectors of Education often have little understanding of the reasons why work with children before primary school should be regarded as equivalent to their own but different in approaches and emphasis. We also know from research (Whitebrook *et al.*, 1989) that the better educated the staff, the higher the children's later achievements.

The discrepancies between the levels of education and training, possible training routes – and some 'dead ends' – for early years staff in one country compared with another, or for those working with children in different age groups should make parents, politicians and educarers keen to engage in debate and development. Here in the UK, for example, several of us have been grappling with the notion of a 'climbing frame' of interlinked education and training possibilities for some years now and there are those who believe we should simply start again from scratch.

The wealth of information packed into this publication will be greatly valued not only in the countries discussed but most widely in both hemispheres. Let us hope the outcome will be an enhancement of the status of young children – and of the status of those who work with them.

Tricia David
Professor of Early Childhood Education
Canterbury Christ Church College
December 1996

Preface

International migration and job mobility are facts of modern life affecting both families with young children and professionals. Interest in the 'European dimension' of organized childcare and education is growing. What are the features of early childhood education in Denmark, Luxembourg or Italy? Is nursery provision in these countries similar to that in the UK, Sweden or Germany? Do Finnish, Dutch or Austrian 4-year-olds attend the same kind of provision in their different countries? Who works in kindergartens, nurseries or playgroups in Greece or Ireland? What kinds of qualifications are needed for work with young children in France or Spain? Is staff training in Belgium the same as in Portugal?

These questions are of interest not only to parents who need or wish to move from one country to another but also to an increasing number of professionals: staff in the early childhood workfield; employers and administrative officers; tutors in training institutions; and researchers, lecturers and students.

Those looking for detailed information on childcare and education services and particularly on staff training for work with children in the whole range of provision outside the compulsory school system will find surprisingly little material. This was the main reason for initiating a project at the State Institute of Early Childhood Education and Research in Munich which was jointly funded by the German Federal Ministry of Family, Senior Citizens, Women and Youth, the Bavarian Ministry of Education and the Bavarian Ministry of Social Affairs.

Working with Young Children in Europe provides information on the social context of childcare and education services in Austria, Belgium, Denmark, Finland, France, Germany, Greece, Ireland, Italy, Luxembourg, The Netherlands, Portugal, Spain, Sweden and the UK. It documents the major kinds of provision for young children, and describes the training of staff working in early childhood services. It also includes material on provision and staff training for work with school-age children outside school hours. In addition, crosscutting themes and issues on training, provision and policy have been drawn out for comparative analysis.

Crossnational studies help us to see our own system in sharper focus, to become more aware of possible and necessary developments. Despite the different traditions and systems between countries, a number of common issues and challenges will be facing most countries during the coming years. These include the need to

- conceptualize and organize early childhood services both as educational provision for children and as a social support system for families;
- improve levels of provision for children under 6, and particularly for children under 3 years of age and for school children outside regular school hours;
- recognize the two sides of decentralization and diversification of services: on the one hand as a means of regulating services according to local needs and on the other as a trend towards privatization based on budget considerations which endangers equal access to provision; and
- develop criteria and procedures for evaluating the quality of services.

Whilst services are diverse, there is a common line of development in many countries as far as training for work with young children is concerned, in particular with children aged 3–6 years. Apart from Austria, Germany and Italy this training is now part of the higher education system – either at university or at a vocational higher education institution. In a number of countries the upgrading of training took place in the 1970s and 1980s, with a further upgrading to university level just recently. This presents a challenge for those countries whose professional workers are trained at a lower level. And many countries need to question the differences in level and orientation of training for group responsibility with children over and below 3 years of age.

We should like to take this opportunity to thank all those colleagues and experts in the 15 European Union countries who helped us with information and advice. Without their support this book would not have been possible. A comprehensive list of interview partners can be found in Appendix II.

Special thanks go the IFP researchers responsible for this project: Pamela Oberhuemer, Dr Michaela Ulich and Monika Soltendieck. Their initiative and enthusiasm in retrieving the necessary information and building up a Europe-wide network of experts were boundless. Gabriele Leonhardt's assistance with translation work and with the systematization of the many documents in different languages was much appreciated. Finally, our thanks go to the Federal Ministry for Family, Senior Citizens, Women and Youth, the Bavarian Ministry of Education, Culture, Science and the Arts, and the Bavarian Ministry for Employment and Social Affairs, Family, Women and Health for their funding support.

Prof. Dr. Dr. Dr. W.E. Fthenakis
Director, State Institute of Early Childhood Education and Research (IFP)
Munich, October 1996

PART I
CHILDCARE AND EDUCATION SERVICES IN EUROPE: A SURVEY OF PROVISION AND STAFF TRAINING

1

Introduction

STAFFING – A KEY QUALITY FACTOR IN CENTRE-BASED SETTINGS

Childcare and education services outside the compulsory school system – and particularly services for young children – are currently expanding in many countries. The demand for professional workers will inevitably increase. According to a growing body of research evidence, staffing is one of the key quality factors in centre-based settings. (Phillips *et al.*, 1987; Powell and Stremell, 1989; Whitebrook *et al.*, 1989). Current studies in the UK are also researching aspects of this link (Blenkin *et al.*, 1994, 1995; Pascal *et al.*, 1995) Decisions made about staffing will be decisions made about the quality levels of services. Who works with young children in Europe? What kinds of qualifications are expected? What are the objectives and contents of training for work in this field?

The purpose of a project based in Munich at the State Institute of Early Childhood Education and Research (IFP) and jointly funded by federal and local government was to collate data from the 15 European Union countries on the training and workplace settings of personnel working with children from birth to 14 years outside the compulsory school system. We chose this particular frame of reference – and not just the early years – because the education and care of school-age children outside school hours have become an issue in several European countries. Expansion of services, quality standards and adequate staff training are some of the questions that have been raised.

CHANGING FRAMEWORK FOR JOB MOBILITY

It is well known that the European Union is a potential framework for facilitating job mobility between member states. In the fields of education and social work there are directives for assessing the formal level of qualifications from other countries. Because of the new dimension that this framework in principle offers in terms of job definition and job aspirations, there is a growing need in the eduction and social service sectors for information about these fields of work in other countries. Workers wish to be able to gauge their employment chances. They wish to know what kinds of employment are open to them and what the salient features of different workplace settings are. Tutors in initial training institutions and in-service programmes wish to be able to inform their students about childcare and education services in other countries. Administrators and decision-makers are interested in systems and policies. Employers need background information in order to make informed decisions when appointing staff from other countries. However, there is surprisingly little systematically collated data detailing information on the wide range of personnel in early childhood and out-of-school services in the EU countries, on their training and the different fields of work open to them. This book provides an extensive survey of these areas.

RESEARCH PROCEDURE

How did we set about collating the necessary data? A first step was a set of questions addressed to the national ministries of education and social welfare. We looked at legislation, official reports, research studies, national and regional guidelines on provision and training, and at the specific programmes of individual training institutions. In some cases we commissioned a supplementary report by a recognized expert in the field. The other major source of information were consultations with a range of key informants representing different areas of expertise. In each country, in 1994 and 1995 we interviewed officials in ministries, lecturers at training colleges and centres, researchers in the field, representatives of professional organizations and practitioners (a list of the commissioned reports and interview partners can be found in the appendices).

The interviews were an invaluable part of the research process and essential for accessing relevant data. The one-to-one exchange was important not only to gain information but also to clarify terminology and to be able to 'make sense' of the data, because – as we all know – similar terms and labels sometimes express quite different things in different countries. *Kindergartens* in Germany are different institutions from the *jardins d'enfants* in France; an educator – *educadora* in Portugal – has a different kind of training from an educator (*éducateur* in Luxembourg) and so on. Both forms and objectives of provision and professional profiles have developed according to specific traditions within the individual countries. We have tried to contextualize these concepts and, in order to avoid misunderstandings we have used key terms in the original language.

ABOUT THIS BOOK

Working with Young Children in Europe presents 15 country profiles, each divided into three sections: A. Social context of childcare and education services; B. Forms of provision; and C. Staff training. Section A describes the general context of childcare and education services outside the compulsory school system, the way the system is organized, how it has developed over the years, and what the current levels of provision for various age-groups are. It also refers to issues and trends. Section B gives an overview of the objectives and features of different types of provision, i.e. of the workplace settings of personnel, and describes major forms of provision in some detail. Section C then focuses specifically on staff training, with extensive tables outlining the main features of training and the range of workplace settings available to specific professional groups. These are supplemented with details on the structure and content of courses, and – where possible – information on in-service training and professional issues.

In order to place the detailed, country-specific data in a wider context, three initial chapters provide a conceptual framework for comparisons across countries. These focus on

- objectives and features of provision;
- staff training and professional issues; and
- current trends and policy developments.

REFERENCES

Whitebrook, M., Howes, C. and Phillips, D. (1989) *Who Cares? Child Care Teachers and the Quality of Care in America.* Executive summary, National Child Care Staffing Study, Oakland, CA.

Blenkin, G. and Yue, N. Y. L. (1994) Profiling Early Years Practitioners: Some First Impressions from a National Survey, *Early Years*, Vol. 15, no. 1, pp. 13–22.

Blenkin, G. M., Whitehead, M. R., Hurst, V. M., Rose, J. A., Burgess-Macey, C. and Yue, N. Y. L. (1995) Principles into Practice: Improving the Quality of Children's Early Learning. Interim Report, Year Two (June 1994 to May 1995). Early Childhood Education Research Project, Goldsmiths College, University of London.

Pascal, C., Bertram, A. D. et al (1995) *Evaluating and Improving the Quality of Learning in Early Childhood Settings: A Professional Development Programme,* Amber Publications, Worcester.

Powell, D. R. and Stremmel, A. J. (1989) The relation of early childhood training and experience to the professional development of child care workers, *Early Childhood Research Quarterly,* Vol. 4, no. 3, pp. 339–356.

2

Objectives and features of provision in the 15 EU countries

LOOKING BACK: PROVISION PRECEDES PERSONNEL

A look at the history of extrafamilial care in Europe reveals a common underlying thread. Provision has always preceded personnel. Institutions for children have been created according to the social needs of specific periods in time, and questions concerning the preparation of staff for work in these institutions have always been a second step.

Social changes over the past 150 years – industrialization, the resulting separation of family and workplace, increasing numbers of mothers in the labour force, changing family structures, growing educational aspirations for children – have led to the establishment of different forms of institutionalized childcare and education and to the emergence of different professional groups engaged in work with children in these settings. This trend – first provision, then personnel – can still be observed today. New definitions of the role of provision based on changing expectations and needs usually lead to a redefinition of training for work in that provision. This of course is not a one-way process, but a question of interplay between provision and training. Reform of training similarly influences the management and content of childcare and education programmes and the general quality of provision.

In this chapter we shall focus primarily on provision for children before they enter compulsory schooling. A shorter section at the end of the chapter will refer to provision for school-age children.

COMMON AND VARYING STRANDS OF DEVELOPMENT

Extrafamilial care for children has similar roots in most European countries. With the onset of female employment in industrial centres in the early nineteenth century, daycare institutions were set up as a reaction to changing family patterns and structures. The main objectives of these early institutions were child protection and custodial care. The concept of early childhood *education* – combined with specific training for educational work – followed later, significantly influenced in most European countries by the ideas of Friedrich Froebel, and later by Montessori, Decroly and others. Over the years, some form of educational provision for young children – in its manifold national and cultural variations – came to be generally accepted policy in most countries for the two or three years preceding compulsory schooling. At the same time this classic type of educational provision has developed in some countries into a system of family-oriented and community-oriented 'educare' which includes children under the age of 3 years, whereas in other countries the shift has been towards providing preprimary schooling for *all* children from the age of 3 up to statutory school age – often with certain characteristics of compulsory schooling. Generally speaking, the education and care of children under 3 years have not developed as part of 'preschool education'. It was seen (and still is in many countries) primarily as a response to deficits in family care.

These broad lines of development – with individual differences between countries – tie up with approaches towards training. They also yield a matrix for comparing different systems.

TWO-TIER SYSTEMS: 'CARE' AND 'EDUCATION'

In many EU countries the period of early childhood has traditionally been divided into two stages – mainly around age 3 – with distinct training routes for each stage: an educational orientation for work with the older children and a paramedical or social care orientation for work with the younger children.

Early childhood services in Belgium provide an example of a clear-cut division between two age-groups. The Flemish, French and German-speaking communities are each divided into a daycare sector for children under 3 years of age and preprimary schooling for children aged $2^1/_2$–6 years. This division runs along conceptual, political and administrative lines, and has a long tradition. Training and provision for the 3–6-year-olds, officially regulated by the state, had been fully developed by the turn of the century, whereas provision and suitable training for children under 3 years of age have only very recently appeared on the political agenda.

In Belgium, almost all children attend preprimary schooling (*kleuteronderwijs, école maternelle, Vorschule*), which takes children from $2^1/_2$ to 6 years. Attendance is not compulsory, and is free of charge. Centres are mainly located on school premises and come under the administrative reponsibility of the respective Community Department of Education. The system is highly regulated and uniform in terms of staffing and organization. Staff complete a three-year higher education training specifically for this age-group. Opening hours are identical to those of school (usually from 8.30 a.m. to 11.30 a.m. and 1.30 p.m. to 3.30 p.m.), which means that some children need additional facilities before and after school and in the school holidays. The guiding principles and the organizational structure of provision and training for this age-group are in their main thrust educational. The child's parents, their specific needs or their participation in the programme are not a primary goal and frame of reference for educational work in this institution.

Daycare for children under 3 years of age is a different matter. Provision is the responsibility of the respective Community Ministry for Family Affairs, parents pay a fee, and regulations and organizational structure are less centralized and standardized. Day nurseries are primarily looked upon as institutions for custodial care in the absence of family care, and not as an educational opportunity for children regardless of their family situation. In spite of recent reforms and an ongoing discussion, training for work in this field is still predominantly in the paramedical tradition.

This division of early childhood into two distinct and separate systems of provision and training – a 'daycare system' and a 'preschool system' – also applies to France, Italy, Luxembourg, The Netherlands, Portugal, Greece, the UK and Ireland, although in different ways.

France, like Belgium, has two separate systems: one for children from $2\frac{1}{2}$ to 6 years with a similarly high rate of provision and clear educational objectives, the other oriented towards care for children under 3 years of age. Training requirements are higher than in Belgium for both age-groups, but still located within two separate career paths: training for work with infants and toddlers is paramedical in orientation, whereas staff in preprimary centres (écoles maternelles) are trained as teachers, completing a university degree and a two-year professional qualification for work in preprimary and primary schooling.

Greece and Portugal – and to a certain extent the UK and Ireland – have parallel systems, one line following the preschool educational tradition, the other line more that of custodial care for specific target groups – with longer opening hours and more consideration of social and family needs.

A MORE UNIFIED APPROACH

Other countries have developed a more unified approach. Denmark is one example. A guiding principle of Danish policy is the idea of quality 'educare', with highly qualified personnel for all age-groups. Institutional childcare in developmentally appropriate surroundings is regarded not only as an educational and social opportunity for children but also as a forum for parent participation and community orientation. Personnel are trained at a higher education level as social pedagogues (paedagoger), with a career path and professional self-image very different from that of schoolteachers.

Finland, Spain, Germany and Austria are all countries which combine characteristics of both strands of development – in different ways. In Finland, children up to the age of 7 attend daycare centres organized around a concept of parent and community-oriented educare. Within the institution, however, paramedically trained personnel tend to work with the youngest children and qualified preschool educators with the older children. The training for preschool educators was upgraded to university level in 1995. Arguments for this move focused on the need for a more academic training which eventually should be integrated or at least inter-related with training for primary school teaching. Thus we have a dual frame of reference: on the one hand a holistic view of early childhood services for all age-groups based on the concept of educare, on the other a tendency to single out preschool educators and to relate their work, training and status to that of primary school teaching.

Finland and Sweden are exceptions in Europe concerning legal entitlement to a place in childcare provision in that they include children under 3 years of age (unlike other countries with a legal entitlement such as Germany and France). In Sweden this applies to children from 18 months onwards whose parents work or study. In Finland entitlement is from birth. The Childcare Act 1990 was a reaction to the high employment rates among mothers with very young children and the questionable conditions surrounding private, non-regulated family daycare. Both countries have in this way chosen to upgrade the social status of provision for the under 3s. However, this status boost was not primarily educationally motivated, but oriented towards parental needs. Spain was the first country to adopt a nationwide policy of early childhood *education* for children from birth to 6 years.

Childcare and education services in Spain were traditionally divided into the two 'classical' categories, each with its own system of provision and training. The Education Reform Act 1990 (LOGSE) provided a new framework for the entire Spanish education system. The period of 'early childhood education' now extends from birth to 6 years and comes under the overall responsibility of the national Ministry of Education. In spite of a division into two cycles (birth to 3 years, and 3–6 years), the goals are similar. For both cycles workers with group responsibility should be qualified early childhood teachers with a three-year university-level training. Even for the very youngest children, institutional childcare is defined as a chance for education, and not merely as a service for children in need. This policy decision is all the more impressive in the context of the low level of maternal employment in Spain. Although financial constraints are currently restricting effective implementation, this is still a forward-looking policy.

Germany and Austria follow different strands of development. On the one hand there is a clear-cut division between the two age-groups. Provision is generally age divided, with *Kindergarten* starting officially at age 3. The level of provision for children under 3 years of age is very low (among the lowest in the EU), and it has low political priority – provision is discussed as a necessity related to maternal employment and not as an educational opportunity for young children. On the other hand both age-groups come under the responsibility of the same ministerial authorities (in both countries social welfare). In Germany, the *Kindergarten* is not a 'preprimary' institution along Belgian or French lines, its educational philosophy is more family and community oriented, and activities are less structured and teacher centred. In addition, an increasing number of institutions are now open to children from birth to 6 years, and several pilot projects have been established which are combining early childhood provision with care and leisure facilities for school-age children, catering for the 0–10 or 3–12 age-range, with flexible, mixed-age grouping among the children, and an active policy of parent participation. The training of educators (*Erzieherinnen*) does not only prepare for work in *Kindergarten* but is also a broad-base course covering a wide age-range. It is not related to the training of schoolteachers, and educators follow quite a different career path.

LINKS BETWEEN PREPRIMARY AND PRIMARY SCHOOLING

In most EU countries compulsory schooling begins at age 6, in some at age 5 or even 4, and in the Scandinavian countries children start school when they are 7 years old (see Table 2.1).

However, the term 'statutory school age' is somewhat confusing if we consider the actual practice of school attendance in some countries. In The Netherlands, for example, although compulsory schooling starts at 5, most 4-year-olds attend school. This is also the case for a growing number of 4-year-olds in the UK. And in Luxembourg, preprimary schooling itself is compulsory, starting at age 4. On the whole, in countries with a lower school starting age, both services and training for children below that age tend to be less developed and regulated and more in the hands of private agencies compared with countries which have chosen a later age for school entry. In both Luxembourg and The Netherlands, for example, daycare for children under the age of 4 is privately organized, and supervised by the Ministry of Social Affairs; some institutions are completely private, with very few official regulations that can be legally enforced. The training of personnel is more within the tradition of social work. In The Netherlands, workers in the

Table 2.1 Compulsory school starting age in the EU countries

Age in years	Country
4	Northern Ireland (UK)
5	England, Scotland, Wales (UK) The Netherlands
6	Austria Belgium France Germany Greece Ireland Italy Luxembourg (preprimary education compulsory from age 4 since 1992) Portugal Spain
7	Denmark Finland Sweden (numerous pilot projects experimenting with school entry at 6)

welfare sector have either a broad-based training with no specific focus on childcare, or they have a lower level of general education and are specifically trained for work with children up to the age of 4 years through a two-year on-site training.

The transition from kindergarten or preprimary schooling into school is often discussed as a 'critical' passage. Trying to improve this transition, and with it educational opportunity for all children, has in several countries led to a growing conceptual link between preprimary and primary schooling. One reason for introducing compulsory preschooling in 1992 in Luxembourg was to offer ethnic minority groups (30 per cent of the population) more educational opportunity. France and Belgium have introduced so-called 'cycles of learning', one of which bridges the transition from the *école maternelle* into primary schooling. In Finland 'learning modules' for the 5 and 6-year-olds have been developed for use in both daycare centres and schools. The country with the most obvious conceptual link between preprimary and primary schooling is The Netherlands. Here, preschool education was integrated into the compulsory school system in 1985, and the training for kindergarten educators was likewise amalgamated with that of primary schoolteachers.

PLAYGROUPS – A VIABLE ALTERNATIVE?

In some countries playgroups have become an established form of provision, notably in the UK, The Netherlands and Ireland. In most cases they were originally established during the 1960s as a conceptual alternative to existing provision. In the mean time they play a significant role in the overall pattern of services as a result of low levels of publicly funded provision. Another country in which playgroups are common is Finland. In this case they were initially established after the Second World War by the Lutheran Church and still play an important role in overall provision, and the Lutheran Church has its own training institutions for work in these groups.

Playgroups are generally parent-managed groups. Children attend two or three times a week for two to three hours at a time. They cannot therefore be classified as regular provision in the way that a classical kindergarten or daycare centre would be. The general aim is to provide an environment for children to make social contacts, to learn through play and to offer parents more opportunities for active participation in decision-making and management.

In The Netherlands, playgroups now come under the responsibility of local authorities and have to fulfil similar requirements to daycare centres concerning group size. One of two workers must be professionally trained at the intermediate vocational level, whereas in the UK and Ireland playgroup leaders may complete a course of up to 200 hours' duration, but they are not obliged to do so.

SERVICES FOR CHILDREN UNDER 3

In most countries the level of publicly funded provision for children under 3 years of age is generally low and differences between countries considerable. Whereas in Denmark there are publicly funded places either in centres or family daycare for nearly half the relevant age-group, and in Belgium for around 30 per cent, in Ireland, Austria, Germany and the UK levels are very low, at around 3 per cent (excepting the eastern part of Germany, where the coverage rate is much higher). The majority of children under 3 in almost all countries are cared for either by family members or within other private family daycare arrangements. Both policy and public opinion concerning out-of-home care for this age-group vary considerably. In countries such as The Netherlands, the UK, Ireland, Austria or Germany, caring for very young children outside the home is still considered to be a private matter, something which working parents have to arrange themselves, and something which is essentially not 'good' for young children. In contrast, countries such as Finland, Sweden or Spain have – as previously mentioned – integrated this kind of provision into legislation, with increasing emphasis on the educational role of services for very young children.

The main forms of publicly funded provision for this age-group are centre-based settings either just for children under 3, or for a wider age-range including children under 3, or family daycare. In some countries, much of this provision is also privately run.

Day nurseries, or crèches, were originally established for the care and protection of children in need. Publicly funded provision is usually on a full-day basis, under the overall responsibility of the Ministry of Social Welfare (in Spain and Sweden the Ministry of Education), and is fee-paying on an income-related basis. Admission criteria are oriented towards defined social needs (e.g. lone-parent families), although the need for this kind of provision far outnumbers available provision. In many countries the need for a more explicitly educational approach both in centre programmes and staff training is being discussed. Dissatisfaction with the traditional paramedical orientation of day nurseries in France was one reason for the establishment of alternative, parent-run groups for this age-group (*crèches parentales*). Parents prefer educationally trained staff (*éducateurs*) to run these groups, rather than the paediatric nurses (*puéricultrices*) who are usually in charge of the publicly funded day nurseries. In northern Italy, in municipalities such as Reggio-Emilia and Pistoia, day nurseries of a 'new kind' – widely acclaimed in educational circles – have developed. Part of their approach includes close co-operation with parents and other professionals in the local community.

In general there is a growing interest in more flexible systems. A number of research studies in different countries have indicated that parents with children under 3 years of age have more varied needs concerning care arrangements than parents with older children. Public funding support for private, parent-run initiatives is seen to be one way of broadening and improving the options available, as is the introduction of regulatory measures for family daycare.

Scandinavian policies have aimed at this kind of flexibility. Even within the system of family daycare in Denmark, Finland and Sweden there are a number of different options, ranging from the traditional arrangement in the provider's home to co-ordinated groups of family daycare providers (as also in Portugal and France).

The development of centre-based care for this age-group needs to be seen in the wider context of parental leave and other family support measures (see the European Commission Network on Childcare publications for detailed, country-by-country accounts). In Germany, for example, extending parental leave to a period of three years was considered an alternative to expanding centre-based provision for the under 3s. In professional circles, however, this is considered to be only one of the necessary options.

CARE AND RECREATION FACILITIES FOR SCHOOL-AGE CHILDREN

Provision for children outside school hours and during holiday times is in many countries an area which has been awarded only scant attention in the past. Usually loosely regulated, if at all, it comprises a range of varying services for which there are few reliable statistics or sources of information, and in most countries there is no single professional group in the field which could stimulate debate or make proposals for necessary innovations. The European Network for School-Age Children (ENSAC) has been trying to check this imbalance at a European level.

Types of provision vary according to the length of the school day. In Austria, Denmark, Finland, Germany, Greece and Sweden schools close down at around lunchtime or soon after. Although all these countries – except Greece – offer some form of regulated provision for after-school care, only Denmark and Sweden provide a reasonable number of places. In Germany and Austria there are established centres (*Kinderhorte*) for this age-group, but levels of provision are minimal (although much higher in the eastern part of Germany than in the western part), and generally this kind of provision tends to be low in public esteem.

In countries with full-day schooling provision is also varied. France and Belgium provide organized, 'wrap-around' arrangements which are financed by local social service authorities. Otherwise, most services are on a voluntary basis, or there is no form of organized provision at all (e.g. in Ireland). Due to the pressing need for places, the role of voluntary organizations in this area has grown considerably in some countries over the past few years (e.g. Kids' Clubs Network in Britain).

Services for school-age children can be categorized as follows:

• Separate centres for school-age children which are regulated (e.g. in

Germany, Sweden, Denmark) and employ specially trained staff.

- 'Wrap-around' arrangements on school premises (before and after-school hours, during the mid-day break), usually fee-paying, and supervised by a variety of qualified and non-qualified, paid and voluntary staff.
- Admission of school-age children into age-integrated centres for 0–10-year-olds or 3–12-year-olds, as in Denmark and in pilot projects in Germany.
- Provision for school-age children within family daycare.
- 'Open-door' community provision (e.g. youth centres, adventure playgrounds, media libraries), variously staffed with qualified workers and voluntary helpers.
- Various types of holiday schemes during school holidays, staffed mostly by personnel with a (very) short-term training.

With the growing need of care for school-age children, some 'open-door' recreation facilities tend to be used as regular services (without the necessary changes in staff and provision). In some countries out-of-school provision is being expanded mainly in social priority areas as a support measure aimed at improving the integration of marginalized groups (as in The Netherlands, Luxembourg and Portugal).

3

Who works with young children?
Staff training and professional issues

Who works with children in childcare and education services? What kind of training is required? What are the similarities and the differences between countries in this respect? This chapter outlines overall training and professional issues, focusing in particular on professional groups working with children before compulsory school age. Shorter sections will deal with personnel in out-of-school services for school children and with auxiliary staff.

Table 3.1 depicts the main professional group in each country working with the largest number of children in publicly funded early childhood centres. Training is categorized according to academic level, length, age-group specialization and whether staff are also qualified as primary school-teachers.

LEVEL AND LENGTH OF TRAINING

In many countries, a reform of the training required to work with young children in the years prior to school entry was first discussed in the context of a widespread educational debate during the 1960s. This debate centred around those professional groups working with children during the two or three years before official school starting age, in many countries the 3–6-year-olds. Over the past 20 years or so training schemes in many countries have been reorganized and upgraded. Table 3.1 shows that the vast majority of staff with group responsibility in publicly funded early childhood centres are trained at higher education level: in Finland, France, Greece, Ireland, Spain and Sweden this training takes place at universities; in Belgium, Denmark, Greece, Luxembourg, The Netherlands and Portugal at vocational higher education institutions. (In Greece there are two parallel systems of training for two different kinds of early childhood centre.) The minimum length of training is three years. France requires the highest formal academic level: *professeurs des écoles* who work in the state-run *écoles maternelles* have to complete a three-year university degree (*licence*) before being granted entry to a two-year professional course of training held at university institutes. The training schemes with the lowest formal requirements are the five-year post-

Table 3.1   Personnel in main form of publicly funded early childhood provision in the EU countries

Country/early years worker	Level of training	Length of training in years	Age-range covered by training in years	Does training qualify for work in primary schools?
Finland (*lastentarhanopettaja*)	University	3	0–7	No
France (*professeur des écoles*)		5 (3 + 2)	2½–11	Yes
Greece* (*nipiagogos*)		4	3, 5–6	No
Ireland (*national teacher*)		3	4–11	Yes
Sweden (*förskollärare*)		3	0–7	No
Spain (*maestro de EGB especialista en educación infantil*)		3	0–6	No
UK (*teacher*)		4	3–11	Yes
(Italy**)		(4)	(3–6)	(No)
Belgium (*institutrice de maternelle/ kleuterleid(st)er/Kindergärtnerin*)	Vocational higher education institutions	3	2½–6	No
Denmark (*paedagog*)		3½	0–100	No
Greece* (*vrefonipiagogos*)		3½	0–6	No
Luxembourg (*instituteur de l'éducation préscolaire*)		3	4–6	No
The Netherlands (*leraar basisonderwijs*)		3	4–12	Yes
Portugal (*educador/a de infância*)		3	0–6 (mainly)	No
Germany (*Erzieherin*)	Secondary, level II	3	0–27	No
Austria (*Kindergärtnerin*)	Secondary, level I	5 (with A-level equiv. only 2)	3–6	No
Italy***	Secondary, level I	5	0–100	No

Notes:
    *Different training routes for work in 1) half-day kindergartens and 2) full-day centres.
    **University-level training endorsed by law in 1990; reform plans not yet implemented.
    ***New five-year broad-based training since 1992.

14 course leading to the award of *Kindergärtnerin* in Austria, the five-year post-14 training as *assistente di comunità infantile* in Italy, and the post-16 training as *Erzieherin* in Germany at intermediate vocational level. In Italy a law passed in 1990 set the framework for upgrading training for work in the *scuola materna* to university level, but these plans have not yet been implemented.

On the whole, the general trend has been to raise formal entry requirements and the length of training. On the other hand, it is necessary to point out that in countries with a comparatively underdeveloped system of publicly funded early childhood centres outside the state school system (such as the UK, Ireland, The Netherlands) playgroups fulfil a substantial role in the provision of places for 2–4-year-olds, and here the staffing requirements are completely different, as is also the case in private, for-profit provision. In the UK, for example, the Children Act 1989 for the first time empowers local authorities to provide training for those working in childcare services, but this requirement is not binding, and there are no basic specifications of the training needed to achieve acceptable standards of provision. Playgroup workers *may* be trained teachers or nursery nurses whose children attend the group, but this is a matter of chance. They *may* have attended one of the courses (up to 200 hours) run by the playgroup umbrella organization (in the UK the Preschool Alliance), but again, this is optional.

In most EU countries, however, the majority of children attending provision during the two years prior to school – and in some countries also younger children – are in groups with staff trained at a high level.

TRAINING FOR SPECIFIC AGE-GROUPS: BROAD OR NARROW?

We have already seen that the common dividing line in provision for children under and over 3 years of age is generally accompanied by a distinction between the training considered necessary for working with very young children and that needed for working with children in preprimary provision. There is a fairly clear split between 'care' and 'education' and provision comes under the responsibility of *either* welfare *or* education authorities. This is currently the case in Belgium, France, Ireland, Italy, Luxembourg, The Netherlands, Portugal and the UK. Training for work with the younger children has lower entry requirement demands, and often has a paramedical or social care orientation. Training for work with children in the two or three years preceding school entry is educational in thrust, and mostly there are strong training links with the school system. Greece has a *parallel* system, both of provision and training. Pedagogues working in the half-day kindergartens (*nipiagogia*) are trained for the 3–5 age-range in a four-year university degree course; personnel for the full-day early childhood centres (*paediki stathmi*) are trained for the age-group 6 months to 5 years in a three-and-a-half year course at a vocational higher education institute. Staff in both forms of provision are paid the same, but have very different conditions of work.

Other countries – mostly those where all provision comes under the responsibility of *either* welfare *or* education – have introduced a single system of training for all age-groups prior to compulsory schooling. Austria, Denmark, Finland, Germany, Spain and Sweden now have – with different emphases – such a unified approach.

Related to the issue of a separate or unified system of training is the emphasis accorded to a specific age-group within that training. In Belgium, for example, preschool teachers are trained specifically for the 3–6 age-group, or in Luxembourg for work with 4–6-year-old children. Denmark, by contrast, trains its *paedagoger* to work not only in all forms of early childhood services but also with school-age children in out-of-school provision and in a wide range of services for children and adults with special needs. Up until 1992 Denmark had three separate training programmes in the socioeducational field: one for kindergarten educators, one for educators working in after-school and leisure-time facilities, and one for educators working with children and adults with special needs. These three strands have now been amalgamated into one training programme lasting three and a half years, including 15 months in work placements.

A similar kind of broad-based training are the schemes for the *éducateur* and *éducateur gradué* in Luxembourg, two recently upgraded professional categories for working in services for children *and* adults, or the new profession of *assistente di comunità infantile* in Italy. Another case is Germany: educators (*Erzieher*) are trained to work with a wide age-range of children in both preschool and out-of-school settings. Generalization is seen to be a key quality factor in all these cases. By contrast, in Greece, Luxembourg and Belgium a high degree of specialization is considered necessary for quality work with young children.

ALIGNMENT WITH MAINSTREAM TEACHER TRAINING OR SEPARATE IDENTITY?

The need to raise the professional and public status of early childhood practitioners and the question of how this can best be achieved is a common topic of debate in many countries. Is the answer a high-level and specialized system of training for work in early childhood provision, separate from teaching training, as in Sweden? Or a broad-based approach for a wide range of age-groups outside the compulsory school system, as in Denmark or Germany? Or is integration into mainstream teacher training, which generally enjoys a higher status than early childhood education, the preferable solution?

The UK, The Netherlands, France and Ireland have chosen the latter model: joint training for preprimary and primary schooling. This qualifies for work with an age-group ranging from 4 to 12 in The Netherlands and Ireland, from 3 to 11 in the UK and from 2 to 12 in France. While this approach in principle grants staff in non-compulsory settings the same status as schoolteachers, in practice it is not without its problems and is currently being debated by professionals in these countries. The question being asked is: are the specific goals and methods of early childhood education as they have developed over the years being streamlined and adjusted to a more curriculum-oriented, systematic and teacher-centred learning in primary school? In The Netherlands for instance this issue has been debated for more than ten years now. It has been questioned whether the original idea of the Education Reform Act 1985, which envisaged a fusion of nursery and primary schooling embodying principles of *both* systems, has really been implemented successfully. Some critics maintain that early childhood education has lost its 'place' within the new system.

Similar arguments can be heard in the UK and France. In England and Wales, for example, the introduction in 1988 of a National Curriculum into schools and subsequent government requirements concerning training have radically changed the nature of teacher education. Traditional school subjects now have a firm place in the training curricula. Strategies for 'teaching to teach' seem to have become more important than considerations of children 'learning to learn'. It seems that in a situation where training for work in non-compulsory education services has to compete for 'space' with the statutory education system, the chances are slim that it will be awarded the necessary focus. This leaves us with a question mark as to whether this alignment with the mainstream education system really is the best way of raising both the quality and status of early childhood education.

COURSE CONTENT

In most EU countries, higher education institutions have considerable autonomy in the development of curricula for the early childhood professions. This makes it difficult to attempt any generalized observations on the content of courses. A further problem is that common terms for areas of study such as 'developmental psychology', 'education', 'professional studies' may imply different approaches and contents. In order to analyse the content of courses more effectively, it would be necessary to study reading lists and seminar topics, which was not possible within the wide remit of our study. However, it was possible to detect certain common features. Most courses for work in specifically educational provision have – predictably – a broad education focus which includes education-related disciplines such as psychology, sociology, history and (less often) philosophy. Most focus additionally on a number of specified curriculum areas such as music and movement, physical education, artwork or health education. Sweden includes socially and politically relevant areas of learning such as environmental protection and intercultural learning and also professional issues (professional role, image, status, conditions of work, etc.) as clearly defined components of training. The focus on general education and the inclusion of foreign languages varies from country to country. Most countries offer English. Luxembourg, for example, also offers Portuguese because of the large number of Portuguese immigrants living in the country. The Stockholm Institute of Education in Sweden even offers a four-year early childhood studies course with English as the language of instruction – aimed to attract both Swedish students and students from abroad.

The more broadly based sociopedagogic training routes also differ from country to country. In Luxembourg, for example, the training as *éducateur* has a strong special needs and remedial focus, with much space allocated to the integration of marginalized children and adults 'at risk'.

Time spent in work placements – *practica* – is usually integrated into the courses, with the longest period occurring during the final year. In some training schemes, however, a sustained period in a work placement takes place after completion of the college-based component, e.g. to become a *técnico superior en educacion infantil* in Spain or an *Erzieherin* in Germany. Work placements in another country are now an integrated part of training schemes in Denmark and Sweden.

Another interesting phenomenon is the increasing role of research in training. In the four-year course in preschool pedagogy in Greece or in the three-year training as 'preschool teacher' in Sweden, for example, learning about research methods and carrying out small-scale research are an integral part of course content. University staff are expected to carry out research, and may involve their students in research studies. Stronger links between research, development work and training will inevitably have a positive effect on early childhood professionals' self-image and status. Through the increasing number of courses offered at university level, the field of early childhood education and care is gradually becoming a sustained focus of university-based research with potential effects on innovation within the field. In countries where the training system for childcare and education services is not integrated into the tertiary level of education (e.g. Austria and Germany), applied research and development work in this field are not so widespread.

PROFESSIONAL ROLES: SCHOOLTEACHER? EARLY CHILDHOOD SPECIALIST? SOCIAL NETWORK EXPERT?

Staff training programmes for early childhood services reflect different aims and objectives concerning those services. For example, the funding commitment towards training, the level, length and appropriateness of training, and – in some cases – the discretionary nature of training altogether, are all indicators of the overall goals of a particular society concerning the education and care of its youngest children. Similarly, as we have argued, training programmes reflect traditions and priorities in the area of early childhood provision. Some emphasize the educational function of early childhood services and consider this to be a right for *all* children from the age of 3 or 4 up to compulsory schooling. This is the case for example in France, Luxembourg, Belgium and The Netherlands. Very often this line of argument ties up with the goal of equal educational opportunity – especially for children of ethnic minorities or underprivileged families, i.e. for groups associated with school failure. It is argued that these children will have a better chance if nursery and primary education are part of one system, thus allowing for a smoother transition adapted to individual needs and levels of competency. In this sense, preschool institutions are seen as an vehicle for preparing children for school – if not exclusively, then at least primarily. Training prepares students to become *teachers* (both for preprimary and primary schooling), as in France, the UK, The Netherlands and Ireland, or *early childhood specialists*, as in Belgium, Greece, Spain – experts in working with children, transmitting knowledge and cultural traditions in accordance with a well defined curriculum framework.

Another line of argument emphasizes the importance of a distinct period of early childhood provision separate and different from compulsory primary education. Holistic approaches towards learning, the importance of play and creativity, parent participation, family and community orientation with matching regional diversity and informal, decentralized structures are some of the ideas and goals of these services. Training schemes such as those in Sweden, Denmark or Finland reflect an understanding of early childhood services as a framework both for educational work with children and for social support for families where the chief caregivers – mother or father or both – work or study. Within this approach, institutions for children of preschool age are often seen to have a multipurpose role and are viewed as an integral part of the community infrastructure, liaising where necessary with local organizations and services, and open to the needs of both children and parents. In Denmark and Sweden, for example, following measures of decentralization, local institutions have been accorded a great deal of autonomy. Lead educators are responsible (in Denmark in close collaboration with parents) for decision-making on the allocation of funding and resources within the institution as well as for developing the educational programme, organizing teamwork and defining work tasks. Accordingly, subject areas such as communication studies, adult education and social management theories have been included in the initial training courses for *paedagoger*.

The professional profile for workers with this broader remit – education, care, social and community work and so on – is not so clearly defined, and moreover it tends to adapt to changes in society as reflected in the local needs of communities. Whereas preschool teachers in the *écoles maternelles* in Belgium or France are primarily responsible for the children in their group during 'class times', the tasks demanded of social pedagogues are wider ranging. In Finland, for example, early childhood professionals (*lastentarhanopettaja*) are responsible for various tasks in the community, such as offering support and advisory services for family daycarers, admitting children who are not registered on a permanent basis, holding information sessions for parents in the area, etc. The desired professional role is not so much the early childhood specialist or teacher, but rather the *social network expert*, with a clear educative function, but with a very different professional self-image from that of a teacher.

STATUS AND CAREER PROSPECTS

Some of the problems associated with the integration of training for non-statutory education services into mainstream teacher training have been mentioned. One obvious advantage of this solution concerns the status factor of pay. In some countries – the UK, France, the Netherlands – staff working with preschool-age children in publicly funded education services are paid the same as teachers working with older children. Despite this, staff working with young children still tend to have a lower public and professional status than staff working with older children, a view confirmed in a number of interviews during the course of our research.

Chances for mobility (horizontal and vertical) within a certain professional group are one way of enhancing attractiveness, besides enhancing motivation to stay within the profession. Continuity and stability are important factors for mobilizing professionals to work for improvements within their own profession.

In Greece, kindergarten pedagogues are state employees with a secure job and chances for promotion. However, unemployment is one of the most serious problems facing this profession. Students who have completed the four-year university course for work in kindergartens currently have to wait up to nine years before being accepted into public service. In Greece there are also considerable status differences *within* the professional groups working with young children. Whereas workers in full-day centres are paid the same as their colleagues in half-day kindergartens, they have almost eight hours a day contact time with the children compared with four hours a day in the kindergartens.

What is the key factor for developing a strong professional identity? Public presence is certainly one of the relevant issues. In Spain the professional organization Rosa Sensat has been particularly effective in drawing public attention to professional issues. In Denmark over 90 per cent of professionals in childcare and education services are members of the trade union organization BUPL, an unusually high level of professional commitment.

WHAT ABOUT MEN?

The early childhood professions have traditionally been women's professions, and the participation of men in this work remains an issue. We cannot enter into that debate here, but should like to point out that some training schemes do draw more men than others. One is the Danish scheme for *paedagoger* introduced in 1992, which is proving to be an immensely popular training option for both women *and* men. This could well have something to do with the generally high status accorded to professional childcare in Denmark. Two other points in its favour are that job prospects are currently very good, and the fact that the award allows a good deal of mobility and side-stepping within the profession. Another aspect could concern the broadly defined framework of the profession, which potentially creates the basis for developing a professional culture and profile appealing to both women and men.

AUXILIARY WORKERS IN CHILDCARE AND EDUCATION SERVICES

What is the role of auxiliary workers in the early childhood workfield? Again, there are considerable differences between countries. With reference to the main forms of provision, three patterns of staffing emerge:

- Professionals with group responsibility are supported by a qualified ancillary worker who has completed a (mostly two-year) post-16 full-time training scheme, such as the *nursery nurses* in UK nursery schools, the *Kinderpflegerin* in German kindergartens or the *barnskötare* in Swedish early childhood centres.
- Professionals with group responsibility are assisted by paid, non-qualified auxiliaries who are expected or obliged to attend courses offered by the local authorities, such as the assistants in the French *écoles maternelles* or in the Danish daycare centres.
- Professionals with group responsibility who are not assisted by paid or voluntary helpers, such as teachers in the *junior infant* and *senior infant classes* in Irish primary schools, kindergarten pedagogues in Greece or qualified staff in the *scuola materna* in Italy.

Spain is an exception concerning entry requirements for the training of auxiliary staff. The Education Reform Act 1990 stipulates that senior childcare workers should have a university entrance qualification in order to be admitted to the 15-month course of training.

A recent development in some countries is the trend towards replacing training schemes focusing on childcare alone (and, it is argued, on a limited choice of workfields) with broad-based schemes for work in a variety of social care and sociopedagogic settings. Examples are to be found in Finland and The Netherlands, and in some regions (*Länder*) in Germany.

In parent-run groups, co-operation between professionals and parents both in the management and programme development of services is matter of fact. In Germany a number of pilot projects have pointed towards the need for closer collaboration between professionals, parents, self-help groups and freelance workers in mainstream centres. This is a general direction which in future years will presumably call for a new understanding and essentially a redefinition of professional roles.

STAFF IN PROVISION FOR SCHOOL-AGE CHILDREN

Only a few countries have developed training schemes for work with school children outside regular school hours. Among these, Sweden is the only country with a specific course of training just for this work, and certainly the only country to offer training at university level. Recreation pedagogues (*fritidspedagoger*) complete a three-year course of studies similar (but separate) to that of the early childhood educators in Sweden. In Denmark, Germany and Austria there is also focused training for work in this field. However, this is not offered as a separate specialism, but is integrated into broad-based courses, generally for a much wider range of ages and workplace settings. In France there are several qualification routes to become an *animateur*, who works with children in care services offered as 'wrap-around' provision outside official school hours and opening times, but none of these can be compared in length or depth to the Swedish course of study.

As the need for provision in this area becomes more pressing, there is growing awareness for the need for trained professionals, e.g. in Flanders (Belgium), where staff requirements are only loosely regulated. A number of new courses of study for work in this area are being introduced at individual colleges (e.g. the playwork qualifications in the UK), but – except for the countries mentioned – these have not been conceived within any overall framework for qualifying personnel and regulating staff requirements in this area.

4

Current trends and policy developments

Are there issues and innovative trends in the field of childcare and education services which are relevant across countries? This is a difficult question to answer, as a glance at the country profiles and their multifaceted traditions in this field will show. Particular issues always need to be contextualized within the specific historical developments and present-day circumstances. Nevertheless, there are a number of discernible trends which – with varying degrees of priority – are of common interest. In this chapter we shall summarize main lines of development and raise some questions for future debate.

PROVISION FOR 3–6-YEAR-OLDS: COMMON POLICIES OF EXPANSION AND UNIVERSAL COVERAGE

In all EU countries there has been a significant expansion of early childhood provision for children from about the age of 3 up to compulsory school age over the past 30 years. In some countries, as in Denmark, a comprehensive system of services was first developed during this period of time. In other countries, as in France, there had long been a tradition of publicly funded services for children of preschool age which was consequently expanded into a system of almost universal coverage. Today it has become perfectly acceptable – and desirable – for 4 and 5-year-old children to attend early childhood centres for at least three or four hours a day, if not longer. According to the specific situation in individual countries, established forms of provision tend to be recruiting ever younger children (in Germany and Spain 3-year-olds, in France and Belgium $2^{1}/_{2}$-year-olds). All countries are expanding provision, in particular those which have until now had a low level of provision for this age-group, such as Portugal.

SERVICES FOR CHILDREN UNDER 3 YEARS OF AGE AND FOR SCHOOL CHILDREN

Most countries do not offer enough publicly funded places for children under 3 years of age. Even though public pressure has decreased in some countries following the introduction of longer parental leave arrangements, the demand for places is generally considerably higher than the number of available places. Recognition of the importance of this kind of provision in the form of appropriate legislation has only been made in a few countries, notably Denmark, Finland, Sweden and Spain, and parts of Germany and Italy. Traditional forms of service are being criticized for their strong paramedical and weak educational orientation both in the training of staff and the programme of activities. There is also a growing interest in more flexible options which parents can choose and use according to their varying needs. Prosposals for improving services include state subsidies for voluntary, non-profit providers, and official regulation and training of family daycarers.

In many countries both professionals and parents are expressing dissatisfaction with the current state of provision for school-age children. Staff training for work in these services is also being critically examined. Only a few countries – France, Belgium, Sweden, Denmark – offer a substantial number (although not enough) of publicly funded places. In many countries parents have to rely on voluntary agencies (sometimes with state funding support) to take the initiative. Required training for this work is regulated only in a few cases, and only Sweden and Denmark require training at a higher education level for this kind of work.

DEBATES ON THE 'RIGHT' AGE TO START SCHOOL

In some countries school entry age is being debated, and with it the question of appropriate programmes for 4–6-year-olds. The starting age is 6 in most countries. In some countries arguments for lowering the school starting age are related to the issue of equal opportunity for socially disadvantaged children (e.g. Portugal). A similar discussion in Luxembourg resulted in the introduction of compulsory preprimary schooling as from the age of 4 in 1992. In Sweden, where children customarily enter school at the age of 7, there are moves to lower the age to 6. Finland is retaining 7 as the starting age for compulsory schooling, but has developed specific modules for work with 5 and 6-year-olds, either in daycare centres or in schools. In countries in which many, in some cases nearly all, 4-year-olds attend schools (The Netherlands, Ireland, the UK), the appropriateness of the learning experiences offered to these very young children is an issue of controversial debate. It is questioned whether staff are adequately trained to work with this age-group. The transition from predominantly child-centred and activity-oriented forms of learning at the preprimary stage to the more systematic and structured demands of school is a common issue in many countries, and one which in France and in parts of Belgium has led to the introduction of 'learning cycles' extending over the whole period of preprimary and primary schooling.

DECENTRALIZATION POLICIES – MATCHING PROVISION TO LOCAL NEEDS?

In a number of European countries there has been a move towards decentralization of services. Such moves are generally linked with arguments concerning the advantages of matching provision to local needs, and of developing a more 'client-friendly' system with diversity of choice. A closer look at the implementation strategies used, however, reveals a number of divergent policy aims (both between countries and within countries). The terms 'decentralization' and 'delegation' can mean quite different things, depending on both the current political climate and the historical context of specific childcare and education systems.

Let us look at Portugal and Spain for examples of what we mean by this. After decades of authoritarian and centralistic regimes (Salazar and Franco), state-issued regulations related to services for young children tend to be judged by specialists in the field as overly directive, as measures which hinder grass-roots initiatives and involvement at a local level. At the same time, as is the case in Portugal, professionals argue equally vehemently against politically motivated delegation of responsibility which – in the face of economic constraint – favours the privatization of services and market-driven policies, i.e. a withdrawal of state responsibility for early childhood care and education. It is argued that effective policies concerning the improvement of quality standards and the necessary expansion of services need to be decided on at a national level. In Spain, too, the whole process of decentralization is a controversial issue in professional circles. On the one hand the Education Reform Act 1990 (LOGSE) is considered to be a progressive piece of legislation; on the other hand the state-supervised implementation of the Act is at odds with the development of autonomous regions and democratic involvement at a local level. Similar issues are also being debated in Italy. Some favour a centralized administration, others would like to see more delegation of power to local communities. These contradictory positions are adversely affecting co-operation at various levels between state authorities, municipalities and the Church.

In countries such as The Netherlands decentralization is considered by some politicians to be a key move in introducing market-driven policies to expand provision for the 0–4 age-group. Creating 'diversity of choice' and 'client-friendly provision' are common arguments of those who favour this development. Experts in the field, however, are critical about this low-profile role of the state and call for more responsibility and regulation concerning quality standards of services. Similar arguments can be heard in professional circles in the UK and Ireland concerning provision for the under 5s.

5

Austria

Monika Soltendieck

[A] SOCIAL CONTEXT OF CHILDCARE AND EDUCATION SERVICES

AT A GLANCE

- Federal constitution with nine provinces (*Bundesländer*).
- Statutory school age: 6 years.
- Kindergartens for 3–6-year-olds (approx. 70 per cent coverage rate).
- Since 1962: legislation and policy concerning childcare and education services outside the compulsory school system the responsibility of each province.
- Very low levels of provision for children under 3 years of age and school-age children.
- Parental leave extended to two years in 1990.

Austria is a federal republic with nine provinces (*Bundesländer*). Each province is responsible for the development and implementation of legislation and policy on childcare and education services outside the compulsory school system. Services for both children under 6 years of age and for school-age children are the responsibility of the national (federal) Ministry of Family Affairs and the regional youth and family welfare authorities.

Traditional types of provision are kindergartens (*Kindergärten*) for 3–6-year-olds, nurseries (*Kinderkrippen*) for 0–3-year-olds and school-age centres (*Horte*) for 6–10-year-olds. Whereas the number of kindergartens has steadily increased since the 1970s, reaching a coverage rate of approximately 70 per cent, the level of provision for both nurseries and school-age centres is very low.

Historical roots

The first institutions for children were founded at the onset of industrialization during the early nineteenth century. Kindergartens based on the ideas of Pestalozzi and Froebel followed later, and in 1872 the first course of professional training for kindergarten educators was established. During the period of Nazi rule the number of kindergartens grew and all large companies were obliged to provide workplace nurseries. The latter were abolished in 1957, combined with the introduction of a six-month maternal leave. In 1962, responsibility for kindergarten legislation was delegated to the individual provinces (*Bundesländer*). Since this time the national (federal) Ministry of Education and Cultural Affairs has been responsible only for the training and employment conditions of kindergarten personnel.

Mothers in the labour force – levels of provision

In 1993, 64 per cent of mothers with children from 0 to 15 years were in gainful employment, 40 per cent on a full-time basis (European Commission Network on Childcare, 1996). This is the highest rate of employment in the EU after the Scandinavian countries (Sweden, Denmark, Finland) and Portugal. The length of parental leave was extended to two years in 1990.

The number of kindergartens doubled between the 1920s and the 1950s. Really significant expansion started in the 1960s, and between the 1970s and the 1990s the number doubled yet again. Today approximately 200,000 children attend 4,212 kindergartens (1994) – a coverage rate of 70 per cent of 3–6-year-old children, whereby the number of 5-year-olds attending is significantly higher (88 per cent) than the number of 3-year-olds (31 per cent).

Attendance rates at day nurseries for children under 3 years of age are minimal by comparison and regionally uneven. Across the country there are places for only 3 per cent of 0–3-year-olds, whereas in Vienna approximately 10 per cent of this age-group have a place in a daycare centre. If mothers decide to return to work at the end of the two-year maternal leave, seeking suitable childcare arrangements is a real problem, since kindergartens do not accept children before their third birthday.

The level of provision for school-age children is also low – on average only 6 per cent of 6–10-year-olds attend a publicly funded centre, and 60 per cent of these places are in Vienna.

Current issues and trends

Demand for expanded and more flexible childcare arrangements

Childcare has become a political issue and parents are demanding not only more provision altogether but also more provision adapted to their specific needs. Longer and more flexible opening hours, a shorter registration procedure and a reduction of group size are just some of the current demands.

Half-day kindergartens (which account for almost a quarter of all kindergartens) do not cover the hours necessary for most part-time jobs. The fact that a number of kindergartens close down during mid-day (approximately 23 per cent), and that hours of work often do not match opening hours means that more and more parents have to seek private childcare arrangements for the 'in-between' times.

The lack of suitable provision for all age-groups has resulted in parents opening groups more appropriate to their needs. These self-organized initiatives cater for children from birth up to 15 years.

Acute shortage of kindergarten personnel

Although the five-year training scheme is popular – 500 candidates had to be turned down in 1993 – there is an acute shortage of kindergarten educators in almost all regions. This was one reason for the 1994 revision of the entry procedure for training, and since then the number of trainees has increased considerably. Nevertheless, it is assumed that staff shortage will become even more acute in the years to come because of the pressure concerning expansion of provision.

[B] FORMS OF CHILDCARE AND EDUCATIONAL PROVISION

AT A GLANCE

- Since 1962 each of the nine provinces (*Bundesländer*) has its own kindergarten legislation; regulations differ from province to province.
- Day nurseries for 0–3-year-olds; parent-managed centres for 0–15-year-olds.
- Steady expansion of family daycare provision.

Table 5.1 illustrates the various forms of provision for children aged 0–15 years.

Day nursery (*Kinderkrippe*)

Day nurseries are full-day centres for 0–3-year-olds. The majority of children attending are in fact 2 years old, since this is the cut-off point following parental leave. Nurseries are generally set up and managed by the municipalities. In each group there are 10–15 children and four workers – two fully qualified kindergarten educators and two non-qualified workers – who arrange their times of work in shifts according to the opening hours.

successfully completed 12 years of schooling with a school-leaving certificate (*Matura*), or candidates aged at least 20 years with several years' work experience in the social sector are also eligible to qualify for work in kindergartens. These candidates attend a two-year course (*Kolleg*) for which a qualifying examination is required in social studies, German, history, English, biology/environmental studies and an optional subject.

In-service training and promotion

In-service seminars for kindergarten educators are held at local authority education institutes, provided both by the state and other providers. In general they are not compulsory (certain seminars are obligatory in only one of the nine provinces). The range of provision and the conditions for secondment vary. In some regions personnel are guaranteed three to four days' secondment and a further two to three days during holiday times, whereas in others there are no regulations concerning in-service training.

In principle, kindergarten educators have a number of promotion chances: as kindergarten director, inspector for kindergartens or tutor in professional studies at a kindergarten training college. However, promotion requirements and career chances vary from *Bundesland* to *Bundesland*.

Specialist kindergarten educator for work with handicapped children (*Sonderkindergärtnerin*)

Qualified kindergarten educators may complete a supplementary training for work with children with special needs. Candidates are seconded for 10 hours per week to attend the two-year part-time course. Course content focuses on work with children with mental and learning handicaps, behavioural disorders, speech and hearing impairments, physical handicaps, and with blind children.

Despite this extra training, there is little difference between the conditions of work and pay of specialist educators and those trained for work in mainstream kindergartens. There is a staff shortage for work in this field.

Family daycare providers

A number of courses for the professionalization of family daycarers have been developed recently. These training schemes are held by private organizations. Length of training varies between four and twelve units (weekends, half-day and evening sessions). The professional organization for family daycarers in Lower Austria demands a more rigorous scheme of training covering 81 units in educational and developmental psychology, play, teaching styles, legal and medical issues, nutrition and physical care. Participants receive a certificate on completion of the course.

REFERENCES AND SOURCES

Diemert, K.- P. (1995) Von den einjährigen 'Bildungscursen für Kindergärtnerinnen' zur fünfjährigen 'Bildungsanstalt für Kindergartenpädagogik' bzw. zum 'Kolleg für Kindergartenpädagogik', in G. Knapp (ed.) *Kindergarten und Familie als Lebens- und Erfahrungsraum 'Politik für Kind-ge-Rechte Strukturen'*. Böhlau, Vienna and Cologne.

Faßmann, H., Aufhauser, E. and Münz, R. (1988) *Kindergarten in Österreich*. Ministry of Social Affairs, Vienna.

Hartmann, W. (1995) Österreichischer Kindergartenbericht des Charlotte Bühler-Instituts, in G. Knapp (ed.) *Kindergarten und Familie als Lebens- und Erfahrungsraum 'Politik für Kind-ge-Rechte Strukturen'*. Böhlau, Vienna and Cologne.

Knapp, G. and Salzmann, G. (1995) Institutionelle Voraussetzungen im österreichischen Kindergartenwesen mit besonderer Berücksichtigung Kärntens, in G. Knapp (ed.) *Kindergarten und Familie als Lebens- und Erfahrungsraum 'Politik für Kind-ge-Rechte Strukturen'*. Böhlau, Vienna and Cologne.

Österreichisches Statistisches Zentralamt (ed.) (1994) *Die Kindergärten (Kindertagesheime), Annual Report 1993/94*. ÖSZ, Vienna.

Schattowitz, H., Denk, G. and Kränzl-Nagl, R. (1994) *Kinderbetreuung in Österreich*. Österreichisches Institut für Familienforschung, Vienna.

Stoll, M. (1995) Das Kind im Spannungsfeld zwischen Familie, Kindergarten und Arbeitswelt, in G. Knapp (ed.) *Kindergarten und Familie als Lebens- und Erfahrungsraum 'Politik für Kind-ge-Rechte Strukturen'*. Böhlau, Vienna and Cologne.

6

Belgium

A SOCIAL CONTEXT OF CHILDCARE AND
EDUCATION SERVICES

*[This chapter is based on commissioned reports submitted to the State
Institute of Early Childhood Education and Research (IFP) by Arlette
Delhaxhe (1994), Ferre Laevers (1995) and Gentile Manni (1994). See
Appendix I]*

AT A GLANCE

- Three communities (French, Flemish, German), each with responsibility for education and childcare services since 1989.
- A long tradition of institutionalized, publicly funded early childhood education centres with high levels of provision for approximately 95 per cent of 3–6-year-olds.
- Two separate administrative systems – welfare and education – with different structures and responsibilities: preprimary schooling for the 3–6-year-olds; welfare services for children under 3 and for school-age care and recreation.
- Statutory school age: 6 years.

Over the past two decades Belgium has developed into a federal state. Today it comprises

- three regions: Flanders, Wallonia, Brussels;
- three communities: French, Flemish, German; and
- four language areas: French, Dutch, German and Brussels as a bilingual area (French/Dutch).

Each community is responsible for childcare and education services in the region. Despite the federal structure, the systems are similar. The following account focuses on the French- and Flemish-speaking communities; the system

Transitions

Both entry into preprimary schooling and the transition to primary school are the focus of current debate. One question being asked is whether preprimary teachers are adequately trained to work with children aged 2$^1/_2$ years, particularly since most 2$^1/_2$ and 3-year-olds are in large groups – a development which has been the focus of critical discussion in professional circles. Concerning the transition to primary school, one solution towards improving continuity at present being discussed is the introduction of an integrated course of training for both preprimary and primary teachers.

B FORMS OF CHILDCARE AND EDUCATIONAL PROVISION

AT A GLANCE

- Preprimary schooling for 2$^1/_2$–6-year-olds; almost universal coverage; majority of preprimary centres attached to schools but with own educational programme.
- General approach in preprimary schooling structured, teacher-centred programme; pilot projects in Flanders with more child-centred approach.
- Paramedical tradition of provision for 0–3-year-olds focus of critical debate.
- Debate and research on issues of care and recreation provision for school-age children (particularly in Flanders).

Preprimary schooling (*kleuterschool/école maternelle/Vorschule* or *Kindergarten*)

Centres for preprimary education come under the responsibility of the Department of Education of the respective community. Opening hours are usually from 8.30 a.m. to 11.30 a.m. and 1.30 p.m. to 3.30 p.m., excepting Wednesday afternoons when centres are closed. Children are admitted at the age of 2$^1/_2$ and are usually grouped according to age. There are some mixed age-groups, but these are not common. Compulsory schooling begins at age 6. Staff in charge of a group are trained preschool teachers (*institutrice de maternelle/kleuterleid(st)er/Kindergärtner/in*) with a three-year training at tertiary level.

In the French-speaking community, one post for a qualified member of staff is allocated to groups of up to 19 children, for groups of 20–25 children one and a half posts, and for groups of 26–38 children two posts. On average there are 18 children in a group, but there are also considerable variations. Groups of 2¹/₂–3-year-olds may sometimes have more than 30 children at the beginning of a school year, and for this reason families prefer to register their children in the spring. The preschool teacher may be supported by a nursery assistant (*puéricultrice*). The inspectorate (part of the compulsory school system) have both an advisory and an inspection role.

In Flanders, group size may vary between 8 and 35 children, the average being 19. A trained preschool teacher (*kleuterleid(st)er*) has group responsibility, and there are seldom auxiliary staff.

Educational programme

The main objectives of preprimary schooling are similar in all three communities. These centre around the all-round development of children's social, cognitive and emotional potential. Church-run establishments also place importance on religious education. In the context of an educational programme emphasizing individual independence and group co-operation, preprimary schooling also explicitly aims to prepare children for school. Psychomotor and fine-motor development and linguistic competence are considered to be particularly important in this respect. The official guidelines emphasize the importance of a 'harmonious' transition from preprimary to primary schooling.

The French-speaking community is gradually adopting an approach introduced in France some years ago which divides both preprimary and primary schooling into three 'cycles' of learning. (This approach is explained in more detail in the chapter on France.) Just recently, however, questions have been raised concerning the appropriateness of the education offered the very young children in preprimary centres. Are staff adequately trained to meet the needs of 2¹/₂-year-old children in group settings? How far does the programme of activities and the general rhythm of school life take into account the situation of the youngest children? These are questions which need to be addressed.

Laevers (1995) describes the situation in Flanders as follows: despite the range of activities which takes place during the course of a day, the daily routine tends to be very structured. The teacher plays a central role in the preparing, selecting and organizing of activities, and written plans and reports are made of each day's work. In this teacher-centred programme, children's self-initiative is not of prime importance. This analysis of current practice was the starting point for an action research project in collaboration with practitioners based on the concept of 'experiential learning' (see Laevers, 1995, for a summary of this approach). A major aim of the project is to help teachers observe children more closely and to learn to see tasks, activities and situations from the child's perspective. The art of observation is systematically trained in order to help teachers understand children's interests and emotional needs more fully.

Table 6.1 Childcare and education services for children aged 0–6 years

Form of provision	Age of children/coverage rate*	Opening hours	Administrative responsibility
École maternelle/ kleuterschool/kinder- garten (preprimary centres)	2¹/₂–6 years 2¹/₂-year-olds: 70.2% 3-year-olds: 97.6% 4-year-olds: 99.3% 5-year-olds: 99.6%	8.30 a.m.–12.00 p.m. 1.30 p.m.–3.30 p.m. except Wednesday afternoons	Community Ministry of Education
Crèche/kribbe/Krippe (day nursery)	0–3 years	10–12 hours daily	Community Ministry of Social Welfare/state-funded organizations** • ONE • Kind en Gezin • DKF
Prégardiennat/ peutertuinen (daycare centre)	1¹/₂–3 years some children up to age 6 No information on coverage rates	10–12 hours daily	See above
MCAE – maison communale d'accueil de l'enfance ('community children's centre') – only a few of this type of centre, mostly in rural areas in the French-speaking community	0–6 years Coverage rate for 0–3-year-olds (including family daycare): approx. 30%	10–12 hours daily	Community Ministry of Social Welfare

Notes:
*European Commission (1995a); European Commission Network on Childcare (1996).
**ONE – Office de la Naissance et de l'Enfance (French-speaking community); Kind en Gezin (Flemish-speaking community); DFK – Dienst für Familie und Kind (German-speaking community).

Services for children under 3 years of age

There are three types of centre for children under 3 years of age:

• *Crèche/Kribbe/Krippe* for 0–3-year-olds.
• *Prégardiennat/peutertuinen* for children from 18 months to 3 years.
• *Maison communale d'acceuil de l'enfance (MCAE)* – community childcare centres for 0–6-year-olds (in the French-speaking community).

All these services are open for at least 10 hours daily. Staff with group responsibility in all three types are usually nursery workers. Larger centres are required to employ medical nurses and social workers, and medical nurses often hold the post of centre manager.

The community childcare centres are a relatively new type of service provided particularly in rural areas. They offer between 12 and 18 regular places and accept children from birth to compulsory school age. Children may also attend on a non-regular basis, or just for a few hours, providing parents with a flexible service which they can use according to their specific needs.

Care and recreation provision for school-age children

There is no overall policy concerning care and recreation provision for school children. The issue of after-school care is one which has long been neglected in Belgium and is now gaining more attention. Most facilities are provided by schools, but these have been established more as a result of pressing need rather than as planned strategy. Staff may be teachers, parents, nursery workers or other 'helpers'. None have specific qualifications for this kind of work, and there is no official programme of aims and activities. Holiday schemes, usually supervised adventure playgrounds, are staffed by 'mentors' who have completed a training scheme of 60–120 hours. They are not planned as a regular form of provision during holiday times, but are increasingly taking on this role. A further form of provision are so-called children's clubs, which have recently been expanded due to targeted funding by the Community Departments of Employment. These centres tend to have a sociopedagogic, playwork approach distinct from the mainly custodial approach of school-based facilities. Some daycare centres for children under 3 also accept school children outside regular school hours, but they cannot provide the room requirements needed for school children, nor are the staff trained to work with this age-group.

[C] STAFF TRAINING

AT A GLANCE

- Three-year training for preprimary teachers at higher education level.
- Two-year training for nursery workers at intermediate vocational level.

Under debate:

- Upgrading of nursery worker training with more focus on education issues.
- Training of personnel in out-of-school provision for school-age children.

The administrative split in services for 0–6-year-olds between 'education' for the 2¹/₂–6-year-olds and 'welfare' for the 0–2-year-olds is also reflected in the qualifications required for work in these two different sectors. Staff in preprimary centres are trained as preprimary teachers, staff in centres for younger children may be nursery workers, medical nurses or social workers. There are no formal training requirements for family daycarers.

Preprimary teacher

The three-year training of staff for work in preprimary centres takes place at vocational colleges of higher education specializing in teacher education (*Instituts Supérieurs de Pédagogie/Pedagogisch Hoger Onderwijs/Pädagogische Hochschule*) (see Table 6.2 for entry requirements).

Current course content in the French-speaking community includes the following:

- Academic subjects: Dutch, French, mathematics, art, music, movement and sport, history, geography.
- Professional studies: education, psychology, methods, classroom management, media technology, verbal expression.
- Social studies (familial, cultural and economic context of early childhood education).

All training modules include educational and didactic aspects of the subject-matter, aiming to integrate theory and practice. Work placements are spread over the three years, taking up two weeks in the first year, four weeks in the second year and twelve weeks in the third year of study.

The following is an example of course content in a Flemish training college (hours per week in the first, second and third years in brackets):

- religion (2, 2, 3).
- education (8, 9, 5).
- professional competence (2, 2, 0).
- Dutch (4, 3, 1).
- mathematics (1, 1, 1/2).
- environmental studies (2, 2, 1/2).
- home economics (1, 0, 0).
- health education and care (1, 1, 0).
- physical education (4, 3, 1).
- art education (4, 3, 1).
- music education (4, 3, 1).
- media education (0, 1, 0).

Work placements cover four weeks during the first year, eight weeks during the second year and sixteen weeks during the third year of study.

In 1994, preprimary teachers were awarded the same salary status as primary schoolteachers. In Flanders, the entire professional status and training

Table 6.2   Staff in childcare and education services

Professional title	Initial training/professional qualification	Fields of work
Instituteur/institutrice de maternelle/ kleuterleid(st)er/ Kindergärtnerin ('preprimary teacher')	*Entry requirements*: 12 years (general or vocational) schooling, upper secondary-education school-leaving certificate. Applicants with vocational certificate: 1 extra year *or* equivalent qualification. *Training*: 3 years at a college of higher education (*Institut Supérieur d'Enseignement Pédagogique/Pedagogisch Hoger Onderwijs/Pädagogische Hochschule*) – *Études de l'Enseignement Supérieure non-universitaire de type court/HOBU – Hoger Onderwijs Buiten Universiteit* – non-university higher education ('short type') *Award*: Diploma	*École maternelle/ kleuterschool/Kindergarten* (Preprimary schooling for 2¹/₂–6-year-olds)
Puéricultrice (not comparable with the more highly qualified *puéricultrice* in France) *kinderverzorging/ Kinderpflegerin* (nursery worker)	*Entry requirements*: 10 years general secondary school *Training*: 2 years upper secondary level (vocational branch) *Award*: Certificate	*Crèche* (0–3 years) *prégardiennat* (day nursery for 1¹/₂–3-year-olds) MCAE – *maison communale d'acceuil de l'enfance* (community children's centre, mostly in rural areas) *École maternelle*, as auxiliary worker, mostly with 2 and 3-year-olds Centres for handicapped children and elderly people
Assistante sociale/ maatschappelijk werk(st)er (social worker)	*Entry requirements*: 12 years schooling (general or vocational) with upper secondary-school leaving certificate. Applicants with vocational certificate: 1 additional year *or* equivalent award. *Training*: 3 years at higher vocational education institution – *Études de l'Enseignement Supérieure non-universitaire de type court/HOBU – Hoger Onderwijs Buiten Universiteit* – non-university higher education ('short type') *Award*: Diploma in social work	Diverse sociopedagogic work settings As part-time worker in day nurseries (large day nurseries are legally required to appoint an *assistante sociale*)
Infirmière/verpleegkundige/Krankenschwester (nurse)	*Entry requirements*: 12 years schooling (general or vocational branch) with upper secondary-school leaving certificate. Applicants with vocational certificate:	Day nurseries (as director) – large day nurseries are legally required to appoint an *infirmière/ verpfleegkundige*

Table 6.2   continued

Professional title	Initial training/professional qualification	Fields of work
	1 additional year *or* equivalent qualification *Training*: 3 years at a higher vocational education institution *Award*: *Infirmière graduée*	Hospitals and other forms of medical care
Infirmier/infirmière social(e)/sociaal verpleegkundige ('social nurse')	*Entry requirements*: 12 years schooling (general or vocational branch) with upper secondary-school leaving certificate. Applicants with vocational certificate: 1 additional year *or* equivalent qualification *Training*: 4 years at a higher vocational education institution *Award*: *Infirmière graduée sociale*	Social care/sociopedagogic work settings Part-time work in large day nurseries
Éducateur/opvoeder ('educator')	*Entry requirements*: 12 years schooling (general or vocational branch) with upper secondary-school leaving certificate. Applicants with vocational certificate: 1 additional year *or* equivalent qualification *Training*: 3 years at a higher vocational education institution *Award*: Diploma	Remedial and sociopedagogic work settings, mostly with school-age children

Note:
Care and recreation provision for children outside regular school hours is not generally staffed with qualified personnel.

of preschoolteachers is currently being debated. Three proposals have been made. To

- extend the length of training to four years;
- make courses more 'academically rigorous' in co-operation with universities; and
- introduce a common training for all teachers (preprimary, primary, secondary), with appropriate age-group specialization within that training.

Nursery worker (*puéricultrice/kinderverzogster/Kinderpfleger/in*)

Nursery workers with a two-year post-16 training are the largest group of qualified staff in all forms of daycare centres for children under 3 years of age (see Table 6.2 for details of entry requirements). Course content focuses mainly on social and medical care and home economics, but also includes subject areas such as music and art education and applied psychology. Work placements account for over half the two-year training scheme, and these usually take place in hospitals.

Both training and status of nursery workers have been criticized in professional circles in connection with debates on the quality of services in the welfare sector (Clymans, 1994; Humblet, 1994a; Manni, 1994). The strong practical orientation, with little dovetailing between theory and practice, and the heavy focus on paramedical care as opposed to education are the major weaknesses of the scheme, it is argued. Lack of career prospects is another issue which has been taken up particularly in the French-speaking community. Nursery workers are not allowed to take on management posts within centres, nor to contribute towards the training of prospective nursery workers. College tutors are usually medical nurses with at least five years' work experience and a supplementary examination award.

In both the Flemish and French communities there are special training courses for work in daycare centres for women wishing to re-enter the labour force after periods at home or of long unemployment. Nursery workers are involved in the on-site training component of these courses. Again, these measures have been heavily criticized because of the potential danger of undermining the already precarious professional status of nursery workers through the availability of cheaper, less qualified personnel.

REFERENCES AND SOURCES

Clymans, G. (1994) Le projet de reforme des études de puériculture. Mobilisation des acteurs et processus de décision. Unpublished thesis, Université Catholique de Louvain.

Delhaxhe, A. (1994) 'L'éducation préscolaire en Belgique' and 'La formation initiale des enseignants des écoles maternelles'. Report commissioned by the State Institute of Early Childhood Education and Research, Munich. EURYDICE, Brussels.

Deven, F. (1993) Flanders, in *Annual Report 1992, European Commission Network on Childcare*. Commission of the European Communities, Brussels.

Hindryckx, G. (1994) La journée d'un enfant de quatre ans en Communauté Française de Belgique, in F. Laevers (ed.) *Defining and Assessing Quality in Early Childhood Education*. University Press, Leuven.

Humblet, P. (1994a) Wallonia, in *Annual Report 1993, European Commission Network on Childcare*. Commission of the European Communities, Brussels.

Humblet, P. (1994b) Programme 1993. Les activités extra-scolaires: garde ou accueil? Unpublished MS, Ecole de Santé Publique de l'ULB, Brussels.

Laevers, F. (1995) *Early Childhood Education in Flanders*. Report commissioned by the State Institute of Early Childhood Education and Research, Munich. University of Leuven, Leuven.

Manni, G. (1994) *Formation du personnel et modes d'accueil des enfants de moins de trois ans en Communauté Française de Belgique.* Report commissioned by the State Institute for Early Childhood Education, Munich. University of Liège, Liège.

Ministère de l'Emploi et du Travail, Secrétariat de la Commision du travail des femmes et Ministre des Affaires sociales et de la Santé de la Communauté française et VBJK et NDO (eds.) (1993) *Accueil extra-scolaire. Une nouvelle approche. Guide pour un accueil centré sur l'enfant.* Vyncke, Ghent.

Peeters, J. (1994) Problem areas in Flemish childcare, in Resource and Training Center for Childcare (VBJK) and Department of General Psychology, University of Ghent (eds.) *Working Towards Better Childcare.* Vyncke, Ghent.

Vandenbroeck, M. (1994) School-age childcare: a state of affairs, in Resource and Training Center for Childcare (VBJK) and Department of General Psychology, University of Ghent (eds.) *Working Towards Better Childcare.* Vyncke, Ghent.

7

Denmark

SOCIAL CONTEXT OF CHILDCARE AND EDUCATION SERVICES

AT A GLANCE

- Statutory school age: 7 years.
- Well co-ordinated system of publicly funded childcare and education services.
- High employment rate for mothers with young children.
- Comprehensive social support measures for families.
- Decentralized administrative structures.
- Childhood policies integrated into related policy areas.

Denmark has a well co-ordinated system of high-quality childcare provision with a combination of full-day nurseries and kindergartens, age-integrated centres and out-of-school facilities, and publicly funded family daycare. This wide range of options helps families to combine parental responsibilities with employment outside the home. Since the passing of childcare legislation in 1964, the number of centres has increased rapidly, not only for the 3–7-year-olds (school entry age in Denmark is 7 years) but also for children under 3 years of age and for school children in out-of-school hours. Despite this expansion, there are still not enough places to satisfy the current demand, i.e. there are long waiting lists in some regions. The Danish government has pledged its support in providing a place for every child over the age of 12 months as from 1996. Although not backed by legislation, many local authorities have acted on the recommendation.

Denmark, a country with 5.6 million inhabitants, is divided into 275 municipalities, each responsible for providing, administering and inspecting all forms of publicly funded childcare provision. Within this framework, individual centres have considerable autonomy. The goal of this decentralized model is to cater for individual and regional needs through participatory processes. Childcare issues are high on the political agenda at a local level.

Daycare centres – historical development

The first institutions in Denmark for the out-of-home care of children were established about 170 years ago. A steadily increasing number of kindergartens based on Froebelian theories were set up during the second half of the nineteenth century alongside more custodial establishments. Around 1890 an attempt was made to combine these two forms of early childhood institutions into full-day folk kindergartens, which received a public subsidy for the first time in 1919. By 1950, 800 centres (nurseries, kindergartens, after-school facilities) had been established. However, the most significant phase of expansion took place during the last 30 years.

Parental employment, levels of provision

Alongside Sweden, Denmark has the highest rate of employed mothers in the EU. In 1993, 76 per cent of women with children aged 0–10 years were employed outside the home, 28 per cent in part-time jobs (European Commission Network on Childcare, 1996). In more than 40 per cent of families with young children both mother and father work 39 hours or more a week. At the same time, interviews with parents in Denmark have shown that full employment for both parents is not considered the ideal situation either for mothers with small children or for fathers. Both would prefer more part-time work for both parents, combined with more time with their children (Langsted and Sommer, 1993, p. 146).

One specific result of this ongoing 'quality of life' debate has been the issuing of new regulations concerning parental leave. In addition to the former 10 weeks parental leave (and 14 weeks maternity leave), each parent is now entitled to take between 13 and 56 weeks leave for the care of their children. Parents who take advantage of the childcare leave receive a basic compensation of 80 per cent of the payments during maternity and parental leave. Both mothers and fathers have an individual, non-transferable entitlement to this leave. Leave can be taken any time during the first eight years of the child's life.

In 1995, 48 per cent of children aged 0–3 years attended publicly funded services: 58 per cent were with family daycarers, and the remainder in day nurseries or age-integrated institutions. In the 3–6 age-group, 82 per cent attended publicly funded services, two thirds in kindergartens and a quarter in age-integrated institutions. Some 7 per cent were with family daycarers (European Commission Network on Childcare, 1996).

Policies for children – an integrated approach

In 1988, an important move was made to include policies for children in all spheres of political decision-making. An interdepartmental committee was set up, with representatives from 15 different ministries. The mission of this committee is to give issues concerning children and families crossdepartmental consideration and to develop appropriate action plans.

B FORMS OF CHILDCARE AND EDUCATIONAL PROVISION

AT A GLANCE

- Age-integrated centres for 0–6-year-olds or 0–12-year-olds alongside the more traditional age-ranges in centres.
- Since 1993: legislation giving parents the right of say in decisions concerning organization and content of centre programmes.
- Almost all 6-year-olds attend preschool classes attached to primary schools.
- Centres have considerable autonomy (including management of budget).
- Family daycare – a publicly funded service.
- Highest levels of provision in the EU for children under 3 and school-age children.
- General move towards locating care and leisure facilities for school children on school premises.

The most common forms of provision in the preschool and out-of-school sectors are day nurseries (*vuggestuer*) for children aged from 6 months to 2 years, kindergartens (*børnehaver*) for the 3–6-year-olds and out-of-school centres (*fritidshjem*) for children between 7 and 10 years, sometimes up to the age of 14 years. In recent years an increasing number of age-integrated institutions (*aldersintegrerede institutioner*) have been established for children of different age-ranges: birth to 6 years, 2–10 years, 3–12 years, birth to 14 years. All the above-mentioned forms of provision are regulated by the national Ministry of Social Affairs (*Socialministeriet*). Administrative responsibility is usually delegated to the municipalities. About one third of all provision is run by non-municipal organizations which receive state subsidies (Jensen, C., 1994, p. 144). Two further forms of provision outside the compulsory school system are regulated not by the Ministry of Social Affairs but by the national Ministry of Education (*Undervisningsministeriet*). These are the preschool classes (*børnehaveklasser*) for 6-year-olds attached to primary schools, and out-of-school facilities on school premises (*skolefritid-*

sordninger) for children aged 7–12 or 14 years. Publicly subsidized family daycare is seen as an equally important childcare option in Denmark. Family daycare providers are part of an organized system run by the social services department of the municipalities. Table 7.1 lists the various forms and main features of provision.

Administration and management of daycare centres

Both central and local government in Denmark are very reticent concerning guidelines and regulations for the running of daycare centres, and centres are accordingly granted a great deal of autonomy and responsibility. Staff, parents and children are involved in decision-making processes. Decisions are taken at three levels: by the local authority committee, by the centre committee and

Table 7.1 Childcare and education services for children aged 0–14 years

Form of provision	Age of children/ coverage rate*	Opening hours	Adminstrative responsibility
Vuggestue (day nursery)	6 months–2 years (11.6%)	10–12 hours per day	Ministry of Social Affairs/local authorities
Børnehaver (kindergarten)	3–5 years (49.2%)	12 hours per day 6.00 a.m.–6.00 p.m.	Ministry of Social Affairs/local authorities
Aldersintegrerede institutioner (age-integrated centre)	6 months–12 or 14 years 0–2 (10%) 3–5 (25.4%) 6–9	Full day	Ministry of Social Affairs/local authorities
Børnehaveklasser (preschool class attached to primary school)	5–6 years (approx. 98%)	4 hours, mornings only	Ministry of Education/local authorities
Fritidshjem (care and leisure centre for school-age children)	6–10 or 14 years (6–9 (59.3%**)	After school hours (1.00 p.m. onwards)	Ministry of Social Affairs/local authorities
Skolefritidsordninger (school-based care and leisure facilities)	6–10 or 14 years	Before and after school hours	Ministry of Education/local authorities
Dagpleje (family daycare)	0–6 years (sometimes older) 6 months–2 years (33.5%) 3–5 (5.7%)	Contract agreement	Local authorities

Note:
*Figures for 1995, Ministry of Social Affairs, Copenhagen 1996.
**Figures for *all* kinds of publicly-funded centres for 6–9-year olds.

by the director of the centre. Formalized parental participation was increased in 1993. All daycare centres now have an elected committee of parents and staff representatives, with parents comprising the majority. The committee decides on the educational objectives and activities of the centre, on the allocation of funds, and advises the local authority committee on staff appointments. It is not responsible for decisions concerning individual children. The head of the centre is responsible for the educational and administrative work of the centre and ensures that decisions made by the centre committee are carried out.

Day nurseries (*vuggestuer*)

Children under the age of 3 may either attend a day nursery (about 11 per cent of the age-group) or – more often – they will be looked after by a family daycare provider (about 30 per cent). Day nurseries are open for 10–12 hours per day and accommodate between 30 and 40 children. The children are generally in mixed age-groups. Group size may vary between 8 and 12 children who are cared for by one or two qualified staff and one or two helpers, depending on the centre and the municipality. Each child is assigned a particular member of staff who is responsible for the daily rituals such as changing nappies, washing and being put to bed. The centres aim to provide a stimulating and caring environment.

Kindergartens (*børnehaver*)

Most kindergartens are open 10–12 hours a day, usually from around 6.00 a.m. until 6.00 p.m. In urban areas up to 80 per cent of the children attend on a full-time basis. Mixed age-groups are becoming the accepted form. There are normally three adults present in a group of 20 children for at least half the day, and for the remaining time two adults. About 50 per cent of staff working in daycare centres are fully qualified (up to 1992 as a kindergarten educator, as from 1992 as a 'pedagogue'). Ancillary staff have no formal qualifications, although they generally attend courses run by the local authority.

Education and care are part of an integrated concept of 'educare'. The underlying principles of Danish kindergarten philosophy can be traced back to the ideas and theories of Froebel and Montessori, with adaptations to Scandinavian culture. Self-initiated play is considered to be very important for the children's overall development. A major educational goal is to help children realize that they can actively influence what goes on in their immediate surroundings. This democratic principle is even anchored in the official guidelines. Daycare centres are to create a framework – together with parents *and the children* – which supports the independent development of each child. Further the *children must be listened to* and – according to their age and ability – value should be placed on the *participation of children* in the planning of activities. This is how they learn about the interdependence of influence and responsibility – not only for themselves but also for the community (Boelskov, 1993, p. 5).

Handicapped children attend mainstream centres wherever possible. They are either integrated into the group, or are members of an additional group attached to the centre.

Age-integrated centres (*aldersintegrerede institutioner*)

The first age-integrated centre was opened at the beginning of the 1970s. In the mean time about 20 per cent of children up to the age of 9 registered in publicly funded provision attend this type of centre (Jensen, J.J., 1993, p. 37). In recent years a fundamental restructuring process has taken place, and many day nurseries and kindergartens have been transformed into centres for children from 6 months to 6 years. Some centres take children up to the age of 10, 12 or even 14 years, and for at least part of the day the children are in groups with a wide age-range. However, it is the centres for children up to compulsory school age which have spread most rapidly, and it could well be that these will prove to be the most popular form of provision in future. Interviews with staff suggest that the level of job satisfaction in these age-integrated centres is high (Jensen, J.J., 1993).

Preschool classes (*børnehaveklasser*)

The great majority (95 per cent) of 6-year-old children attend a preschool class before starting school at the age of 7. These classes attached to the primary schools are open mornings only for four hours. Staff trained to work in preschool and out-of-school facilities ('pedagogues') often work in a preschool class in the morning and in after-school facilities on the school premises in the afternoon. This ensures continuity for the children and they are spared the walk – often under heavy traffic conditions – to another centre. Since 1989 it is possible to organize a so-called 'co-ordinated school start' (Vilien, 1993, p. 30). About half of all primary schools have adopted this model, which involves the preschool class co-operating closely with the first two grades of primary school, e.g. through across-class project work.

Daycare centres for school children

Daycare facilities for school children are run by professionally qualified 'pedagogues', either in separate centres (*fritidsjhem*) or directly on the school premises (*skolefritidsordninger*). It is the school-based provision – initially set up during the 1980s – that has spread most rapidly during the last few years (partly because of economic reasons) and which is expected to become the most accepted form of provision in the future, with pedagogues and not the head of school in charge. Programme emphasis is on creative and cultural

university entrance requirement acquired by the successful completion of upper secondary education. The remaining 80 per cent of candidates have various 'other' qualifications, such as vocational qualifications of some kind,

Table 7.2   Staff in childcare and education services

Professional title	Initial training/professional qualification	Fields of work (rank order indicates frequency)
Up to 1992 there were three separate training schemes: Børnehavepaedagog ('kindergarten educator')	*Entry requirements:* 12 years' schooling *or* diverse other possibilities (see entry requirements for *paedagog*) *Training:* 3 years at a seminary (= non-university higher education institution specializing in this field of training)	Educational and social care establishments for children and young people: • kindergarten • age-integrated centres • preschool classes attached to primary schools • day nurseries • out-of-school leisure centres • school-based care facilities • leisure facilities/youth clubs
Fritidspaedagog ('leisure time educator')	*Entry requirements:* 12 years' schooling *or* diverse other possibilities (see entry requirements for *paedagog*) *Training:* 3 years at a seminary (= non-university higher education institution specializing in this field of training)	Educational and social care establishments for children and young people: • out-of-school leisure centres • age-integrated centres • school-based care facilities • kindergarten • preschool classes attached to primary schools • leisure facilities/youth clubs • day nurseries • 24-hour care for children and young persons
Socialpaedagog ('social care worker/special needs')	*Entry requirements:* 12 years' schooling *or* diverse other possibilities (see entry requirements for *paedagog*) *Training:* 3 years at a seminary (= non-university higher education institution specializing in this field of training)	Special needs services for children, young people and adults

In 1992 the above-mentioned three schemes were integrated into one training programme for the new professional qualification of paedagog:

Table 7.2   continued

Professional title	Initial training/professional qualification	Fields of work (rank order indicates frequency)
Paedagog ('pedagogue')	*Entry requirements:* Minimum age of entry: 18 years	Educational and social care establishments for children, young people and adults. Childcare provision includes:

Paedagog
('pedagogue')

Entry requirements:
Minimum age of entry: 18 years

1. 12 years' schooling with higher secondary examination (*Studentereksamen*) *or* HF-eksamen (examination award of equivalent institution *or* HH-eksamen (higher vocational) *or* HTX-eksamen (higher technical) *or* GIF (higher secondary course for refugees))
or
2. 9 years' schooling plus 2 passes in HF-subjects (Danish and one other subject) plus at least two years work experience
or
3. completed apprenticeship *or* EFG/HG-eksamen *or* a specialist training of at least 2.5 years *or* the entrance examination for a social and health training *or* 12 years' Rudolf Steiner schooling
or
4. secondary examination of another country

Candidates are admitted according to a quota system:

- quota 1 (20% of intake): candidates with the highest grades in the upper secondary examination
- quota 2 (80%) of intake): 'other' candidates take a qualifying examination and must fulfil the requirements (2), (3) or (4) above. These may include: general personal qualifications and experience, e.g. work experience, vocational training, exchange visits abroad, residence abroad; relevant professional experience, e.g. work in a social institution, community work, work in leisure facilities, co-operation with parents, committee work; relevant examination subjects, i.e. single subject at HF or 10th grade level, e.g. in Danish, drama, philosophy, handicraft, home economics, sport, media studies, music, ecology, psychology, sociology

Training:
3.5 years (41 months) at a higher education institution specializing in this scheme of training

Educational and social care establishments for children, young people and adults. Childcare provision includes:

- day nurseries
- kindergarten
- age-integrated centres
- preschool classes attached to primary schools
- out-of-school leisure centres
- school-based care facilities
- leisure facilities/youth clubs

Special needs services for children, young people and adults, e.g.:

- hospital children's ward
- residential care for children and young people
- residential care for the handicapped
- portage schemes
- diverse services for adults, e.g. drug users, alcoholics

Educational administration and consultancy

relevant work experience or particular life experience (such as living abroad for a time). This means that the average age of students is higher than in most other countries where the school leavers predominate. Those embarking on a career are on average around 28 years of age. The new training scheme is not only enormously popular (in 1993 more than 80 per cent of candidates had to be turned down) but it is also an option chosen by men.

The training lasts three and a half years (41 months) and includes integrated workplace experience (12 weeks unpaid in the first year of study, 26 weeks paid during the second and third years). The on-site placements are selected in three different workfields. In some training institutions the course can be attended on a part-time basis. This is often the option chosen by childcare assistants who have five years' work experience in a centre.

The course forms a theoretical and practical basis for work with children, young people, adults and the elderly, including persons with physical, psychological and social handicaps. During the course of study it is possible to specialize within certain subject areas and workplace settings. Topics for in-depth study are chosen collaboratively by students and teaching staff within the framework requirements of the course. Teaching and learning methods are diverse and adaptable. The emphasis is on projects and teamwork.

A particular focus of this training lies in strengthening the individual and communicative abilities of the students. Key competences for the profession – such as decision-making, flexibility, creativity – are both illustrated and fostered in a variety of concrete practice-based situations. The emphasis is on learning by 'doing' rather than on the acquisition of formalized knowledge. *Paedagoger* are generalists rather than specialists.

The subject areas studied are as follows (hours per semester in brackets):

- Education and psychology (30).
- Social theory and health education (20).
- Cultural and physical activities (40): Danish; music; sport and movement; craft and design; drama; ecology studies; other topics.
- Communication (10): organizational theory; leadership.

The reform was also used to extend the international dimension of training. During the fifth semester students spend several weeks in a work placement abroad. In addition, contacts with other European countries are encouraged by means of study tours, exchanges of training staff and international seminars.

The professional award at the end of the course of study opens up the possibility of work in a wide range of settings:

- Childcare provision of all kinds.
- Special kindergartens and groups in mainstream centres for handicapped children.
- 'Open institutions' such as family centres or advisory centres – in close

collaboration with social workers, psychologists and other specialists.
- Hospitals with a children's ward.
- The admissions office in regional social services departments
- The co-ordination and professional supervision of family daycare services.
- Residential care for children and young people.
- Residential care for the severely handicapped.
- Home visiting.
- Advisory services for drug users.

In-service training and professional development

In-service training is provided by national institutions (such as the Royal Danish School of Educational Studies or the School for Advanced Training of Social Pedagogues), the professional organization BUPL and the local authorities. Those interested in taking up a course at the Royal Danish School may apply to be seconded from work for one day a week over a period of two and a half years. All branches of BUPL hold courses, e.g. courses of 30 hours on leadership for centre directors.

The course of professional study at the Royal Danish School focuses on different theoretical approaches during the first year, and during the second year participants study an option of their choice and write a dissertation. While the certificate (*cand. paed.*) is not officially recognized by the government, it does carry weight in practice. Most professional advisers employed by the local authorities have completed one of these courses, for example. The Royal Danish School has 13 local branches.

On-site in-service training can also be arranged if the director of the centre considers this appropriate. A major goal of the courses offered by the local authorities is to strengthen the effectiveness and the autonomy of the daycare centres by enhancing the leader's decision-making and conflict resolution skills.

A system of professional support through advisers or consultants has not been developed everywhere. Only 75 of the 275 municipalities employ advisers. These professionals have both an advisory and inspection mandate. Advisers are normally childcare professionals with long years of experience, including that of directing a centre. They have usually completed a course of further study at one of the national centres for in-service training. The advisers also aim to support the autonomy of the centres. Centres may apply for sessions with an independent consultant if this is considered necessary.

Career structure

Career prospects for *paedagoger* are currently very good. This may be the significant motivating factor for the choice of this profession. The number of students rose from 3,500 in 1992–3 to 4,300 in 1993–4. At present there are around 60,000 persons employed in the fields of childcare and social care,

15 per cent of them being men. Full-time *paedagoger* work a 37-hour week. In childcare services, around 32 hours are spent in direct contact with the children. The director of a centre works for 20 hours with the children, the deputy director some hours more.

'Pedagogues' receive a salary similar to that of other professional groups in public education and care services (e.g. primary schoolteachers, social workers, nurses). At the start of his or her career a *paedagog* is responsible for a group of children. After some years' experience it is possible to be appointed as deputy director, or even as the head of a centre. Directors are paid according to the size of the centre, i.e. the number of children attending.

Paedagoger with job experience who have completed a course of further study may apply for a post in social administration with the local authorities. This may involve being responsible for the admissions to daycare centres, or co-ordinating family daycare services in the municipality – two posts which all local authorities allocate. They are also eligible for educational consultancy posts where these are available. Over 90 per cent of staff in childcare services are members of the professional organization BUPL.

REFERENCES AND SOURCES

Boelskov, B. (1993) Altersübergreifende Kindergruppen (0–12 Jahre) in Dänemark, in P. Oberhuemer (ed.) *Blick auf Europa – Tageseinrichtungen für Kinder. Sonderheft der Zeitschrift Theorie und Praxis der Sozialpädagogik, TPS–extra*, Vol. 13, pp. 5–7.

Corsini, A. (1991) Family day care in Denmark: a model for the United States? *Young Children*, Vol. 46, no. 5, pp. 10–15.

Danish Ministry of Education (1995) *The Educator Training Programme*. Ministry of Education, International Relations Division, Copenhagen.

Danish Ministry of Social Affairs (1993) *Social Policy in Denmark. Child and Family Policies*. Ministry of Social Affairs, Copenhagen.

Frøbelseminariet (1993) *Course Profile*. Frøbelseminariet, Copenhagen.

Jensen, C. (1994) Fragments for a discussion about quality, in P. Moss and A. Pence (eds.) *Valuing Quality in Early Childhood Services. New Approaches to Defining Quality*. Paul Chapman, London.

Jensen, J. J. (1993) Denmark, in *Annual Report 1993, European Commission Network on Childcare*. Commission of the European Communities, Brussels.

Jensen, J. J. (1994) Denmark, in *Annual Report 1994, European Commission Network on Childcare*. Commission for the European Communities, Brussels.

Langsted, O. and Sommer, D. (1993) Denmark, in M. Cochran (ed.) *International Handbook of Child Care Policies and Programs*. Westport, Conn. and London, Greenwood Press.

Lauridsen, S. K. (1993) The training of childcare and social care workers in Denmark – an educational challenge. Jydsk Paedagog-Seminarium, Risskov.

Qvortrup, J. and Christoffersen, M. N. (1991) *Childhood as a Social Phenomenon. National Report Denmark. EUROSOCIAL Reports* Vol. 36. European Centre for Social Welfare Policy and Research, Vienna.

Rogvi, K. à (1993) Parents and services, in *Parental Employment and Caring for*

Children: Policies and Services in EC and Nordic Countries (conference report). Danish Ministry of Social Affairs, Copenhagen.

Vilien, K. (1993) Provision for preschool children in Denmark, in T. David (ed.) *Educational Provision for our Youngest Children: European Perspectives.* Paul Chapman, London.

8

Finland

[This chapter is based on a commissioned report by Pirjo Honkavaara (Central Union for Child Welfare, Helsinki) submitted to the State Institute of Early Childhood Education and Reseach (IFP) in December 1995. See Appendix I for further details.]

[A] SOCIAL CONTEXT OF CHILDCARE AND EDUCATION SERVICES

AT A GLANCE

- High level of maternal employment on a full-time basis compared with other EU countries.
- Well developed system of publicly funded centre-based provision and family daycare.
- Since 1990: legal entitlement to a place in publicly funded services for 0–3-year-olds; statutory right extended to include 4–7-year-olds in 1996.
- Statutory school age: 7 years.
- Comprehensive social benefits for families, both for extrafamilial childcare arrangements and for family-based care.
- Trend towards decentralization and delegation of responsibility to municipal authorities.

Finland gained independence in 1917, having been first under Swedish and then Russian rule for many years. Even today, around 10 per cent of the Finnish population speaks Swedish as a first language, and Swedish is still an official language.

Development of provision: historical background

Kindergartens were introduced to Finland by Hanna Rothman, a pioneer early childhood educator who studied in Berlin. On her return to Helsinki in 1888 she opened the first kindergarten based on Froebel's educational philosophy. The Froebel approach was to have a strong influence on subsequent developments, even to the present day. The first course of professional training for work in kindergartens was launched as early as 1892, and in 1919 kindergarten educators founded the first professional association in Finland for early childhood education.

Kindergartens were initially maintained by charities and sometimes through municipal subsidies. A framework for the public funding of kindergartens was created by the Finnish Child Welfare Act 1936. Other kinds of public facilities for children were established at the beginning of the twentieth century. The first public play schemes and holiday camps were founded in 1906, and in 1908 hospitals began to offer play therapy sessions for children in their care. Playgroups and play schemes expanded rapidly during the 1940s. The Lutheran Church in particular reacted to the growing need for provision which could not be met by the publicly funded centres. Even today, church-run playgroups for young children constitute an important part of the Finnish childcare system.

Urbanization, female employment

Industrialization reached Finland comparatively late compared with other European countries. The transformation from an agricultural to an industrial society started during the 1940s, and by the 1960s this was leading to radical changes in Finnish society. A massive wave of migration from the rural areas in the north to the industrial centres in the south affected large parts of the population. The rapid growth of the urban population combined with the large numbers of mothers at work resulted in tremendous problems concerning the daytime care of children. Many mothers had to resort to leaving their children with private childminders operating under low-standard conditions. This crucial situation triggered off public debate on the quality of care for very young children, and finally led to the legislation which guaranteed all children under 3 years of age a place in publicly funded provision.

Finland had a comparatively high participation rate of mothers in the labour force. However, with the onset of recession in the early 1990s, the number of unemployed rose significantly, peaking at 20 per cent of the labour force, and affecting women in particular. In 1993 the employment rate of mothers with children aged 0–10 years was 63 per cent, with only 8 per cent working part time (European Commission Network on Childcare, 1996).

Legislation and family support measures, provision

Finland has for many decades considered itself a welfare state. Over the years a comprehensive range of social benefits has been introduced to help support families with children. Legislation in the mid-1980s set out to improve children's status in society. Since the Child Law Act 1983 all children are equal before the law, independent of the legal status of their parents; they are allowed access to both parents in the case of divorce; and all forms of corporal punishment (also by parents) are forbidden. Children aged 0–3 years were granted an individual, statutory right to childcare provision. This can be a place in a daycare centre, a place in publicly funded family daycare or parents receive a childcare allowance if they prefer to care for their child at home. Since January 1996 all children below statutory school age (7 years) have this entitlement. This comprehensive system of publicly funded support allows parents to choose the childcare option most suited to their particular needs. They can also combine different forms with one another if they so wish.

In 1994, 21 per cent of the age-group 0–3 years attended publicly funded services. Of these a little more than half (53 per cent) attended centres the remainder family daycare (European Commission Network on Childcare, 1996).

Compulsory schooling starts at age 7 in Finland. Six-year-olds sometimes attend a kind of 'preschool class' attached either to a daycare centre or a school. Daycare centres are open for children from birth to compulsory school age. Of children under the age of 7, 55 per cent attend centre-based provision (Ministry of Social Affairs, 1995). Over 60 per cent of children aged 4–6 years attend a playgroup organized by the Lutheran Church. Family daycare is a popular option for children under 3. Provision for school children is scarce, and generally not regulated. In contrast to the early childhood sector, after-school care has not received much attention. Deficits in this area have only just recently become a target of public debate.

Administrative responsibility

At a national level the Ministry of Social Affairs and Health is responsible for   childcare and education services outside the compulsory school system. For some years now there has been a move away from centralized regulation and responsibility for the funding, management and monitoring of services, which has been gradually transferred to the regional and local authorities.

Current issues and trends

Welfare state – recession – decentralization – privatization

Recession started to affect Finland at the end of the 1980s. In a country accustomed to full employment the rate of unemployment rose to almost 20 per cent. There is widespread concern that cuts in public funding and increased privatization of services will lead to a dismantling of the welfare state. Finland's entry into the European Union in 1995 was also seen by some as a threat to the high level of social benefits which Finland had achieved. Cuts are also feared in the area of childcare provision.

Transition to school – school entry age

In connection with Finland's entry into the European Union, there has been talk of lowering the statutory school age from 7 to 6 years. A number of alternatives are being discussed. An interministerial group (Education and Social Affairs) is currently developing a system of 'didactic units' for 6-year-olds which can be implemented either in daycare centres or in preschool classes attached to schools.

Provision for school children

Out-of-school provision has not been systematically developed in Finland. One reason is that funding allocated to the local authorities for childcare has been used primarily for provision for young children, since it was in this area that public pressure was greatest.

Changes in training

Training schemes for work in the early childhood and out-of-school field are currently under review. Initial training for work in daycare centres was upgraded to university level in 1995, one argument being the need for greater interconnectedness between training and research. Beyond this, there are plans for joint course units for early childhood educators and primary schoolteachers. Some professionals approve of this move, others see a danger in stressing the academic side of training while neglecting the specific needs of young children.

Another area of reform concerns the training of auxiliary staff. For example, training courses for nursery nurses (*lastenhoitaja*) have changed their focus on childhood and child welfare to a more broadly based social care and community work qualification (*lähihoitaja*) for work with different age-groups in diverse settings. Changes in the training for playgroup leaders represent an even more radical move away from a specific focus on work with children. There is a trend towards accepting any kind of relevant vocational qualification (e.g. as a carpenter), and it is up to the employing organization to provide workplace-relevant training sessions.

In general, specific training schemes and a centralized regulation of vocational training are losing significance. In future it will be more important to have a completed apprenticeship of any kind, even if it is not specifically related to the workfield in question. This also applies to the field of care and education services. One reason is to give employers more choice when considering applicants; another is to give employees more choice of work options. There is also a move towards making the whole process of training more flexible through the introduction of a system of module units which can be combined in a variety of ways.

B FORMS OF CHILDCARE AND EDUCATIONAL PROVISION

AT A GLANCE

- Full-day early childhood centres for 0–7-year-olds.
- Playgroups run by the Lutheran Church, mainly for 4–6-year-olds.
- Different kinds of publicly funded family daycare regulated by municipal authorities.
- Curriculum and methodology in early childhood centres based on the Froebel tradition, with mixed age-grouping and community orientation.
- Every third member of staff in centre-based care must be a trained educator.

Table 8.1 illustrates the main forms of provision in Finland: local authority and private daycare centres (for 0–7-year-olds), the Lutheran Church playgroups and family daycare.

Daycare centres are the most common form of provision in the cities, whereas family daycarers are more widespread in rural areas. Mobile kindergartens are provided in sparsely populated areas, offering sessions mainly for 5–7-year-olds. At the beginning of 1994 approximately 63 per cent of publicly funded places were in centre-based care and 37 per cent in family daycare. The number of family daycare places has decreased in recent years, and the number of places in centres has increased. All children up to compulsory school age are statutorily entitled to a place in publicly funded provision.

The playgroups for 4–6-year-olds run by the Lutheran Church do not provide the full-day care offered by the centres.

Daycare centres (päiväkoti)

Most daycare centres are provided by the municipalities. However, the local authorities may fall back on private sector provision if their own resources are insufficient to satisfy the demand. In the past centres were traditionally divided into two age bands, with children under 3 years of age grouped together, and the 3–7-year-olds in mixed age-groups. Today some centres

Table 8.1 Childcare and education services for children aged 0–7 years

Form of provision	Age of children in years/coverage rate*	Opening hours	Administrative responsibility
Päiväkoti (early childhood centre); also: • 'open-door' centres for family daycarers, parents and children; • 'mobile kindergartens' in sparsely populated areas	0–7-year-olds (*c.* 55%)	At least 10 hours per day Some for 24 hours a day for parents working shifts	Ministry of Social Affairs/local authorities
Päiväkerho (playgroup)	Mostly 4–6-year-olds (66%) Some school-age children	2–3 hour sessions on 3–4 mornings Some afternoon groups	Lutheran Church
Perhepäivähoito (family daycare); also group meetings on municipal premises	Mostly 0–7-year-olds	Individual arrangements	Local authorities

Note:
*Figures for coverage rate: Ministry of Social Affairs, 1995.

prefer a wider age mix, particularly if siblings attend the centre. Most children under the age of 3 in centres have a full-time place.

Daycare centres are open for 10 hours per day, a few for 24 hours a day (for parents working shifts). They provide full-day and part-time education and care. Some centres offer special programmes for 6-year-olds, and some take school children during after-school hours.

So-called 'open-door' centres exist alongside the regular provision. These are primarily for children in family daycare or for children looked after at home by their parents. A qualified member of staff (usually an educator) organizes activities for children and parents; these include lectures and workshops for parents and family daycarers on child-rearing and child development.

Educational activities

Early childhood education in Finland has been strongly influenced by the Froebel tradition. Only a few (private) centres adhere to a different approach (e.g. based on Montessori or Steiner).

Finnish and Swedish are the two official languages in Finland. Swedish children are entitled to instruction in their mother tongue. Local authorities are obliged to organize provision in the appropriate language, i.e. Finnish, Swedish or Lapp.

Today's daycare centres generally function as a kind of neighbourhood centre for the region. Alongside regular provision, activities are also provided for children attending on an hourly basis. Providing a forum for parents and family daycarers and other community-oriented work are also important tasks.

Wherever possible, handicapped children are integrated into mainstream groups – based on a calculation of two daycare places for one disabled child.

Staffing

Staffing regulations were laid down in the 1973 Childcare Act and also apply to private centres. Each centre has a manager or director who is a trained educator (*lastentarhanopettaja*) or social educator (*sosiaalikasvattaja*) – both have a three-year training at tertiary level. The manager is usually responsible for a group of children and is exempted from this duty only in very large centres. The manager is also responsible for the supervision and co-ordination of local family daycare providers. Auxiliary staff are generally trained nursery assistants or paediatric nurses (*lastenjoitaja*), or community carers (*lastenohjaaja*). Specialist trained staff, most of them peripatetic, are also employed to help children with special needs.

Under present legislation, daycare centres are obliged to employ at least one suitably trained person for not more than seven children over the age of 3 in full-time care, and at least one suitably trained person for not more than four children under the age of 3. At least one in three staff must be a trained kindergarten educator or social educator. Maximum group size is 12 for children under 3, and 20 for the 3–7-year-olds (12 for mixed-aged groups from 0 to 7). The preschool classes for 6-year-olds take up to 25 children.

Family daycare

Family daycare in Finland is part of the publicly funded system of childcare provision. Of the costs for organized family daycare, 42 per cent are funded by central government and local authorities. Parents pay an income-related fee to cover the remaining costs. Private family daycare is indirectly subsidized through childcare benefits.

Most family daycare providers are employed by the local authorities; privately employed childminders have to have an official licence. Providers may take up to four children under 6 years of age, including their own children, and one school-age child. Organized family daycare providers are given a training of around 250 hours by the local authorities and receive regular supervision.

Family daycare is a popular childcare option in Finland (Karlsson, 1995, p. 32). In 1992, 42 per cent of all children under the age of 7 in publicly funded provision were in family daycare.

Besides family daycare either in the child's home or in the provider's home there is a so-called 'three-family model' in Finland. Children and provider spend one week at a time in the home of the three families involved. Family daycare can also be organized in groups. This entails two to three childminders jointly looking after the children in their care on premises supplied by the local authority.

Family daycare providers are entitled to the same social benefits as other employees: paid holidays, parental leave, sick leave, pension rights, etc. Persons in organized family daycare sign an agreement that they are willing to stand in for other providers in the case of sickness, holidays or training leave. Of the providers employed by municipal authorities, 81 per cent are members of the union for local government employees (Karlsson, 1995, p. 33). Self-employed childminders negotiate their conditions of service directly with the parents.

Playgroups (*päiväkerho*)

Playgroups run by the Lutheran Church have existed for over 50 years. Children attend for a few hours on three or four mornings a week, occasionally in the afternoon. They cater mainly for the 4–6 age-group, but some are attended by younger and older children. Over 60 per cent of the 4–6-year-olds attend a playgroup. This number is so high because it includes not only children normally looked after by their parents but also children in family daycare, and sometimes children attending a daycare centre, too. Playgroups are also often used as a form of after-school care for school children during the first few years of school.

Church playgroups are an accepted part of life in Finland. Although the number of regular church-goers is small, about 90 per cent of the population are members of the Lutheran Church and pay church taxes. Children from non-Lutheran families also attend the playgroups.

Staff employed are occasionally qualified educators, but more often nursery assistants or paediatric nurses. The Lutheran Church maintains 10 colleges to train people for work in early childhood and community services.

Community facilities for children of all ages

Most out-of-school leisure time facilities are non-regulated. Municipal 'play centres' for all age-groups are quite common – generous outdoor playspace combined with supervised indoor activities. Children under 4 years of age have to be accompanied by an adult. The emphasis in recent years has changed from an exclusive focus on activities for children: many centres are now called 'family parks'. Staff are usually 'play park leaders' (a non-regemented course of training), but may also be early childhood educators, paediatric nurses, youth workers or people interested in handicrafts or sport.

C STAFF TRAINING

AT A GLANCE

- Training courses at all levels under review.
- Initial training as early years educator now at university level (since 1995); courses heavily oversubscribed.
- Introduction of broad-based courses at the intermediate level which include a whole range of social care activities rather than emphasizing child-related work.
- Introduction of more flexible vocational qualification schemes and training arrangements, e.g. for playgroup workers.
- Course of training (250 hours) for family daycarers.

Initial training for staff working with children in non-statutory settings is currently undergoing radical changes. There are two major trends: one is the upgrading of tertiary-level courses (early childhood educator, social educator); the other represents a move away at intermediate level from specialist training courses (e.g. in childcare) to more broadly based social and healthcare qualifications. Table 8.2 outlines the main professional qualifications needed to work in the field. It also documents recent changes.

Early years educator (*lastentarhanopettaja*)

Initial training

Before 1995 educators completed a three-year course of training at a non-university higher education training college. This was then replaced by a university-level course of studies. This is not a radical change, since many training colleges had co-operated closely with universities since the mid-1970s. However, training is now officially integrated into the university system.

This is a popular training option and heavily oversubscribed. Currently, only one in four or five applicants is successful in obtaining a place. While entry requirements have remained the same, as have the length and the main objectives of training, entrance examinations are changing considerably. School-leaving certificate grades still count towards initial selection. However, in the second round applicants have to complete a series of proficiency tasks successfully including a set essay, various interviews and a supervised visit of 15–20 minutes in a daycare centre.

In terms of content, the amount of academic work has increased, combined with a decrease in the practical side of training. Practical placements now comprise 10–15 per cent of the course, i.e. 10–15 weeks. Course content of the new module system is broader than that of the former training scheme. The course comprises 120 units which are weighted as follows:

- Education (35): theory (15); curriculum studies (20).
- Methods of early childhood education (35).
- Professional studies (27): psychology and sociology (15); practical placements (12).
- Subsidiary studies (e.g. social policy) (15).
- Language and communication (8).

Another new feature is the opportunity to complete an additional course of a further 40 units which qualifies early years educators for work in the lower grades of primary school.

In-service training, further studies, professional status

In-service training is not obligatory. Courses provided by the local authorities are free of charge; those offered by other organizations (e.g. professional associations, universities) require a tuition fee. Courses are well attended, including the fee-paying seminars outside working hours, even though attendance does not necessarily raise promotion chances or result in higher pay.

Traditionally, promotion prospects for early years educators included centre management, the supervision of family daycarers or administrative work for the local authorities. They could also complete a one-year course to qualify as a special needs educator. The upgrading of initial training has brought with it the additional possibility of qualifying as a primary school-teacher. It also means that students can continue their academic studies if they so wish.

Both early years educators and schoolteachers are public sector employees, and both professional groups are organized in the same union. However, educators earn less than their colleagues in primary schools. Despite upgrading and integration at university level, a general climate of recession and high unemployment means that this situation is unlikely to change in the near future.

Social educator (sosiaalikasvattaja)

The Childcare Act 1973 had implications concerning the personnel structure and training of staff for work in childcare and education services. Besides early childhood educators, staff trained as social educators may now also work in daycare centres. In the 1970s the course focus – traditionally residential care – broadened to include early childhood and out-of-school provision.

Training takes place at colleges of social welfare – tertiary-level institutions – and lasts three or four years (see Table 8.2). Compared with the initial

Table 8.2   Staff in childcare and education services

Professional title	Initial training/professional qualification	Fields of work
Lastentarhanopettaja (educator, early years)	*Entry requirements:* 12 years' schooling plus leaving certificate; entrance examination *Training:* Before 1995: 3 years at a non-university higher education institution; award: *lastentarkanopettagan futkinto* Since 1995: 3 years' university studies; award: *kasvatustieteen leandidaatti*	Usual field of work: daycare centres for 0–7-year-olds; sometimes: after-school care; occasionally: teaching in first 2 grades of primary school
Sosiaalikasvattaja ('social educator')	*Entry requirements:* Completion of 12 years' school with leaving certificate *Training:* 3 years at 'College for social work professions'	Sociopedagogical work settings, usually as manager or director e.g. residential homes for children and young people, youth centres, occasionally daycare centres
Lastenjoitaja (nursery nurse – up to 1992) *Lähijoitaja* (social carer – post-1992)	*Entry requirements:* Minimum age: 17 years; completion of 9 years' schooling *Training:* 2 years, 6 months at 'college for social work professions'; training lasts only 1 year, 6 months if candidates have completed 12 years of schooling; change from specialist training (before 1992) to broad-based training (after 1992)	Social care and sociopedagogical settings, e.g. hospitals, daycare centres, youth centres, rehabilitation centres, work with families and aged
Erityislastentar-hanop ettaja (special needs adviser)	*Entry requirements:* Completion of 12 years' schooling with leaving certificate; entrance examinations *Training:* as for educator (*lastentarhanopettaja*), plus one additional year	All kinds of settings for children with special needs
Lastenohjaaja (playgroup leader/leisure-time educator)	*Entry requirements:* 9 years' compulsory schooling *Training:* After 1989: 2 years, 6 months' vocational training in Church training college (reform in process); before 1989: 300-hour course	Mainly playgroups run by the Lutheran Church

training for early years educators, the course puts a stronger emphasis on family and social work issues. Course content is weighted as follows:

• Social welfare (43 units): social work; care and education of children of different ages; residential care, children with special needs.

- Education and psychology (17 units): development and education of children; practical placements in day nurseries, residential homes, etc.
- Social sciences (10 units): social policy; sociology; economics.
- Supplementary subjects: health education, health administration; expressive arts.

Practical placements, which are integrated into the study programme, account for about one third of the total course.

State-enrolled paediatric nurse (*lastenjoitaja*)/community care worker (*lähihoitaja*)

The training course for paediatric nurses was restructured in 1994 and now qualifies for the broader-based social and healthcare profession of 'community care worker'. Until this change, paediatric nurses were trained at healthcare colleges.

The new training scheme (see Table 8.2) is an intermediate-level social and healthcare qualification which also entitles access to higher education. It aims to provide a broad-based qualification which will permit more job market flexibility (both for employers and employees). As a consequence, childcare, development and education play a less important role in course content. The basic course now consists of three main areas of study:

- Care and caring (20 units).
- Development, support, guidance (15 units).
- Rehabilitation (15).

These are supplemented by specialist subjects (20 units), one of which focuses on the care and education of young children. Other areas of specialization include work with the elderly, work with the disabled, combined mental health, crisis and substance abuse work, emergency care, nursing and caring, and dental hygiene.

Practical studies and work placements in a variety of welfare and health institutions and non-institutional settings account for a further 25 units.

Playgroup leaders (*lastenohjaaha*)

Playgroup leaders generally receive training at one of the Lutheran Church colleges. The initial 350-hour scheme has now been extended into a full-time programme of two and a half years' duration. In some ways it is similar to the community care worker qualification, with a stronger emphasis on religious development and pastoral care. Currently, there is a move towards accepting qualified apprentices for work in playgroups.

Family daycarers

The majority of family daycarers are employed by the local authorities. An obligatory, 250-hour course of training was introduced in 1980 which had to be completed either before starting the job or within the first six months of employment. In the case of a shortage of providers, local authorities pay the costs of tuition; otherwise providers are expected to cover expenses themselves. Since 1994 the training of family daycare providers has been integrated into the new community care worker training scheme (see above). Course content includes topics such as childcare, creative activities, psychology, social policy, nutrition and hygiene.

REFERENCES AND SOURCES

Central Union for Child Welfare and the Association of Kindergarten Teachers (1988) Special issue, 100 years of kindergartens in Finland. *Children in Finland*, Vol. 2. Central Union for Child Welfare, Helsinki.

Children's Day Care in Finland (1995) Unpublished MS. Ministry of Social Affairs, Helsinki.

Honkavaara, P. (1995) *Day Care and Early Childhood Education in Finland*. Report commissioned by the State Institute of Early Childhood Education and Research, Munich. Central Union for Child Welfare, Helsinki.

Huttunen, E. (1992) Children's experiences in early childhood programs. *International Journal of Early Childhood*, Vol. 24, pp. 3–11.

Huttunen, E. and Turunen, M.-M. (1993) Finland, in M. Cochran (ed.) *International Handbook of Child Care Policies and Programs*. Greenwood Press, Westport, Conn. and London.

Huttunen, E. and Tamminen, M. (1989) *Day Care as Growth Environment*. The National Board of Social Welfare in Finland, Government Printing Centre, Helsinki.

Karila, K. and Ropo, E. (1994) Expertise and the context: a case study of the relations between persons' expectations and the culture of the working environment. Paper given at the 23rd International Conference for Applied Psychology, Madrid, July.

Keskinen, S. (1990) *Connections between Internal Models and Working Satisfaction, Stress at Work and Occupational Identity in Day Care Personnel*. Department of Psychology, University of Turku.

National Board of Education (1992) *National Core Curriculum for State Enrolled (Paediatric) Nurse Education*. NBE, Helsinki.

9

France

AT A GLANCE

- Long tradition of public sector early childhood education.
- Widespread acceptance of the *école maternelle* as an educational institution for 3–6-year-olds.
- Legal entitlement to a place in an *école maternelle* for children aged 3 years up to school entry age at 6.
- Almost all 3, 4 and 5-year-olds and over a third of 2-year-olds attend an *école maternelle*.
- Tax benefits for families to subsidize childcare expenses.

The well established system of publicly funded early childhood education in France has a long history (Plaisance, 1994). The predecessors of the *écoles maternelles* – the *salles d'asile* – were founded in 1825 and officially integrated into the public education system under the responsibility of the Ministry of Education as early as 1881. Staff in the *écoles maternelles* were given equal status with primary schoolteachers in 1921. The Education Act 1975 ensured 5-year-olds legal entitlement to a place in an *école maternelle*, and this was extended to include 3 and 4-year-olds in 1989.

Today the *écoles maternelles* are an accepted way of life for young children in France. Levels of provision are the highest in the EU countries for the 3, 4 and 5-years-olds. In recent years, 2-year-olds have also been admitted to the *écoles maternelles*, and in the mean time over one third of this age-group attend (35 per cent in 1993–4). As state-funded, public education institutions, parents do not have to pay a fee. In terms of equality of opportunity this is a remarkable achievement. France invests considerably in childcare and education services in the years preceding formal school entry compared with most European countries. The few *écoles maternelles* which are run privately also receive state subsidies.

Alongside the *écoles maternelles* there are a number of other services for children, in particular for children under 3 years of age, which also receive state subsidies. Nurseries and organized family daycare are jointly funded by regional family allowance funds (*CAFs – caisses d'allocations familiales*), by local authorities and the regional *département*, as well as through parental fees.

Administratively, France has a split system of services: whereas the *écoles maternelles* are the responsibility of the Ministry of Education, institutions for the under 3s come under the auspices of the national Ministry of Social Affairs, Health and Towns, and leisure-time facilities for school-age children under the Ministry of Youth and Sport.

In France the level of employment of women with a child under 10 years of age is 59 per cent. The majority work full time; only 14 per cent have part-time jobs (European Commission Network on Childcare, 1996).

Current issues, trends

Two-year-olds in the école maternelle

The issue of admitting 2-year-olds into the *école maternelle* is a matter for controversial debate. Those in favour of this procedure argue along the lines of the importance of group socialization and of providing less privileged children with an early start in the education system. Opponents emphasize the importance of the mother–child relationship for a child's healthy development and of the role of the mother at home. Another aspect which is criticized is the fact that the teachers (*professeurs des écoles*) working in the *école maternelle* are not specifically prepared for working with very young children. The fact is that the number of 2-year-olds in the *écoles maternelles* is growing steadily, although regional differences are considerable. Areas designated educational priority zones (*zones d'éducation prioritaires*) offer the highest number of places.

Introduction of 'cycles of learning' into the public education system

As from 1990 the French preprimary and primary school system has been organized along new lines. There are now three stages or cycles of education covering the age-range 2 or 3–11 years. The overall aim is to emphasize individual learning processes, to improve the transition into formal schooling and to avoid class repetitions. The first cycle concerning social, emotional and cognitive skills includes the 2–4-year-olds in the *école maternelle*. The second cycle covers the last year in the *ecole maternelle* and the first two years in primary school and focuses on literacy and numeracy. The third cycle, covering the last three years in primary school, then focuses on a consolidation of literacy and numeracy skills. Professionals in the early childhood field are concerned that this new system, which was introduced in 1992, will lead to an undue formalization of learning experiences in the *école maternelle* and that elements of play and creativity will be squeezed out of the early childhood curriculum (Goutard, 1993; Noel, 1993).

B FORMS OF CHILDCARE AND EDUCATIONAL PROVISION

AT A GLANCE

- Universal educational provision for children aged 3 years to school entry age: *école maternelle* dominant institutional form.
- Wrap-around provision for both preschool and school-age children outside regular school hours.
- Variety of provision (public, voluntary, private) for approx. 20 per cent of children under 3 years.
- Organized family daycare system.

Table 9.1 gives an overview of the various childcare and education services for children from birth to age 14.

École maternelle (preprimary schooling)

The *école maternelle* is the dominant form of provision, with high coverage rates (see Table 9.1) and a full-day service throughout the school year – but not during school holidays. Classes are normally same age-groups divided into *la petite section* (2 and 3-year-olds), *la moyenne section* (4-year-olds) and *la grande section* (5-year-olds). Average class size in 1993–4 was 27.4, staffed by a teacher (*professeur des écoles*) and for at least half of the day by an auxiliary who is trained on the job (*agent spécialisé des écoles maternelles – asem*). There is a support system for a certain number of *écoles maternelles* in a particular region, staffed by a psychologist, a social worker and a remedial educator (*éducateur spécialisé*).

The three official objectives of the *école maternelle* are *scolariser, socialiser* and *faire apprendre et exercer*, i.e. to prepare children for school life, to foster social relationships and to help children 'learn how to learn'. The curriculum is defined according to four broad areas of experience: physical activities; communication activities, oral and written expression; artistic and aesthetic activities; and scientific and technological activities (Goutard, 1993, p. 47). Active parent participation is uncommon.

short-term training (see Table 9.2). However, qualifications are not binding for this work. *Animateurs* also work on the school premises during the two-hour lunch break in schools. They may also work in leisure-time centres (*centres de loisirs sans hérbergement*) for school-age children up to age 17.

C STAFF TRAINING

AT A GLANCE

- Staff (teachers) in the *écoles maternelles* (*professeurs des écoles*) trained for both preschool and primary school education: two-year training following three-year university degree.
- Training for work with younger children predominantly in the paramedical tradition.

Table 9.2 gives an overview of the different kinds of personnel employed in early childhood and out-of-school provision. While these are varied, staff and training basically fall into two distinct groups: those working within the education system in the *écoles maternelles* and those working in other forms of service outside the education system. Education staff are trained as teachers (*professeurs des écoles*) for both preschool and primary school. Staff in services within the welfare system are predominantly trained in the paramedical tradition (*puéricultrices, auxiliaires de puéricultures*). However, there is now a tendency to employ more staff with an educational (but not teaching) or remedial background (*éducatrices de jeunes enfants; éducatrices specialisées*) – not just in the 'kindergartens' but also in nurseries. Staff in out-of-school provision have a completely different kind of training – mostly short-term courses in leisure work. The initial and in-service training of teachers, of 'educators' and of *puéricultrices* is now described in more detail.

Teacher (*professeur des écoles*)

Initial training

Teachers working in the *écoles maternelles* are qualified schoolteachers, trained for work with the 2–11 age-range.

The three-year university course, ending with the *licence* award, comprises a two-year general studies section (*formation pluridisciplinaire*), ending with the *DEUG* award, and one-year's in-depth study in a particular subject. The two-year professional training includes

- studies in education, philosophy, history of education, sociology, psychology;

Table 9.2 Staff in childcare and education services

Professional title	Initial training/professional qualification	Fields of work
Up to 1991: *institutrice/institueur* ('teacher') as from 1991–2: *professeur des écoles* ('teacher')	*Entry requirements*: Up to 1991: • *baccalauréat* (university entrance qualification) • *DEUG* (*diplôme d'études universitaires générales 7* = award after a two-year general studies course at university • qualifying examination As from 1991–2: • *baccalauréat* • *licence* (= award following a three-year university degree course) • entrance examination *Training*: Up to 1991: 2 years at an *école normale* (= non-university higher education teacher training college) As from 1991–2: 2 years at an *IUFM* (*institut universitaire de formation des maîtres*) = training institute for teachers with university status. The *IUFM* are associated with a university or several universities as an *académie* *Award*: CAPE/*professeur des écoles* (*certificat d'aptitude au professorat des écoles*)	*École maternelle* (nursery school/preprimary schooling, 2.5–6 years) *École élémentaire* (primary school, 6–11 years) Training covers the age-group 2–11 years, i.e. nursery and primary schooling
Éducatrice/éducateur de jeunes enfants ('educator of young children'/ nursery worker)	*Entry requirements*: Up to 1992: • *baccalauréat* (university entrance qualification) or equivalent • entrance examination Since 1993: • *baccalauréat* or equivalent • university entrance examination *or* • completion of a two-year training in a social or paramedical profession *or* • qualification as *auxiliaire de puéricultrice* and 3 years' work experience *or* • general examination (*examen de niveau*) and qualifying examination *Training*: Up to 1992: 2 years at a non-university training institution specializing in this particular training scheme As from 1993: 2 years, 4 months (1,200 hours)	*Crèche collective* (nursery, 0–2 years) *crèche parentale* (parents' co-operative, 0–4 years) *jardin/jardinière d'enfants* ('kindergarten', 2/3–6 years) *halte-garderie* (sessional care, 6 months–6 years) *halte-garderie mobile* (mobile provision in rural areas) Further fields of work: • child protection centres for babies and older children • remedial centres • children's wards in hospitals • mother–child clinics • toy libraries • centres for psycho-social care etc.

Table   9.2   continued

Professional title	Initial training/professional qualification	Fields of work
	Award: *Diplôme d'état d'éducateur de jeunes enfants*	
Éducateur spécialisé (remedial educator)	*Entry requirements*: • minimum age 30 years • award as state-registered educator (*éducateur de jeunes enfants*) or • masters degree (*maîtrise*) • work experience and experience as supervisor *Training*: 1 year in a training centre recognized by the Ministry of Social Affairs	Remedial centres for children and adolescents
Moniteur-éducateur ('remedial auxiliary worker')	*Entry requirements*: • BEP *(brevet d'études professionelles)* – vocational qualification • qualifying examination *Training*: 1 year *or* (if no vocational qualification) 2 years *Award*: *Certificat d'aptitude à la profession de moniteur-éducateur*	Remedial centres for children and adolescents
Puéricultrice (paediatric nurse)	*Entry requirements*: • *baccalauréat* • *diplôme d'état d'infirmière* (state-registered nurse) (3 years) *or* • *diplôme d'état de sage-femme* (state-registered midwife) (4 years) • qualifying examination *Training*: 1 year at an *école de puériculture* *Award*: *Diplôme d'état de puéricultrice*	*Crèche collective/mini-crèche* (nursery, 0–2 years) *crèche parentale* (parents' co-operative, 0–4 years) *crèche familiale* (registered family daycare, 0–2 years as co-ordinator and supervisor/ advisers) After 5 years' work experience *puéricultrices* can take on a post as trainer and superviser; may also work as head nurse in socio-paramedical settings
Auxiliaire de puériculture (paediatric auxiliary worker)	*Entry requirements*: • minimum age 17 years • vocational qualification *Training*: 1 year at an *école d'auxiliaire de puériculture*	See above

Table 9.2   continued

Professional title	Initial training/professional qualification	Fields of work
	Award: *Certificat d'auxiliaire de puériculture*	
Animateur (leisure-time worker/playworker)	*Entry requirements*: 9 years' compulsory schooling, minimum age 17 years	*Garde/acceuil périsolaire* (out-of-school provision) *centre de loisirs sans hérbergement* (leisure-time centres, 2–17 years) *centre de vacances* (holiday centre)
	Training: Courses lasting several weeks at a training centre recognized by the Ministry for Youth and Sport plus work placements	
	Awards: BAFA *(brevet d'aptitude aux fonctions d'animateur)* BASE *(brevet d'aptitude a l'animation socio-éducative)* (leisure-time worker/playworker) BAFD *(brevet d'aptitude aux fonctions de directeur de centres de vacances et de loisirs)* (director of a holiday centre/leisure-time centre) There is now a diploma award for work in this field:	
	Entry requirements: 12 years' schooling, minimum age 19 years, 2-year training *or* 3 years' work experience *or* 3 years' voluntary work *or* a *BASE* qualification (see above)	
	Training: 5 training modules of 160 hours, work placements lasting 4–8 months	
	Award: DEFA *(diplôme d'état relatif aux fonctions d'animation)*	

- specialists courses, e.g. work in the *école maternelle*, integration of migrant children;
- subject study: French, mathematics, science and technology, geography, sport, art, music;
- preparation for administrative and pastoral tasks within the teaching profession; and
- optional subjects.

The first year of training comprises 1,500–700 hours of study, during which students prepare for the *concours* – a competitive examination including written papers in French, mathematics, a science subject and an arts subject, a practical examination in sport, and an oral examination on workplace experiences during the year. Successful candidates (the failure rate is high) may then proceed to the second year of training, which is spent predominantly in schools. Two 'external' practical placements are also necessary, e.g. in a leisure-time centre or a cultural organization.

In-service training/professional status

Teachers in the *écoles maternelles* are civil servants with equivalent status to primary schoolteachers.

In-service courses are offered by the IUFM, in regional centres for educational research, in other higher education institutions and in the schools themselves. There are courses specifically aimed at teachers working in the *écoles maternelles* – mostly focusing on curriculum issues. Teachers are paid 85 per cent of their current salary during attendance at an officially recognized course. Most courses are certificated. These additional qualifications do not lead automatically to promotion, but they are useful when applying for a new job. Teachers wishing to take on the post of headteacher have to complete a course of several weeks' duration. Most headteachers also have a class of their own. They are seconded from these duties only if the school has eight or more classes. Further opportunities for promotion include work as a teacher educator or as regional inspector for nursery and primary schooling.

'Educator' (*éducatrice/éducateur de jeunes enfants*)

Éducateurs are employed in diverse settings outside the education system (see Table 9.2). Compared with the number of teachers in the *écoles maternelles*, this professional group is relatively small.

Training takes place at one of the 23 specialist training centres in France. These are mainly run by private providers and come under the responsibility of the Ministry of Social Affairs. In 1993 the length of training was extended to 2 years, 4 months and includes the following subject areas (number of hours in brackets):

- Pedagogy and human development (160).
- Education and care (160).
- Child development and educational practice, 0–7 years (240).
- Group management (160).
- Law, economics, social studies (180).
- Professional studies, methods (140).

Some 9 months – in three separate periods – are spent in work placements. One of these placements may be spent abroad.

Qualified 'educators' work predominantly in early childhood education and care services. Over 50 per cent are employed in nurseries, 'kindergartens' and short-term sessional care. A certain tension appears to exist between the two professional groups *éducatrices* and *puéricultrices*. More and more *éducatrices* are applying for the post of nursery director, which traditionally has been the undisputed domain of the *puéricultrices*.

Paediatric nurse (*puéricultrice*)

Paediatric nurses are qualified medical nurses or midwives who have completed an additional one-year specialist training (see Table 9.2). Training comprises the following (number of hours in brackets):

- College-based instruction in healthcare, law, education, sociology, psychology, pathology, nutrition, administration, organization (650).
- Work placements in maternity wards, post-natal clinics, children's wards, nurseries, advisory centres, mother–child centres (710).
- Supervised practical work with appraisal (140).

In-service courses are organized on a regional and national basis by the national association of *puéricultrices*. Table 9.2 gives details of promotion chances.

REFERENCES AND SOURCES

Balleyguier, G. (1991) French research on day care, in E. C. Melhuish and P. Moss (eds.) *Day Care for Young Children. International Perspectives.* Tavistock/ Routledge, London and New York.

Combes, J. (1993) France, in M. Cochran (ed.) *International Handbook of Child Care Policies and Programs.* Greenwood Press, Westport, Conn. and London.

Felix, M. and Ribes, B. (1994) France, in *Annual Report 1993, European Commission Network on Childcare.* Commission of the European Communities, Brussels.

Gempek, P. (1990) Vorschulische Erziehung in Frankreich. Tageseinrichtungen in Frankreich für Kinder von 0–6 Jahren, *Treffpunkt Kindergarten/Forum Sozialpädagogik*, Vol. 9, no. 6, pp. 1–3.

Goutard, M. (1993) Preschool education in France, in T. David (ed.) *Educational Provision for our Youngest Children: European Perspectives.* Paul Chapman, London.

Howes, C. and Marx, E. (1992) Raising questions about improving the quality of child care: child care in the United States and France, *Early Childhood Research Quarterly*, Vol. 7, pp. 347–66.

Journal Officiel de la République Française (1981) Les Modes de Garde de Jeunes Enfants. JORF, Paris.

Leprince, F. (1991) Day care for young children in France, in E. C. Melhuish and P. Moss (eds.) *Day Care for Young Children. International Perspectives.* Tavistock/Routledge, London and New York.

McMahan, I. D. (1992) Public preschool from the age of two: the *école maternelle* in France, *Young Children*, Vol. 47, no. 1, pp. 22–8.

Noël, C. (1993) Regeln und Freiraüme in der école maternelle, in P. Oberhuemer (ed.) *Blick auf Europa – Tageseinrichtungen für Kinder.* Sonderheft der Zeitschrift Theorie und Praxis der Sozialpädagogik, TPS – extra 13, pp. 11–13.

Plaisance, E. (1994) L'éducation préscolaire et les institutions pour la petite enfance en France. Débats et données sociologiques sur les institutions de garde et d'éducation pour les enfants de 0 à 6 ans. Paper given at the 14th Conference of the Deutsche Gesellschaft für Erziehungswissenschaft, University of Dortmund, 14–16 March.

Prein, G. (1995) ErzieherInnenausbildung in Frankreich, in T. Rauschenbach, K. Beher and D. Knauer *Die Erzieherin. Ausbildung und Arbeitsmarkt.* Juventa, Weinheim and Munich.

Wattier, P. and Picard, O. (1992) *Les Métiers de la Petite Enfance.* Bayard, Paris.

10

Germany

A SOCIAL CONTEXT OF CHILDCARE AND EDUCATION SERVICES

AT A GLANCE

1948–1989

- Development of two different systems of childcare provision in the German Democratic Republic (GDR) and the Federal Republic of Germany (FRG).
- In the GDR: centralized political structure; high employment rate among women with young children; kindergarten expansion to universal coverage; high level of provision for children under 3.
- In the FRG: federal political structure; low employment rate among women with young children; expansion of kindergartens in the 1970s, with considerable regional differences in level of provision; low coverage rate for children under 3 and for school-age children; *Subsidaritätsprinzip* – voluntary agencies have priority over public authorities in the establishment of kindergartens and other childcare and education facilities.

Post-1990

- Unification of the two German states in October 1990.
- Federal political structure (16 constituent states).
- Child and Youth Welfare Act 1990: umbrella legislation for childcare and education services in East and West.
- As from 1996: legal entitlement to a place in kindergarten for every child aged 3 years up to school entry age (6 years).

East and West: two childcare systems

The unification of the two German states on 3 October 1990 illustrated in a distinct way how developments and priorities in the field of non-statutory childcare and education are related to a particular social and political context. During the postwar years, the two German nations developed very different models of early childhood services. In the socialist German Democratic Republic (GDR) the participation of women in the labour market was a declared political goal, accompanied by the development of a system of full-day kindergartens and nurseries. This eventually led to universal coverage for children aged 3–6 years and to a high level of provision for children under 3 years of age – higher than in other east European countries. Families and children were linked into a common core of values endorsed by state education programmes. One of the objectives of kindergartens was to educate the 'socialist personality' (Engelhard and Michel, 1993, p. 226).

In the western Federal Republic of Germany (FRG) political responsibility was deliberately decentralized following the experiences of the Nazi regime. Non-statutory childcare and education came under the auspices of the constituent federal states (*Länder*), each having its own legislation and administrative structures. According to the so-called *Subsidaritätsprinzip* – a principle which establishes the priority rights and responsibilities of individuals, voluntary bodies and the state – family support measures such as kindergartens were set up by public authorities only if voluntary agencies (mainly state subsidized welfare organizations run by the Catholic and Protestant churches) were not in a position to do so. Female labour market participation was much lower than in the GDR and mostly on a part-time basis. Coverage rates in kindergartens were considerably lower, and the places offered predominantly part time. Nurseries for the under 3s were almost non-existent outside large cities. Kindergartens catered for little more than 30 per cent of the 3–5-year-olds up until the early 1970s. At this time early childhood education became the focus of extensive curricular and structural reform strategies, resulting in the widespread expansion of kindergartens. Although kindergartens were officially recognized as the first stage of the public education system in 1973, they neither legally nor administratively became part of the statutory education system.

Parental responsibility and the *Subsidaritätsprinzip* are both firmly anchored in the Child and Youth Welfare Act 1990; at the same time this legislation emphasizes the necessity to establish an adequate network of childcare and education facilities and other family support measures. The Child and Youth Welfare Act is now the umbrella legislation for further developments in early childhood and out-of-school provision in both the eastern and western parts of Germany. Responsibility for implementing the wide-reaching goals of the Act lies with the regional governments of the now 16 constituent states.

Levels of provision, maternal employment

Kindergartens have become a widely accepted form of provision. In 1994, there were places available in publicly-funded services for 73 per cent of children aged 3–6^1/$_2$ years in the western *Länder* and for 96 per cent in the eastern *Länder* (Statistisches Bundesamt, 1996). In former East Germany, universal coverage was the norm. In former West Germany, numbers more than doubled between the mid-1960s and the end of the 1970s. This immense rate of expansion stagnated during the 1980s, however, and at the beginning of the 1990s experts talked of the need to create 500,000 new places in the western *Länder* in order to meet the demand. As from 1 January 1996, every child from the age of 3 years up to school entry at age 6 is legally entitled to a place in a kindergarten. However, this obligation could not be met in all regions by the agreed date, and transition procedures have been introduced, with the aim of fulfilling the legal requirements by 1999.

Childcare provision for children under 3 or for children of school age does not enjoy the same public esteem or political priority – at least in the western *Länder*, where day nurseries (*Kinderkrippen*) and other centres cater for only 1.8 per cent of children under 3 years. By contrast, in the former East Germany – shortly before unification – there were places available for 56 per cent of children from birth to 3 years of age. In 1994–5, out-of-school educational daycare facilities (children generally attend school mornings only) were available for only 5.6 per cent of children aged 6–10 years in the western *Länder*, whereas in the eastern federal states the coverage rate for the same age-group was 60 per cent (Deutsches Jugendinstitut, 1996). Even though the extension of parental leave to three years has lessened public pressure concerning the care of children under 3, the coverage rate is still far from satisfactory. It seems that day nurseries and school-age childcare are still officially considered to be institutions for families 'in need' and not part of a necessary comprehensive support system for *all* families.

Maternal employment is much lower in the western part of Germany than in the eastern *Länder*. In 1993, 46 per cent of women in the west with children aged 0–10 years were in the labour force, the majority (28 per cent) in part-time jobs. The employment rate for mothers with children in the same age-group in eastern Germany was much higher at 69 per cent, and most (55 per cent) were in full-time jobs. At the same time, the level of unemployed mothers with children under 10 years of age at 19 per cent was also high (European Commission Network on Childcare, 1996).

Funding and responsibility

Approximately 70 per cent of childcare and education services in the western *Länder* are run by voluntary agencies, mainly welfare organizations associated with the Catholic and Protestant Church. Only 30 per cent are run by local authorities. This contrasts with the situation in the eastern *Länder*, where the majority of institutions come under the responsibility of the municipalities: only 3 per cent are run by voluntary agencies, and approximately 11 per cent of centre-based settings are workplace nurseries attached to large companies. Funding regulations vary from *Land* to *Land*. On the whole, though, kindergartens and other daycare facilities are funded from four sources: the specific provider (*Träger*), parental contributions, local authority funds and state subsidies. Parental fees are income related and vary from agency to agency. On average, parents finance between 10 per cent and 15 per cent of operating costs. This contrasts with the situation in the former East Germany, where childcare and education services were free of charge.

Services run by voluntary agencies are subject to inspection by state authorities. The provider (*Träger*) is responsible for the day-to-day running of the centre, for the employment of staff and for setting down guidelines for the educational programme.

Current issues and trends

Developing provision to match the needs of children and families

Changing family structures and labour market conditions have precipitated debate on the objectives and format of educational and family support services in many European countries. In Germany, the challenges of unification have accentuated this debate. Developing appropriate provision involves – particularly in western Germany – adapting and extending the opening times of kindergartens to match parental wishes. In both east and west it involves extending the age-groups traditionally catered for in kindergartens; it also involves diversifying the programme content. Alongside the concept of kindergartens as a social network and learning opportunity for children, community-oriented approaches are gaining significance: kindergartens as multifunctional institutions, i.e. as a meeting place for parents, as a partner for other social and educational services in the area or as an information exchange centre for childcare issues. Co-operation with parent self-help groups and the inclusion of non-professionals in the professional work of the centres are some of the issues being discussed within the wider goal of creating institutions more open to the needs of the social infrastructure in which they are located (cf. Deutsches Jugendinstitut, 1995).

Legal entitlement to a kindergarten place – will it affect quality standards?

The decision to introduce a legal entitlement to a place in kindergarten for all children as from the age of 3 was made during a time of increasing economic restrictions. This has precipitated controversial debate on the necessary conditions for actually implementing this legal entitlement. Professionals fear a reduction of present quality standards, e.g. by increasing group size and staff–child ratios (cf. Arbeitsgemeinschaft für Jugendhilfe, 1993). Some warn of the danger of a 'two-tier' system, with small, high-quality centres only for those children whose parents can afford to pay the fees. Quality assurance is therefore one of the most challenging issues for the years ahead.

Staff professionalization and career prospects

For many years professionals have been debating the need for a fundamental reform of the training of 'educators' (*Erzieherinnen*) – the largest professional group in childcare and education services (see Section C). A radical reappraisal of the goals, content and the level and length of training, combined with improvements in professional development opportunities and career prospects, are the key issues (cf. Pestalozzi-Fröbel-Verband, 1994). The question of job mobility within the European Union has also influenced the debate. The training of educators in Germany takes place at a lower level than that of professionals in early childhood provision in the majority of European countries and, although German educators are not officially disadvantaged, the lower level of training is seen by some as a practical hindrance.

Since the introduction of the entitlement to a place in kindergarten – and the pledge within the Child and Youth Welfare Act to provide an appropriate number of places for children under 3 and school-age children – job prospects for *Erzieherinnen* in the western *Länder* have improved. However, in the eastern *Länder* the situation is completely different. The radical decline in the birth rate since unification, coupled with the reform of the entire administrative system, has led to the closure of many day nurseries and also some kindergartens. Many *Erzieherinnen* have lost their jobs, or have been forced to take on part-time employment. An entire professional group is having to come to terms with the difficult fact that their jobs are no longer secure and that they no longer enjoy the same kind of social prestige as they did in the GDR. These are factors which at present are obstacles in the development of a new and positive professional self-image.

B FORMS OF CHILDCARE AND EDUCATIONAL PROVISION

AT A GLANCE

- Kindergartens the main form of provision for 3–6-year-olds.
- Different legislative and administrative structures in the 16 constituent states (*Länder*).
- Voluntary agencies predominate as providers in the western *Länder*, local authorities in the eastern *Länder*.
- Move towards expanding kindergartens into centres for children from 0 to 6 years or 3 to 12 years.

Table 10.1 gives an overview of the main forms of provision.

Table 10.1 Childcare and education services for children aged 0–14 years

Form of provision	Age of children/ coverage rate	Opening hours	Administrative responsibility
Kinderkrippe (day nursery)	0–3 years Places available in day nurseries and other forms of provision for 6.3% of children under 3 years of age*	Full day	Ministry of Social/ Youth Affairs in the individual *Länder* Local authorities/ voluntary agencies
Kindergarten (kindergarten)	3–6 years Places available in kindergartens and other forms of provision for 90.7% of children aged 3–6 years and for 77.2% of children aged 3–6½ years*	Varies considerably: • mornings and afternoons (with mid-day closure) *or* • 'prolonged morning sessions' – till about 2.00 p.m. *or* • full day, with mid-day meal *or* • morning and afternoon sessions with different groups of children	Ministry of Social Affairs in the individual *Länder* Voluntary agencies/ local authorities
Altersübergreifende Tageseinrichtung (extended-age centre)	4 months–6 years (mainly in Northrhine-Westfalia) 0–12 years, 3–12 years (pilot schemes)	Generally full day	Ministry of Social/ Youth Affairs in the individual *Länder* Voluntary agencies local authorities (municipalities)
Vorklasse/Schulkindergarten (preschool class, 'school kindergarten')	5 years, 5% (Vorklassen) western *Länder***	Mornings only	Ministry of Education in the individual *Länder* In Bavaria and BadenWürttemberg: Ministry of Social/ Youth Affairs
Kinderhort (centre for school-age children)	6–10 years or 6–12/14 years Places available in school-age centres and other forms of provision for 11.6% of children aged 6–10 years and for 7.9% of children aged 6–12 years*	(Before and) after-school hours, usually until 5.00 p.m.	Ministry of Social/ Youth Affairs in the individual *Länder* Local authorities (municipalities)

Table 10.1   continued

Form of provision	Age of children/ coverage rate	Opening hours	Administrative responsibility
Familientages pflege (family daycare)	0–3 years (occasionally also older children) 1.8% of the 0–3-year-olds, western *Länder** (1990)	Individual arrangements with parents	Ministry of Social/ Youth Affairs/ local authorities voluntary agencies in the individual *Länder*

Notes:
*Figures for 1994: Statistisches Bundesamt, 1996.
**Figures for 1990: (western Länder only), Tietze and Paterak, 1993.

Kindergarten

Kindergartens are the main form of provision for children aged 3–6 years. Within the legal framework of the Child and Youth Welfare Act 1990, kindergartens are institutions with the function of providing both education and care and helping to 'advance the development of the child into a responsible member of society'. Furthermore, 'The programmes and services shall orient themselves educationally and organizationally towards the needs of the children and their families' (Child and Youth Welfare Act, segment three).

During the reform era of the 1970s a specific educational approach for work in kindergartens known as the 'situation-oriented approach' (*Situationsansatz*) was developed. This approach focuses on real-life situations as a starting point for work with children and parents and aims to combine the development of personal and social competence with the mastery of skills and knowledge. Many of the key features of this approach – mixed age-grouping, child-initiated learning, parent participation, community orientation – have become part of everyday practice in kindergartens (Colberg-Schrader and Oberhuemer, 1993, p. 66). At present a new debate about this approach and about educational objectives in general, is under way, precipitated by the search – particularly in the eastern federal states – for new ways of educating children in times of fundamental social change.

Recently there has been a move towards extending the 'traditional' age-group to include children under 3 and over 6 years of age. For children living in the federal state of Northrhine-Westfalia, for example, there are centres where infants as young as 4 months are in a group alongside children up to compulsory school age. Or in the federal state of Thüringen, 2-year-olds have been granted the right by law to attend a kindergarten. A number of innovatory and action research projects are at present developing and evaluating different forms of mixed-age provision (e.g. 0–6 years, 0–12 years, 3–14 years).

For handicapped children there are a number of special kindergartens (*Sonderkindergarten*). There is a gradual move towards integrating handicapped children into mainstream kindergartens. In 1988–9 in western Germany, 2,100 places were available for handicapped children in so-called integrative groups (specially designed kindergarten groups with an average group size of 12–15 children, 3–5 of whom are handicapped). Approximately 21,000 handicapped children are enrolled in special facilities, and roughly the same number attend normal kindergartens.

Preprimary classes/school kindergartens

Some federal states (Hesse, Berlin, Hamburg, Lower Saxony) operate preprimary classes for 5-year-olds which fall under the school system and are free of charge. About 5 per cent of 5-year-olds in the western *Länder* attend this kind of provision. Children who have or are expected to have difficulties in adjusting to school may attend a one-year referral class (*Schulkindergarten*) (see Table 10.1).

Day nurseries (*Kinderkrippen*)

Day nurseries are usually open on a full-day basis and take children from birth to 3 years of age. Whereas the level of provision in the eastern federal states is high compared with other European countries, the coverage rate in the western *Länder* is very low. Demand far outweighs supply. Staff are mostly trained educators (*Erzieherinnen*) or nursery workers (*Kinderpflegerinnen*). In some regions of Germany age-integrated centres for 0–6-year-olds have been established as an alternative form of provision.

Parent-managed centres

Parent-managed groups and centres – originating from grass-roots initiatives in the 1960s, as in some other countries – exist alongside the more traditional forms of provision. They employ paid staff, and parents are involved in daily activities on a regular basis. Opening hours are negotiated with parents. Mother–toddler groups for children under 3 are especially popular because of the lack of publicly funded provision for this age-group.

Care and recreation facilities for school children

The traditional form of after-school provision is the *Kinderhort* for 6–12 or 14-year-olds. Since the school day is short in Germany, usually finishing at lunchtime, these institutions have an important function. However, levels of provision are low – 5.6 per cent in the western federal states for children aged 6–10 years (Deutsches Jugendinstitut, 1996). A number of alternative forms are under discussion, such as providing a meal and homework supervision in schools, or encouraging school children to attend kindergarten groups in the afternoon. Again, as with provision for children below 3 years of age, demand far outstrips the number of available places.

Family daycare

Family daycare has been 'elevated' in status through inclusion in the Child and Youth Welfare Act 1990 and is now officially recognized as an alternative to other forms of provision, in particular for the 0–3 age-group. However, specific regulations are a matter for the individual *Länder*, and these vary. In some regions family daycare organizations receive state subsidies. A professional organization which is trying to introduce a training system for work in family daycare also receives state funding. Most family daycarers (*Tagesmütter*) negotiate directly with the parents concerning their conditions of work. They are not eligible for social benefits.

[C] STAFF TRAINING

(This section was compiled by Dietrich von Derschau. A more detailed report on training in Germany is given in von Derschau (1995) – see Appendix I for further details.)

AT A GLANCE

- Diversity of staff training schemes for work in non-statutory childcare and education.
- No nationally agreed regulations for the various training schemes.
- *Erzieherinnen* ('educators') are the most common professional group in early childhood and out-of-school services.
- *Erzieherinnen* complete a broad-base training for work in a variety of sociopedagogical settings – not only qualified for work in early childhood provision.
- Fundamental reform of training demanded by experts in the field.

Diversity of professional workers and training schemes

Non-statutory childcare and education services are not staffed by one particular professional group. On the contrary, a number of different professionals with very different kinds of training work in kindergartens, day nurseries and school-age childcare. These differences can only be explained in historical terms, they have nothing to do with the specific job demands of the various institutions (cf. von Derschau, 1976). *Erzieherinnen* ('educators'), *Kinderpflegerinnen* (nursery auxiliary workers) and *Sozialpädagoginnen* ('social pedagogues') are the three most widely represented professional groups, and it is on these three groups – and in particular on the educators – that we shall focus in this section.

Table 10.2 gives a synopsis of the training and workplace settings for these three groups. Educators are the largest group, accounting for 55.9 per cent of all workers in childcare and education services (*Jugendhilfe*).

For all these training schemes there are no nationally agreed regulations, although there are framework guidelines (*Rahmenvereinbarungen*) which leave considerable room for individual interpretation. Responsibility for training lies with the *Länder*, and each has its own legislation, training requirements and courses of study. This is also the case now for the 'new' federal states. Before 1990, in the GDR, training for work with children in non-statutory settings was co-ordinated and uniform (cf. Rauschenbach *et al.*, 1995). Professional workers in day nurseries, kindergartens and out-of-school provision were all trained separately. Following unification, the western model of a broad-based training programme was introduced in the eastern *Länder*, and this is now the one unifying feature in all federal states.

Table 10.2   Staff in childcare and education services

Professional title	Initial training/professional qualification	Fields of work
Kinderpflegerin (nursery worker)	*Entry requirements:* 9 years' compulsory schooling or an equivalent school leaving qualification *Training:* Generally 2 years at a vocational school for nursery workers *Award:* *Staatlich geprüfte Kinderpflegerin* (state-registered nursery worker)	Childcare and education services • day nursery • kindergarten • school-age childcare (as an auxiliary worker) Further provision in the fields of social pedagogy and social care (cf. 'educators') Private household (as nanny)
Erzieherin ('educator')	*Entry requirements:* • minimum age 18 years • intermediate school leaving qualification (after 10 years of schooling) or equivalent school leaving qualification • relevant practical experience, e.g. a one-year or two-year preparatory practicum *or* a completed vocational training scheme *or* several years' working experience *or* similar qualifications, e.g.: – 12 or 13 years' schooling with a successfully completed A-level equivalent (*Abitur*) or vocational qualification; – a number of years as a parent in a household with at least one child;	Work with children and young people in: • kindergartens • day nurseries • portage schemes • parents' co-operatives • school-age childcare • youth centres • youth organizations • organizations for handicapped children and adolescents • youth hostels

Table 10.2   continued

Professional title	Initial training/professional qualification	Fields of work
	– a two-year training in the field of social pedagogy or social care at a vocational school for social work (award as *Sozialassistentin* – 'social assistant') *Training:* Generally 3 years: 2 years at a vocational college specializing in social pedagogy plus 1 year supervised work placement in a chosen field (not the case in all federal states). Part-time training also possible. In the *Kollegschulen* (Northrhine-Westfalia) the training lasts 4 years because of a twofold qualification scheme leading both to a professional qualification *and Abitur* *Award:* *Staatlich anerkannte Erzieherin* (state-registered educator)	• children's ward in hospitals • boarding schools • residential care • supervised flats for young people • family support services
Sozialpädagogin ('social pedagogue')	*Entry requirements:* *Fachhochschulreife* (entry requirement for non-university higher education following 12 years' schooling) *Training:* 4 or 4½ years: either 8 semesters (plus 1 examination semester) with an integrated practicum lasting 2 semesters *or* 7–8 semesters full time plus 6 months' work placement. Training takes place at *Fachhochschulen* (non-university higher education institutions) or at polytechnics *Award:* *Staatlich anerkannter Diplom-Sozialpädagogin* (state-registered 'social pedagogue') – award title varies from *Land* to *Land*	Work with children, young people and adults in: • all forms of childcare and education services • family support services • remedial education • leisure education • drug abuse centres • social work services • street work • healthcare • centres for handicapped persons

Note:
The table refers to the three most common professional groups working in childcare and education services.

Educator (*Erzieherin*)

Erzieherinnen are not trained exclusively for work in kindergartens or other forms of preschool provision. Their initial training is broad based and covers a variety of educational and daycare facilities with a wide age-range (see Table 10.2). In 1994 approximately 86 per cent of all qualified *Erzieherinnen* worked in kindergartens, nurseries or school-age childcare.

Training in the former East Germany focused on specific institutions (e.g. kindergartens or day nurseries). In the unified Germany these qualifications are only recognized for the area of specialization. In order to gain full state recognition, educators trained under the former East German system have been required to attend a 100-hour 'adaptation' course covering the knowledge base necessary for working in further areas of childcare and education.

Training takes place at vocational colleges specializing in social pedagogy (*Fachschule für Sozialpädagogik*; in Bavaria: *Fachakademie für Sozialpädagogik*). Of these training institutions, 60 per cent are state run, and approximately 40 per cent are run by the so-called 'free' providers, mainly attached to the Protestant or Catholic Church. Around half the institutions are integrated within larger vocational training institutions (*Berufsfachschulen*).

Entry requirements are diverse (see Table 10.2) and vary from *Land* to *Land*. It has been estimated that about one quarter of applicants have already completed some form of vocational training or have been employed; the remainder complete the one or two-year preparatory practicum.

Training generally takes three years: two years at college (including study visits in different kinds of provision), and one year in a work placement. This third year is supervised by the college and includes 20 days for reflecting on workplace experiences.

Course content

The following is an example of the compulsory subjects of the course content in the state of Bavaria (number of hours during the two-year period in brackets):

- Education (160).
- Psychology (160).
- Sociology (80).
- German (160).
- Social studies (80).
- Biology/health education (80).
- Remedial education (120).
- Children's literature and media education (120).
- Law (80).
- Theology/confessional education/ethics (120).
- Group management/methods (320).
- Art education (160).
- Craft and design (160).
- Music (40).
- Movement (160).
- Sport (160).
- Practical experience in centres (400).

A further 240 hours are spent on the in-depth study of certain compulsory areas. Optional areas include 480 hours for studies qualifying for entry to higher vocational education, and 240 hours in a subject area of choice.

Kinderpflegerin (*nursery worker, childcare worker*)

Kinderpflegerinnen undertake a two-year post-15 training at a vocational school (*Berufsfachschule*) specializing in childcare. Originally *Kinderpflegerinnen* – a professional group with some 130 years' history – were trained as nannies. However, with the gradual increase in centre-based settings over the years, and in particular since the expansion in this field during the 1970s, the training focus has also shifted in this direction. *Kinderpflegerinnen* generally work in kindergartens and nurseries as an auxiliary worker. Some federal states are broadening the training into a general basic training in social care which not only includes childcare but also care of the elderly, family care and remedial work. On completion of these courses, candidates are awarded the title of *Sozialassistentin* ('social assistant'). In both cases it has been argued that the short length of the course and the lack of in-depth study do not prepare candidates adequately for independent work with children and/or adults.

Sozialpädagogin (*'social pedagogue'*)

Since 1971, social pedagogues have been trained together with social workers at *Fachhochschulen* – non-university higher education institutions (see Table 10.2 for formal entry requirements and training structure). The first two years of training focus on general studies in social work and social pedagogy; following this students specialize in a specific area, such as childcare, healthcare, care of the elderly, etc. (see Table 10.2 for the range of workplace settings).

In childcare and education services (kindergartens, nurseries, out-of-school provision, etc.) social pedagogues often manage large institutions, centres for handicapped children or pilot projects. Compared with *Erzieherinnen*, however, they hold a relatively small number of posts in this area: 1.2% in kindergartens compared with 54.1% held by *Erzieherinnen*, 2.8% in out-of-school provision compared with 66.9% (figures for 1994). They may also work as educational advisers for municipal authorities or for the professional welfare organizations run by the Church.

Current issues

Germany is one of the few countries with a broad-based training which reaches beyond the early years. On the whole, the idea is widely accepted. It is argued that

- professional work in the fields of social pedagogy – whether in kindergartens or other childcare settings, youth and community services or residential care – is based on a common theoretical framework;
- this calls for a form of training which allows on the one hand for general studies in the field, and on the other for specialization and in-depth study

in one or two chosen fields, coupled with strategies for transferring this knowledge to other fields of work;

• a broad-based training gives *Erzieherinnen* more chances on the job market and a wider choice of career possibilities. Since educators are now staying in the field longer, this aspect will become increasingly important;

• knowledge of the work in a variety of workfields helps to ensure more continuity and co-operation in the childcare and education workfield; and

• the present move towards expanding the traditional age-groups in kindergartens to include younger and older children will be more difficult to transform into practice without a broad-based training.

What is criticized, however, is that this concept has not been properly put into practice or further developed. Experts consider an extension of the length of training necessary, coupled with a closer dovetailing of college-based training, the workplace components of training and the first two years of employment. What is also necessary is a more coherent approach which combines the early years of professional training and work with a well developed system of in-service education and advisory support throughout professional life. The different training schemes are themselves not connected – neither in a structural, organizational nor curricular sense. Those interested in pursuing the next step up the hierarchical ladder have to start from scratch – their previous qualifications are not considered. For years now, this impermeability has been criticized by professionals in the field. In practice, however, transitions have become even more difficult, and their hierarchical structure is apparent at all levels: entry requirements, status and length of training, career prospects and pay. Yet another area of criticism is the school-like nature of the training. The bureaucratic structure of the traditional vocational school system is often a hindrance in the development of creative, flexible work procedures. On the whole, both the structure and content of training need to be conceptualized more according to the demands of the fields of work for which it aims to qualify.

REFERENCES AND SOURCES

Achter Jugendbericht (1990) Bericht über Bestrebungen und Leistungen der Jugendhilfe. *Bundestagsdrucksache*, 11/6576. Bundesministerium für Frauen und Jugend, Bonn.

Arbeitsgemeinschaft für Jugendhilfe (1993) *Der Kindergarten für alle. Stellungnahme der AGJ zu qualitativen Mindestanforderungen bei der Umsetzung des Rechtsanspruchs auf einen Kindergartenplatz*. AGJ, Bonn.

Bundesministerium für Frauen und Jugend (1994) *Kinder- und Jugendhilfegesetz (Achtes Buch Sozialgesetzbuch)*. Bundesministerium für Frauen und Jugend, Bonn.

Colberg-Schrader, H. (1989) Der Situationsansatz, in Bayerisches Staatsministerium für Unterricht und Kultus (ed.) *Festschrift – 150 Jahre Kindergartenwesen in Bayern*. Ernst Reinhardt, Munich and Basel.

Colberg-Schrader, H. and Oberhuemer, P. (1993) Early childhood education and care in Germany, in T. David (ed.) *Educational Provision for our Youngest Children: European Perspectives*. Paul Chapman, London.

Derschau, D. von (1976) *Die Ausbildung der Erzieher für Kindergarten, Heimerziehung und Jugendarbeit an Fachschulen/Fachakademien für Sozialpädagogik. Entwicklung, Bestandsaufnahme, Reformvorschläge*. Miro, Gersthofen.

Derschau, D. von (1995) *Ausbildung von Fachkräften in vor- und außerschulischen Einrichtungen für Kinder in der Bundesrepublik Deutschland*. Report commissioned by the State Institute of Early Childhood Education and Research. Fachakademie für Sozialpädagogik der Landeshauptstadt, Munich.

Derschau, D. von and Dittrich, J. (1995) *Erzieher/Erzieherin, Blätter zur Berufskunde*, 2-IVA. Bertelsmann, Bielefeld.

Deutsches Jugendinstitut (1993) *Tageseinrichtungen für Kinder. Informationen – Erfahrungen – Analysen*. DJI, Munich.

Deutsches Jugendinstitut (1995) *Orte für Kinder. Auf der Suche nach neuen Wegen in der Kinderbetreuung*. DJI, Munich.

Deutsches Jugendinstitut (1996) *Hort, Schule – und was noch? Betreuungsangebote für Kinder – Eine Bestandsaufnahme*, DJI, Munich.

Engelhard, D. and Michel, H. (1993) Entwicklungen in den Tageseinrichtungen der östlichen Bundesländer seit 1990, in W. Tietze and H. G. Rossbach (eds.) *Erfahrungsfelder in der frühen Kindheit, Bestandsaufnahme, Perspektiven*. Lambertus, Freiburg i.Br.

Heiland, H. (1993) Die Wirkung Fröbels in europäischen Ländern, in P. Oberhuemer (ed.) *Blick auf Europa – Tageseinrichtungen für Kinder, Sonderheft der Zeitschrift Theorie und Praxis der Sozialpädagogik*, TPS extra 13, pp. 36–68.

Neunter Jugendbericht (1994) *Bericht über die Situation der Kinder und Jugendlichen und die Entwicklung der Jugendhilfe in den neuen Bundesländern*. Bundesministerium für Familie, Senioren, Frauen und Jugend, Bonn.

Pestalozzi-Fröbel-Verband (ed.) (1994) *Zur beruflichen Situation der Erzieherinnen in Deutschland. Bestandsaufnahme und Perspektiven*. Profil, Munich.

Rauschenbach, T., Behler, K. and Knauer, D. (1995) *Die Erzieherin. Ausbildung und Arbeitsmarkt* (with M. Schilling, M. Feldmann, O. Filtzinger, G. Prein and G. Römer. Juventa, Weinheim and Munich.

Statistisches Bundesamt (1996) *Statistik der Jugendhilfe, Teil III.1, Einrichtungen und tätige Personen 1994 – Tageseinrichtungen für Kinder*. SB, Wiesbaden.

11

Greece

[Parts B and C of this chapter are based on a commissioned report submitted to the State Institute of Early Childhood Education and Research (IFP) by Konstantin Zacharenakis, Heraklion. See Appendix I for further details.]

A SOCIAL CONTEXT OF CHILDCARE AND EDUCATION SERVICES

AT A GLANCE

- A dual system of half-day kindergartens and full-day centres under different ministries, with varying structural features and two systems of staff training.
- Kindergartens and full-day centres predominantly state-run institutions.
- School starting age: 6 years.
- Considerable regional disparities in levels of provision.

In Greece, there are two parallel systems of childcare and education services up to the age of compulsory schooling (recently raised from 5½ to 6 years). The kindergartens or nursery schools (*nipiagogia*) come under the administrative responsibility of the national Ministry of Education and Religion, and are open for half-day sessions only. The full-day centres (*paediki stathmi*) were originally conceived as provision for the children of working mothers. The management of these services was transferred to local authorities in 1995. At a national level, responsibility for services in the welfare system is shared between the Ministry of Social Welfare and – since 1995 – the Ministry of Internal Affairs. Most kindergartens and daycare centres are state run, but there are also municipal and private establishments.

Not only have differing concepts of 'education' and 'care' led to an institutionalized dichotomy of services for children and their families but there are also two kinds of training for work in these two separate institutions (see Section C). The School Reform Act 1985 envisaged the introduction of full-day compulsory schooling and the integration of kindergartens and daycare centres into combined centres. However, this model has yet to be implemented.

Provision and training: historical background

The early development of institutions for the education and care of young children in Greece was influenced by two strands of educational thought. From 1830 to 1875 French theories were dominant, in particular the works of Carpentier, who considered learning to read and write to be the major tasks of early education institutions. The development of a more comprehensive understanding of preschool education can be traced back to the years between 1860 and 1880, i.e. to the period when Friedrich Froebel's ideas were gaining widespread acceptance in many parts of Europe and beyond. Aikaterini Laskaridou was the chief protagonist of the Froebel movement in Greece. She was also responsible for the opening of the first daycare centre for the children of working mothers in 1901. In 1926 the first state-funded daycare centres were set up, and three years later the first state-funded kindergarten. In the same year, 1929, within the framework of a general educational reform movement, training institutions for practitioners working with young children were founded. From this time right up to the early 1980s training institutions were repeatedly opened and closed, according to the policies and political situation of the time (Makraki-Chryssafidi, 1992). This of course was not without impact on the continuity of development within the training system. With the general upgrading of training to tertiary level in the mid-1980s and the extension of the length of training, there are now hopes for the necessary stabilization and systematization in this field.

Levels of provision

The number of kindergartens (*nipiagogia*) and the number of children attending kindergartens have risen steadily over the past 30 years. Despite the expansion of places and the falling birth rate in recent years, there are still not enough places to meet local needs. In the school year 1990–1, one child in five in the year preceding school entry did not attend a kindergarten. There are also considerable regional variations. Children living in rural areas are more likely to have access to a place than children in the cities and towns (Zacharenakis, 1995, p. 29).

In 1993, around 64 per cent of children aged between $3^{1}/_{2}$ and $5^{1}/_{2}$ attended publicly funded provision. An estimated 76 per cent of these children were in half-day kindergartens, and 24 per cent in the full-day centres and other services. There are no reliable statistics about the levels of provision for children under 3 years of age, but it is estimated that approximately 3 per cent of the age-group attend publicly funded centres (European Commission Network on Childcare, 1996).

Mothers in employment – family support system

In 1993, 44 per cent of women with a child under the age of 10 years worked outside the home, the vast majority (40 per cent) on a full-time basis (European Commission Network on Childcare, 1996).

According to new regulations for the public service sector, mothers with children of preschool age are allowed to work one or two hours per day less than other employed women, depending on the age of the child. Both parents are entitled to a three-month leave during the child's first two and a half years of life. Some 6–10 days annual leave are granted if the child is sick. In the private sector, firms with more than 300 employees are obliged to offer childcare arrangements. Maternity leave is four months in the public sector (two months before and two months following birth) and 50 days in the private sector (Makrinioti, 1992). There is no tax relief system, nor are there any other direct contributions towards child-rearing.

Childcare in rural areas

The rural regions of Greece are confronted with the problem of a dwindling population (Papadimitriou, 1993). Whereas before the Second World War the Greek economy was predominantly based on agriculture, the postwar years witnessed a tremendous exodus to the cities (in particular to Athens) and abroad. Today it is the families in the mountain regions who face the most serious problems concerning lack of infrastructure and developmental planning. For women it is particularly difficult to find suitable employment or to attend any kind of training. Children tend to be cut off and have little or no social contact with children of their own age. The lack of daycare centres and the fact that the extended family is practically non-existent in remote areas have resulted in mothers working on the fields either taking their children with them or leaving them in the care of older siblings. Primary schools are scattered, which means long journeys for many children. A further problem is that the schools do not offer a mid-day meal, and also that there are no after-school care or recreation facilities.

In recent years the private welfare association EOP has helped to alleviate the situation by opening 84 daycare centres and 73 seasonal centres open during the summer months only.

Current issues and trends

Developing provision matched to local needs

The need for childcare services outside the home is growing. However, the system of early childhood care and education in Greece has not yet adapted to the changing role of women (Makrinioti, 1992, p. 15). Childcare remains a priority issue on the political agenda because of the lack of available places. The few research studies that have been carried out in this area illustrate that kindergartens in their present form (short opening times of three and a half hours) are of no great help for working mothers. Families turn mostly to other family members for support during the interim hours; grandparents play a particularly important role in this respect.

An important task during the coming years will be to improve the situation of children and families in rural areas. In this connection the following measures are considered necessary (Papadimitriou, 1993):

- The development of mobile advisory services and provision – medical, social and educational – for children and parents.
- The expansion of daycare centres for children of preschool age and the setting up of facilities for school children.
- The establishment of more seasonal provision in the agricultural and tourist areas.
- The development of a system of family daycare.
- The development of multipurpose centres for children and adolescents.

Training courses for family daycare providers

In order to extend the number of childcare options open to parents, a new training course for potential family daycare providers has been set up with the help of the EU-NOW programme (New Opportunities for Women). The 240-hour course focuses primarily on early childhood development, health education and music and movement.

B FORMS OF CHILDCARE AND EDUCATIONAL PROVISION

AT A GLANCE

- Two separately organized types of institution: half-day kindergartens for 3–5-year-olds and full-day centres for 0–6-year-olds.
- No organized system of out-of-school provision.

Welfare/Ministry of Internal Affairs and are open during school holidays. They provide a mid-day meal. Some centres in Athens are open up to 8.00 p.m., some also on Saturday mornings. Parental fees are graded according to income, with the private centres being considerably more expensive than the state-run or municipal services. Places are issued according to defined criteria of social need. According to the ministry guidelines published in 1984, the aims and content of the centre programme are similar to those of the state-run kindergartens.

C STAFF TRAINING

AT A GLANCE

- Two separate training systems for work with young children.
- For kindergartens: four-year course of studies at university.
- For full-day centres: 3½ years' training at vocational higher education level.
- No training schemes below tertiary level.

In Greece there are two forms of training for work with young children. Kindergarten pedagogues (*nipiagogos*) are trained to work with 3–6-year-old children – either in half-day kindergartens or in the kindergarten section of daycare centres, and daycare educators (*vrefonipiagogos*) are trained to work with children from birth to 6 years in the full-day centres. Table 11.2 outlines the main features of these two training routes and lists the fields of work open to both kinds of professional. There is no specific training for work with school children in out-of-school facilities.

Kindergarten pedagogue (*nipiagogos*)

Initial training

The former two-year training for work in kindergartens was officially upgraded to a four-year university degree course in 1982. Whereas training previously took place in academies specializing in preschool education, kindergarten pedagogues now study in the preschool department of university education faculties. The first courses started in 1984, and there are currently nine locations across Greece. In order to qualify for entry, candidates have to pass a competitive university entrance examination. At present many university courses are oversubscribed, and only one in four potential candidates is actually able to study.

The four-year training includes practical work placements in kinder-gartens. The length and frequency of this part of the training vary from

Table 11.2 Staff in childcare and education services

Professional title	Initial training/professional qualification	Fields of work
Nipiagos (nursery school teacher)	Entry requirements: • higher school-leaving certificate (lykeio) • national entry examination (genikes exetaseis) for university candidates Training: Pre-1982: 2 years in a specialist training institution, qualifying examination of the particular institution (ptichio nipiagogou) Post-1982: 4 years (8 semesters) at a university education faculty (preschool department) Award: Degree (ptichio tou paedagogikou tmimatos nipiagogon) of the university attended; a three-month induction course is obligatory before taking up first post	Nursery school (nipiagogio) – state run, municipal or private – for children aged 3¹/₂–5¹/₂ years Kindergarten section of full-day centre (paedikos stathmos/ paediko kentro) for children aged 36–66 months
Vrefonipiagogos/ vrefonipiokomos (childcare worker)	Entry requirements: • higher school-leaving certificate or vocational certificate • entry examination of the particular training institute Training (state-run institutions): 3¹/₂ years at a polytechnic (TEI – technologiko ekpaedeftiko idrima), including 6 months in a work placement Award: Diploma (ptichio) of the polytechnic attended Training (private institutions): 2 or 3 years at a state-validated institution, 1 or 2 years at a non-registered institution	Daycare centre (paedikos stathmos/ paediko kentro) for children aged 8 months–6 years, occasionally for 0–3-year-olds only

Note:
Primary schoolteachers, social workers, health visitors, healthcare staff and home economics teachers are all occasionally employed in daycare centres.

university to university. Course content includes education, professional studies/methodology, psychology, sociology, Greek language, music, fine arts, foreign languages.

In-service training

In-service training for kindergarten pedagogues is partly obligatory, partly optional. Courses take place in the 14 'regional in-service centres' in the larger towns. There is also an in-service training institute in Athens for staff in nursery schools and primary schools.

Courses are obligatory:

- Before taking up a post in a state nursery school (a three-month course).
- For updating knowledge on specific issues.
- For the dissemination of reform projects.

Staff with the former two-year training can attend a two-year part-time course in order to have their qualification upgraded to the level of a university degree. Kindergarten pedagogues with a university degree can study for a higher degree (master's, doctorate). The in-service institute in Athens (MDDE) offers a two-year course in special education for staff under 40 years.

Kindergarten pedagogues are seconded both for the obligatory and for the optional courses. Supply staff take over their duties. They also receive an additional supplementary benefit for the duration of the course (cf. Zacharenakis, 1993, p. 20ff.).

Career prospects

Unemployment is widespread in Greece, and this has led to a situation where trained kindergarten pedagogues have to wait up to nine years before being officially employed in a regular job. This means that those trained within the new four-year system are only now beginning to enter the system. It also means that many qualified professionals do not actually end up working in a kindergarten, since the long waiting period often necessitates changing to another field of work. Some work in a daycare centre, often as director, until they are able to find a post in a kindergarten.

Kindergarten pedagogues are civil servants in the AT category (degree class). After two years' service they progress from one point on the scale to another, and after a further six years they are promoted to the A category. Kindergarten pedagogues earn the same as teachers in primary and secondary schools. Qualified kindergarten staff can apply for a job as an educational adviser. Advisers are employed by the Ministry of Education and have between 100 and 200 kindergartens in their remit. They do not have inspection tasks. A further promotion prospect is that of administrative head of a school district.

Daycare educators (*vrefonipiagogos/vrefonipiokomos*)

Initial training

Personnel for daycare centres are trained at a polytechnic-type institution of higher vocational education alongside social workers, health visitors and nurses in the faculty of health and social care. The course of study lasts seven semesters, one of which is spent in a practical work placement. Course content (188 hours per semester) is weighted as follows (number of hours per week in brackets):

- Education (39).
- Child care (37).

- Psychology (18).
- Foreign language (12).
- Audio-visual media for young children (11).
- Music (10).
- Music and movement (10).
- Social care (5).
- Children's literature (4).
- Sociology (4).
- Elements of social law (4).
- Paediatrics (4).
- Physical development and nutrition (3).
- Anatomy (3).
- Economics – management of a daycare centre (3).
- Health education – microbiology (2).
- Nutrition (2).
- Developmental paediatrics (2).
- First aid (2).
- Gynaecology (2).
- Educational research (2).
- Organization and management (2).
- Child psychiatry (2).
- Ecology (2).
- Final seminar (3).

Daycare educators are state employees and are paid the same as kindergarten pedagogues, despite the differences in training. The fact that there are two different training schemes for the same broad category of work is a problem in practical terms. Even though daycare educators are paid the same as kindergarten pedagogues, their working conditions are less favourable. For example, they spend eight hours a day in the centre and in direct contact with the children, whereas the kindergarten pedagogues have four hours a day 'contact time'. This has resulted in tensions and status wrangles between the two professional groups and tends to thwart collaborative efforts in the field of early childhood education and care.

REFERENCES AND SOURCES

Dragonas, T., Frangoudaki, A. and Inglessi, Ch. (eds.) (1996) *Beyond One's Own Backyard. Intercultural Teacher Education in Europe.* Society for the Study of Human Sciences, Athens.

Frangos, Ch. (1993) A child development centre (CDC) based on the world of work and everyday life: a case of quality education provision for 2.5 to 5 year old children, *European Early Childhood Education Research Journal*, Vol. 1, no. 1, pp. 41–52.

Frangos, Ch. (1994) The kindergarten as neighbourhood: a project approach for three hundred kindergartens in the framework of university degree equivalence (Greece).

Unpublished paper, University of Thessaloniki.

Kokkinaki, S. K. (1985) Die Ausbildung von Sozialarbeitern in Griechenland, *Soziale Arbeit*, Vol. 36, no. 4–5, pp. 173–9.

Makraki-Chryssafidi, M. (1992) Die Vorschulerziehung in Griechenland, *Treffpunkt Kindergarten/Forum Sozialpädagogik*, Vol. 11, no. 3, pp. 3–8.

Makrinioti, D. (1992) *Childhood as a Social Phenomenon. National Report Greece, Eurosocial Reports*, Vol. 36, no. 12. European Centre for Social Welfare Policy and Research, Vienna.

Markou, G. (1994) Intercultural education in multicultural Greece, *European Journal of Intercultural Studies*, Vol. 4, no. 3, pp. 32–43.

Pantazis, S. (1995) Zur Entwicklung des Kindergartens in Griechenland, *Lernen in Deutschland*, Vol. 15, no. 2, pp. 106–15.

Papadimitriou, V. (1993) Greece, in *Annual Report 1992, European Commission Network on Childcare*. Commission of the European Communities, Brussels.

Papadimitriou, V. (1995) Greece, in *Annual Report 1994, European Commission Network on Childcare*. Commission of the European Communities, Brussels.

Zacharenakis, K. M. (1993) Aus- und Fortbildung von Kindergärtnerinnen in Griechenland, in P. Oberhuemer (ed.) *Blick auf Europa – Tageseinrichtungen für Kinder. Sonderheft der Zeitschrift Theorie und Praxis der Sozialpädagogik*, TPS extra 13, pp. 20–2.

Zacharenakis, K. M. (1995) Fachkräfte in vor- und auserschulischen Einrichtungen für Kinder: Ausbildung und Tätigkeitsprofile – EU-Mitgliedstaat Griechenland. Report commissioned by the State Institute of Early Childhood Education and Research, Munich. University of Crete, Rhethymnon.

12

Ireland

[This chapter is based on a commissioned report submitted to the State Institute of Early Childhood Education and Research (IFP) by Anne McKenna, Dublin. See Appendix I for further details.]

A SOCIAL CONTEXT OF CHILDCARE AND EDUCATION SERVICES

AT A GLANCE

- Statutory school age: 6 years.
- Almost all 5-year-olds and over half of all 4-year-olds in preprimary classes in primary schools.
- Low level of publicly funded early childhood provision outside the school system.
- Low employment rate among mothers with children under 6.
- Very few state-funded family support measures.

Early childhood provision in Ireland is located within a system divided between two independently operating sectors: 'education' and 'welfare'. Early primary education – under the responsibility of the national Department of Education – represents the largest sector. Although compulsory schooling starts at age 6, almost all 5-year-olds and over half of 4-year-olds attend primary school on a voluntary basis. The childcare sector – under the responsibility of the national Department of Health – is an umbrella term to cover all other forms of non-parental care outside the school system, e.g. public sector and private nurseries, workplace nurseries, playgroups and family daycare. There is no established tradition of kindergarten education in Ireland, with separate institutions and training schemes, and there is no organized system of care and leisure facilities for school-age children.

Mothers in the labour force – levels of provision

Ireland – together with Spain – has the lowest rate of maternal employment among the EU countries. In 1993, only 35 per cent of mothers with children aged 0–10 years (compared with 70 per cent and over in Portugal, Denmark and Sweden) worked outside the home (European Commission Network on Childcare, 1996). There are few family support measures to help combine family duties with employment patterns. There are no statutory parental leave arrangements, or leave arrangements to look after a sick child, and maternity leave (ten weeks with the possibility of extending for a further four weeks) is the shortest among the EU countries. In addition, the level of publicly funded provision for children under 3 years of age is very low. In 1993, around 2 per cent of the age-group were enrolled in subsidized provision. Over two thirds of these children attend a community playgroup on a sessional, part-time basis, and only fewer than one third have a full-time place in a nursery. Around 3 per cent of children aged 3–6 years are in provision within the welfare system. Again, most are in part-time playgroups (European Commission Network on Childcare, 1996). Some 99 per cent of 5-year-olds and 55 per cent of 4-year-olds attend primary school on a voluntary basis.

Current issues and developments

Changes in provision and training

Early childhood and out-of-school services in Ireland can be said to be in a process of rapid and far-reaching change (McKenna, 1994c) resulting from demands for increased quantity and quality in childcare provision. The process includes changes in funding, in the support of personnel, in the award of new qualifications and in increased involvement of parents in services. There has also been a noticeable growth in the number of private sector nurseries. Whilst the voluntary sector is lacking in coherence and adequate funding, there are signs of increasing coherence in training and employment policies for publicly financed services at the national level.

The Early Start Programme

In 1994, eight new preschool centres linked to primary schools, each for 60 3 and 4-year-old children, were established in designated areas of disadvantage. Children attend either mornings or afternoons. The centres are managed by the primary school management committee. Each group of 15 children is staffed by a primary schoolteacher and a qualified childcare assistant. This programme is historic in that it is the first national programme for children of preschool age to include components of both 'education' and 'care'. In terms of personnel, it is the first programme to place primary teachers alongside childcare staff.

Decentralization: Regional Educational Councils

Decentralization of school administration is one of the aims for the coming years. The national Department of Education is delegating responsibility to Regional Educational Councils. The aim is to improve the delivery of educational services by making them more sensitive to regional needs, and to involve local communities in education issues. Because of the large number of 4 and 5-year-olds in primary schooling on a voluntary basis, this has implications for parental involvement in services for children not yet of statutory school age.

EU initiatives

EU funding, in particular the NOW (New Opportunities for Women) initiative, has contributed significantly to the development of the childcare infrastructure in Ireland. Various national measures to create jobs in socially disadvantaged areas have also helped these regional developments. However, since these initiatives are all on a project basis, it is difficult to estimate their long-term effects on the national system of provision and training.

B FORMS OF CHILDCARE AND EDUCATIONAL PROVISION

AT A GLANCE

- Majority of 4 and 5-year-olds in preprimary classes in primary schools.
- Publicly funded centres outside the school system only for children 'at risk'.
- Playgroups: a widespread form of provision.
- Increase in number of nurseries run by private agencies.
- No organized out-of-school provision for school children.

Table 12.1 outlines the salient features of services for children aged 0–6 years. The main forms of provision are then described in more detail. In Ireland – apart from a pilot project in Dublin – there are no care and recreation facilities for school-age children on an organized basis, although the need for this kind of provision is growing significantly.

Preprimary schooling – infant classes

Before starting school officially at age 6, children may attend a junior infant class (for 4-year-olds) or a senior infant class (for 5-year-olds) in primary

Table 12.1 Childcare and education services for children aged 0–6 years

Form of provision	Age of children/ coverage rate*	Opening hours	Administrative responsibility
Infant classes (preprimary classes in primary school)	3–4 years (1.3%); 4–5 years (55%); 5–6 years (99%)	$3^1/_2$–5 hours (approx. 20 hours per week)	Ministry of Education
Social service nursery (publicly funded daycare centre for children 'at risk')	0–5 years (2.6%)*	8.30 a.m.–4.30 or 5.00 p.m.	Ministry of Health
Day nursery (private sector provision)	0–5 years (2.5%)**	Full day	Private agencies or local authorities
Playgroup (also Irish-medium playgroups)	2–5 years (6.7%)	Several hours per day	Private agencies
Workplace nursery	0–5 years (0.2%)	Full day	Local authorities

Notes:
*Figures for 1991 (unless stated otherwise), McKenna, 1994.
**Figures for 1992 estimated from advertisements in commercial pages of Irish Telephone Directory (McKenna, 1994).

schools. These classes are usually in the main primary school building and come under the responsibility of the primary headteacher. Classes run for approximately 20 hours per week, from 9.00 a.m. to 12.30 or 2.00 p.m., according to the child's age. Class size varies between 20 and 39 children, the average being 35 children per class with one qualified primary schoolteacher and no auxiliary staff. Attendance is free of charge.

Almost all primary schools are substantially state aided but are established under church or diocesan patronage. As the population of Ireland is predominantly Roman Catholic, the vast majority of these schools (around 93 per cent) are in Roman Catholic ownership. There has been a move in recent years to make provision for non-denominational schools in response to parental demand.

The curriculum for the infant classes is part of an integrated programme extending over the eight years of primary schooling. It includes the following subject areas: Irish, English, mathematics, social/environmental and science education, arts education, physical health education. The official approach emphasizes the integral nature of learning and the importance of child-centred discovery methods of learning. However, experts argue that the average class size does not permit the kind of individualized learning necessary, and that the needs of young children are not given the necessary attention (cf. Hogan and Douglas, 1995).

Social service nursery

The Irish Department of Health funds so-called social service nurseries (sometimes called preschool centres or children's centres) managed by the regional health boards. The remit of the Department of Health is that of caring for children 'at risk' through circumstances of social and economic disadvantage. At the same time, it is also the responsibility of this department to implement the Child Care Act 1991, which regulates services for *all* children and not just for children at risk. In this context health boards are to be given more responsibility concerning the management of services. However, this part of the Act has not yet been implemented.

Waiting lists for a place in a social service nursery are long. Children are admitted from the age of 3 months and may stay in the centre until they are 6 years old. However, most are between 1 and 4 years old, since parents then prefer to send their children to early primary schooling. Centres run on a full-day basis, with opening hours between 8.30 a.m. and 4.30 or 5.00 p.m. In many centres, some children attend mornings, others in the afternoon.

In 1985, regulations concerning registration requirements were issued, and although these are not binding, they are used as a guide in publicly funded services. Requirements include a 'suitable qualification' on the part of personnel, health and safety measures, and recommendations concerning equipment and facilities and adult/child ratios.

Groups are supervised by trained childcare workers (see Table 12.2). The health boards prefer applicants with an award from the Dublin Institute of Technology (see Section C).

Playgroups

Playgroups are the most widespread form of provision for preschool-age children outside early primary schooling. They are open for several hours per day, and children may attend for between one and five sessions per week. The majority are private, and many are run in private homes. Community playgroups are run in community and school halls and are administered by a management committee. There are up to 20 children in one group. Community playgroups are used as placements by the regional health boards for children 'at risk'. However, despite state subsidies, they are generally underfunded and lacking in resources. Playgroups are associated under the Irish Preschool Playgroups Association (IPPA), founded in 1969.

The Irish-medium playgroup movement (An Comhchoiste Reamh-scolaiochta) is an organization to set up, support and monitor Irish-medium playgroups. The aim is to foster the Irish language, and they are marginally better resourced from public funds than their English-language counterparts. Children attend 2–3 hour daily sessions under the guidance of a supervisor.

Family daycare

Family daycare is not regulated. Family daycarers are self-employed and negotiate their conditions of work directly with the child's parents. Within the stipulations of the Child Care Act 1991, family daycarers supervising more than three children under 6 years of age (not counting their own children) will need to be registered and will be subject to inspection. There are no national courses of qualification for family daycarers.

C STAFF TRAINING

AT A GLANCE

- The majority of 4 and 5-year-olds in primary schools on a voluntary basis in classes taught by primary schoolteachers.
- Diverse new (short) training schemes for childcare work outside the official education system.
- Variety of awarding bodies for childcare qualifications.

Teachers of children under statutory school age have the same qualifications as primary teachers of children up to 12 years. They are therefore equal in status and in terms of pay. Workers in childcare services outside the education system may have one of a number of different qualifications awarded by various bodies (see below).

Table 12.2 outlines features of training and the workplace settings of staff in childcare and education services for children aged 0–6 years. There are no regimented courses for work with school-age children, for family daycare or for work in playgroups.

Table 12.2 Staff in childcare and education services

Professional title	Initial training/professional qualification	Fields of work
National teacher (preschool and primary education)	*Entry requirements*: • minimum age 16 years (usual entry age 17 or 18 years) • National Leaving Certificate in 6 subjects (3 obligatory: English, mathematics, Irish) • qualifying examination • interview *Training*: 3 years (pass degree) or 4 years (honours degree) at a college of education (higher education institution attached to a university) *Award*: BEd (Bachelor of Education) or BEd Hons awarded by the university (BEd Hons award at a Trinity College Dublin only)	National school (state-subsidized primary school run by church for 6–12-year-olds, with preprimary classes for 4 and 5-year-olds)

Table 12.2 continued

Professional title	Initial training/professional qualification	Fields of work
Childcare worker	*Entry requirements:* • minimum age 18 years • National Leaving Certificate in at least 5 subjects including English and mathematics *Training:* 2 years at an institute of technology (non-university higher education institution). There is only one institution of this kind in Ireland: the Dublin Institute of Technology. *Award:* Certificate in Early Childhood Care and Education (recognized by the National Council for Educational Awards) After completion of the above-mentioned training scheme it is possible to take a 1–2-year or part-time course at a private college. The various qualifications are recognized by individual organizations (e.g. City & Guilds; National Council for Vocational Awards)	Preschool services (for children aged 0–6 years) e.g. • day nursery/ preschool centre/ children's centre (mostly private centres for 0–6-year-olds) • crèche (sessional care for 0–3-year-olds) • residential centre • workplace nursery • Montessori centre
Nursery nurse/ nursery worker	*Entry requirements:* • minimum age 17 years • National Leaving Certificate • interview *Training:* 2 years at a (private) college of further education *Award:* National Certificate (recognized by the National Council for Educational Awards) *or* Diploma in Nursery Nursing (UK award through NNEB/CACHE – see UK) *or* Diploma in Child Care (UK award through NNEB/CACHE – see UK)	Centres for children aged 0–6 years (see above) Private households as nanny
Montessori teacher	*Entry requirements:* • minimum age 17 years • National Leaving Certificate in 6 subjects • interview *Training:* Diverse training schemes of 1–3 years' duration at private colleges; also distance learning *Awards:* Diverse diplomas and certificates, e.g. • Diploma in Montessori Teaching (3-year course for work with 0–12-year-olds – not recognized by Irish Ministry of Education)	Preschool centres (and private schools) with Montessori programme

Table 12.2 continued

Professional title	Initial training/professional qualification	Fields of work
	• Primary Diploma in Montessori (2-year course for work with 3–6-year-olds) • Nursery (Foundation) Teaching Diploma (2-year course for work with 0–6-year-olds) • Pre-Primary Teaching Certificate (1-year course for work with 3–6-year-olds)	
Playgroup leader	*Entry requirements*: • no formal academic requirements • introductory IPPA course (20 hours) • 1-year work experience in playgroup *Training/Award*: IPPA courses in further education institutions, e.g. • basic course (120 hours) • Diploma in Playgroup Practice (160 hours)	Playgroup (for 2¹/₂–4-year-olds)

Primary schoolteacher (national teacher)

Initial training

There are five colleges for the training of teachers in Ireland, each affiliated to a university. Entrance is based on specified performance within the National Leaving Certificate awarded at age 17 years after five or six years of postprimary education. Applicants should be at least 16 years old and not older than 22 years.

Length of training is three years. In some colleges it is possible to study for a fourth year in order to obtain a higher degree pass (honours award). Work placements take up 18 weeks, 6 weeks per year of study. Course content – comprising academic subjects and professional studies – varies from college to college. Most include the following:

- *Academic subjects*: English; French; Irish; geography; history; mathematics; biosciences; philosophy; music; German.
- *Professional studies*: philosophy of education; history of education; sociology of education; developmental psychology; educational psychology; curriculum studies.
- *Subject methodology*: Irish; English; social studies; environmental studies; science; religion, music; arts and crafts; language arts; physical education.

On successful completion of the course, a degree (BEd or BEd Hons) is awarded by the university to which the college is affiliated.

In-service training/inspection

In-service training is not mandatory. Most training institutions run in-service courses during the summer vacation months. Course participants are granted three days' leave in lieu of time spent on courses during holiday times. In-service training has high priority within the teachers' union – the Irish National Teachers' Organization (INTO). Traditionally INTO have offered one or two-day courses on a variety of topics from administration and management to specific issues on classroom management and learning difficulties. As yet there is no certification of in-service training. One college, the Froebel College, offers a two-year part-time in-service diploma which is recognized by the Department of Education for salary incremental purposes.

The role of primary school inspectors is advisory as well as inspectorial. There are no inspectors specifically designated for early primary schooling.

Training and awards in the childcare sector

There are three national accrediting bodies in the field of training for childcare in Ireland: the Dublin Institute of Technology, the National Council for Educational Awards and the National Council for Vocational Awards.

The Dublin Institute of Technology

The Dublin Institute of Technology was founded in 1992 as a tertiary education organization and is made up of a number of separate colleges which previously operated under the vocational education sector. It offers two courses in early childhood care and education:

1) *Certificate in Early Childhood Care and Education* (see Table 12.2): a two-year, full-time course qualifying for work in preschool centres, day nurseries, playgroups, children in need, travellers' children. Course content covers the areas: human development; society and its institutions; early childhood care and education; personal development and skills of the worker; work placements in settings with children aged 0–7 years.
2) *Diploma in Early Childhood Care and Education*: a two-year part-time course for candidates interested in acquiring organization and managerial skills. Applicants are expected to hold the above certificate or other qualifications deemed equivalent, and to have worked in the field for a minimum of two years. Course content includes: organization and management; professional studies; assessment and management of children; comparative studies; counselling skills; curriculum; family involvement; play; research.

The National Council for Vocational Awards (NCVA)

The NCVA was established in 1991 to develop a comprehensive certification system for a wide range of vocational education and training programmes with particular reference to the education sector. Awards are granted at four levels (Foundation and Levels 1, 2 and 3). A Level 2 award in childcare is at present offered under the rubric of 'Community and health services'. Of the eight modules needed to acquire a National Vocational Certificate Level 2, the three mandatory modules for a childcare award are: child development; early childhood education; health, hygiene, safety. Level 2 is open to candidates who have completed the National Leaving Certificate and a one-year full-time Post-Leaving Certificate course (PLC) in a vocational or community school.

The National Council for Education Awards (NCEA)

The NCEA was established in 1979 to accredit third-level national colleges (e.g. regional technical colleges) outside the university accrediting system. In response to the current concern about expanded preschool services, a number of regional technical colleges have introduced accredited three-year courses in childcare and related areas. At present it seems that most graduates of these courses are entering private sector nurseries.

Private colleges

There are a number of private colleges in Dublin providing training in childcare. A number of these offer the UK City & Guilds award (for work with children aged 0–7 years). Some are Montessori colleges, one of which grants awards from the Association Montessori International (AMI). Graduates of this college are not officially recognized for primary teaching. However, they may work in publicly funded provision for children with special needs.

REFERENCES AND SOURCES

Ardagh, J. (1994) *Ireland and the Irish. Portrait of a Changing Society.* Hamish Hamilton, London.

Douglas, F. G. (1994) *The History of the Irish Pre-School Playgroups Association.* The Irish Pre-School Playgroups Association, Dublin.

Hogan, M. and Douglas, F. (1995) The professional development of early years childhood educators in Ireland and Germany, *International Journal of Early Childhood*, Vol. 27, no. 1, pp. 19–27.

McKenna, A. (1994a) Ireland, in *Annual Report 1993, European Commission Network on Childcare*. Commission of the European Communities, Brussels.

McKenna, A. (1994b) Childcare in Ireland, *Irish Home Economics Journal*, Vol. 4, no. 1, pp. 14–21.

McKenna, A. (1994c) *Personnel in Early Childhood and Out-of-School Provision – Training and Job Profiles. A Survey in EU Countries.* Report commissioned by the State Institute of Early Childhood Education and Research, Munich. European Commission Network on Childcare, Dublin.

National Council for Educational Awards (1992) *Report of Working Party on Social and Caring Studies.* NCEA, Dublin.

Phádraig, M. N. G. (1991) *Childhood as a Social Phenomenon. National Report*

Ireland. EUROSOCIAL Reports, Vol. 36. European Centre for Social Welfare Policy and Research, Vienna.

Working Group on Childcare Facilities for Working Parents (1994) *Report to the Minister for Equality and Law Reform*. The Stationery Office, Dublin.

13

Italy

Monika Soltendieck

[A] SOCIAL CONTEXT OF CHILDCARE AND EDUCATION SERVICES

AT A GLANCE

- Compulsory school entry age: 6 years.
- Split system of education (for the 3–6-year-olds) and welfare (for children under 3 years of age).
- Preprimary education part of the state education system since 1968.
- High coverage rate for the 3–6-year-olds (approximately 92 per cent).
- Low level of provision for children under 3 years of age.

In Italy, services for children under 3 years fall within the responsibility of the welfare system, whereas preprimary schooling for children from 3 years up to compulsory school age at 6 is part of the public education system. Until the end of the 1960s, 'kindergartens' were almost exclusively run by the Catholic Church, and it was not until 1968 that the *scuola materna* was integrated into the publicly funded education system under the responsibility of the national Ministry of Education (Ministero della Pubblica Istruzione).

Levels of provision

In 1969, official curriculum guidelines were published which form the basis for the educational work with children. During the following years the number of 3–6-year-olds attending preprimary schooling increased steadily – from 59.4 per cent in 1970 to 92 per cent in 1990, with considerable regional differences: in the northern provinces 97 per cent of the age-group attend a *scuola materna*, in the south and on the islands of Sardinia and Sicily approximately 75 per cent.

Centre-based provision for children under 3 years has not been developed in the same way. Approximately 5 per cent of the 0–3-year-olds attend a day nursery/crèche. Again there are considerable regional differences, and 75 per cent of the available places are in northern and central Italy. Despite the higher levels of provision in the north, there are still not enough places to satisfy demand. Parents' co-operatives and other self-help groups have sprung up as an alternative. However, the majority of children under 3 years are cared for either by family members or by a self-employed family daycare provider. There is no organized system of family daycare in Italy.

The employment rate for mothers with children under the age of 10 years is 43 per cent (European Commission Network on Childcare, 1996).

Historical review

Daycare centres of a custodial nature were founded in the 1820s. The first establishment for 3–6-year-olds with an explicitly educational approach was a children's home (*asilo di carità*) founded by an abbot, Ferrante Aporti, in Cremona in 1829. Similar institutions spread rapidly across the country, in particular in the northern provinces. Some 30 years later Friedrich Froebel's ideas began to influence thinking in Italian early childhood education, and the first Froebel kindergarten (*giardino d'infanzia*) was founded in 1869.

At the turn of the century, the Agazzi sisters came to have considerable influence on early childhood education. Their approach emphasized the importance of a family-like atmosphere based on the 'motherly' competences of the personnel. The term *scuola materna* – still in use today – is derived from this approach. Some years later, in 1907, Maria Montessori founded the first *casa dei bambini* (children's house). Her concept of the child (famous throughout Europe and beyond) was that of the creative child who learns about the world through self-initiated activity. The educator works 'alongside the child', providing the physical and material environment to help further the child's physical, emotional and cognitive development. However, Montessori centres were shut down during the Fascist regime and – with support from the Catholic Church – the Agazzi philosophy came to be accepted as the official approach to early childhood education. In 1968, kindergartens were integrated into the official education system.

B FORMS OF CHILDCARE AND EDUCATIONAL PROVISION

AT A GLANCE

- Preprimary schooling (*scuola materna*) for the 3–6-year-olds.
- Day nurseries (*asili nidi*) for children under 3 years.
- Very few services for school children outside school hours.

Table 13.1 outlines the main features of the two main forms of provision: preprimary schooling for the 3–6-year-olds and day nurseries for children under 3 years. They are then described in more detail.

Preprimary schooling (*scuola materna*)

Since 1968, the national Ministry of Education (Ministero della Pubblica Istruzione) has been responsible for the administrative guidelines, curriculum and staffing of preprimary schooling. Approximately half of all *scuole materne* are run by the state, the remainder are managed by local authorities or by private (generally religious) organizations. The funding of state-run centres is regulated by law. Local authority or private institutions can apply for state subsidies, or may be entirely funded through public sources. Attendance is free of charge in the state-run centres; parents pay for the mid-day meal only. Approximately half the local authority centres adhere to the same regulations, otherwise parents pay an income-related fee. About 5 per cent of the private kindergartens – those not run by the Church – are 'exclusive' centres which charge high fees (Filtzinger, 1995).

Most centres have between three and five groups; some comprise one group only, others up to nine groups. Group size varies between 23 and 28, and children are normally grouped according to age. Most children attend preprimary centres on a full-day basis. Centres are open during term times only, usually between 08.30 and 16.30 daily, five or six days a week. Centres not run by the state may have longer or shorter opening hours; however, they must be open for a minimum of 24 hours a week.

Nearly all preprimary centres work according to the didactic guidelines published by the ministry in 1969 and revised in 1991 (*nuovi orientamenti*). The revised guidelines emphasize educational objectives within a holistic approach encompassing religious education; emotional, spiritual and social development; play and creativity; cognitive development; language development; art and design; music and movement; physical education; health education.

Table 13.1   Childcare and education services for children aged 0–6 years

Form of provision	Age of children/coverage rate	Opening hours	Administrative responsibility
Scuola materna (preprimary schooling)	3–6 years (approx. 92%)*	8.30 a.m.–4.30 p.m.	Ministry of Education
Asilo nido (day nursery/crèche)	0–3 years (approx. 5%)** In some northern provinces up to 30%	9 hours daily	Ministry of Health

Notes:
*Figures for 1991, European Commission Network on Childcare.
**Cited in Ghedini, 1993.

In the state-run *scuole materne* parents are obliged to attend parents' evenings. In the local authority institutions a number of forms of parental participation have been developed, e.g. as members of the kindergarten board parents can co-operate with staff in developing the educational programme; and as members of the management board they can influence decisions on opening times and new entrants.

Staff/child ratios and hours of work vary according to the type of centre. In the private and municipal centres, staff work 30 hours a week, whereas hours of work in state-run centres have been reduced to 25. Staff are allocated two hours per week for planning, preparation work, co-operation with parents and in-service training.

A law passed in 1982 stipulates that handicapped children should be integrated into mainstream *scuole materne* – and group size reduced accordingly. A qualified special needs teacher (*insegnante di sostegno*) is employed for a minimum of four handicapped children.

Day nursery (*asilo nido*)

In 1971, day nurseries were officially anchored in national legislation and since then *asili nidi* are managed by local authorities and regional government under the overall responsibility of the national Ministry of Health (Ministero della Sanità). The same law defines the main aims of these services as providing support for families in the case of the mother's employment. In 1983 day nurseries were classified as a 'service on individual demand'. Centres are jointly funded through the state, regional and local government or the local authorities. Parents contribute 36 per cent towards the costs on an income-related basis (Filtzinger, 1995).

Day nurseries are open on a full-time basis (usually nine hours daily) for five days a week and 10–11 months a year. Maximum group size is 10, and children are usually grouped according to age (3–12 months, 12–18 months, 18–24 months, 24–36 months). One member of staff is responsible for five to seven children. Staff work 30 hours a week. Six hours daily are spent with the children, and a further six hours per week are allocated for planning, preparation, co-operation with parents and in-service training.

Integrated services and the 'Reggio-Emilia' approach

During the mid-1980s a group of experts, practitioners and politicians developed a vision of a new, more flexible approach towards services for parents and children. Alongside the more traditional nurseries some of the northern regions now also offer integrated services (*nuove tipologie/servizi integrativi*) with a more specifically community-oriented approach. Opening times and times of attendance are flexible, parents and grandparents are encouraged to participate, and there are links with private organizations which offer specific services. This means that the municipalities are no longer the sole managers of services (Ghedini, 1993).

Reggio-Emilia – known worldwide for its innovative work – is one of the municipalities offering this kind of service. Loris Malaguzzi (1920–94) – founder of the Reggio approach – considered the education of young children to be a public task for the community at large: parents, citizens and politicians. A central concept is children's basic right to a broad education, with the arts (theatre, painting, drawing, music) playing an important role.

'Investment in children is a productive investment' is the Reggio credo. Accordingly, 40 per cent of public spending is allocated to education. However, recent economic restrictions in public spending mean that parents and politicians are having to fight to maintain the quality of the 'best centres in the world' (Dreier, 1993).

C STAFF TRAINING

AT A GLANCE

- Reform of training for staff in preprimary schooling, primary schooling and social care work in 1991–2: now five years' post-14 training.
- Equal salary status for preprimary and primary teaching staff.
- Plans to upgrade training for work in the *scuola materna* (and primary schools) to university level endorsed by law (1990) but not yet implemented.

As early as 1974 there were plans to upgrade the status of the staff working in preprimary centres (*insegnanti di scuola materna*) to university level. A four-year academic course of study was endorsed by law in 1990, but this has not yet been implemented in practice. In the mean time, training schemes for staff in preprimary and primary schooling have been reformed at another level, and the new awards are now equivalent to university entrance. Both the training institutions for primary teachers (*istituti magistrali*) and for the social care and education professions (*instituti professionali*) are nearly all state run. Table 13.2 gives an overview of the different kinds of training – both prereform and postreform – for early childhood education and care services. Following this, the three most relevant professional groups are described in more detail.

nurseries or out-of-school provision for school-age children. This is a matter for the municipalities. The few institutions of this kind are mainly for Italian-speaking children in the larger towns such as Bozen, Meran and Leifers.

Staff training

The training of kindergarten educators is the responsibility of the Bozen regional government and takes place in two vocational schools. Overall responsibility lies with the national Ministry of Education in Rome. Course content is similar to that of the state-run *scuole magistrale* (see Table 13.2). Both the German-language/Ladin-language and the Italian-language vocational school offer the new five-year training scheme for work in kindergartens and other fields (*'progetto EGERIA'*) (see Table 13.2). The diploma award qualifies both for work in the designated fields and for university entrance and is officially recognized in other parts of Italy.

Kindergarten educators wishing to complete a supplementary course of training qualifying for work with handicapped children generally choose to do this in Austria. Bozen offers a two-year part-time course of 1,300 hours to this purpose.

Kindergarten educators are public service employees.

Kindergarten assistants are trained in a two or three-year course at a 'vocational school for women's professions' (Innerhofer, 1991).

NOTE

We should like to thank Fiorella Palini (Sprachenschule München) for her networking arrangements and translation work.

REFERENCES AND SOURCES

Corsaro, W. and Emiliani, F. (1992) Child care, early childhood education, and children's peer culture in Italy, in M. E. Lamb and K. J. Sternberg (eds.) *Child Care in Context, Cross Cultural Perspectives.* Lawrence Erlbaum Associates, Hilldale, NJ.

Dreier, A. (1993) *Was tut der Wind, wenn er nicht weht? Begegnung mit der Kleinkindpädagogik in Reggio Emilia.* FIPP, Berlin.

Dreier, A. (1994) Ein Provokateur in Sachen Kindheit, *Theorie und Praxis der Sozialpädagogik*, Vol. 102, no. 3, pp. 167–8.

Edwards, C., Gandini, L. and Forman, G. (eds.) (1993) *The Hundred Languages of Children. The Reggio Emilia Approach to Early Childhood Education.* Ablex, Norwood, NJ.

EURYDICE (1992) The education system in Italy, in *Information Dossiers on the Structures of the Education Systems in the Member States of the European Community.* Commission of the European Communities, Brussels.

Filtzinger, O. (1984) Der Kindergarten in Italien, *Sozialpädagogische Blätter*, Vol. 35, no. 4, pp. 113–19.

Filtzinger, O. (1993) Berufsprofile und Ausbildung sozialer Fachkräfte in Italien, in L.Guerra and G. Sander (eds.) *Sozialarbeit in Italien*. Schäuble, Rheinfelden and Berlin.

Filtzinger, O. (1995) ErzieherInnenausbildung in Italien, in T. Rauschenbach, K. Beher and D. Knauer (eds.) *Die Erzieherin – Ausbildung und Arbeitsmarkt*. Juventa, Weinheim and Munich.

Ghedini, P. (1993) Italy, in *Annual Report 1992, European Commission Network on Childcare*. Commission of the European Communities, Brussels.

Ghedini, P. (1994) Italy, in *Annual Report 1993, European Commission Network on Childcare*. Commission of the European Communities, Brussels.

Innerhofer, W. (1991) Die Ausbildung zur Kindergärtnerin in Südtirol, *Erziehung und Unterricht, Österreichische Pädagogische Zeitschrift*, Vol. 141, no. 10, pp. 855–65.

Macchietti, S. (1987) La scuola materna italiana, in EURYDICE (ed.) *L'anno nell-'educazione e nella formazione. Dati e valutazioni*. Istituto della Enciclopedia Italiana, Rome.

Pistillo, F. (1989) Preprimary education and care in Italy, in P. Olmstedt and D. Weikart (eds.) *How Nations Serve Young Children: Profiles of Child Care and Education in 14 Countries*. High Scope, Ypsilanti, Mich.

Pusci, L. (1993) Preprimary education in Italy, in T. David (ed.) *Educational Provision for Our Youngest Children: European Perspectives*. Paul Chapman, London.

14

Luxembourg

[A] SOCIAL CONTEXT OF CHILDCARE AND EDUCATION SERVICES

AT A GLANCE

- Three national languages: Letzeburgisch, French, German.
- Approx. 30 per cent immigrant population.
- Relatively low number of mothers in the labour force compared with other EU countries.
- Two separate systems of childcare and education: 1) compulsory preprimary schooling for 4–6-year-olds; 2) services for 0–4-year-olds and for older children outside school hours.
- Rapid expansion of services for the under 4s since 1990, in particular for the 0–2-year-olds; state allowance for caring for children at home and in the case of part-time employment of parents.
- Statutory school age: 6 years.

The Grand Duchy of Luxembourg, with a population of 390,000, has been a multilingual country for generations. The three national languages are Letzeburgisch, French and German. Almost 30 per cent of the population are of foreign origin.

Preprimary education

A notable expansion of 'kindergartens' began in the early 1960s. National legislation which came into force in 1963–4 required all municipalities to set up 'kindergartens' and regulated state funding. The terms *éducation préscolaire* ('preschool education') and *jardin d'enfants* ('kindergarten') were incorporated into a national law for the first time. In 1973, the training of staff came under the responsibility of the state, and the entry requirements for training were raised. Further legislation documents the growing significance of preschool education: in 1976 nursery schooling was made obligatory for 5-year-olds, and in 1992 this legislation was extended to include 4-year-olds.

This means that, although the official school-entry age (primary school) is still 6 years, compulsory schooling in effect begins at the age of 4 years. The main difference is that non-attendance during the two years of preprimary schooling is not considered a legal offence, as it is during the primary school years. Compulsory schooling in Luxembourg thus comprises two years' preprimary schooling (*éducation préscolaire*), six years' primary school (*enseignement primaire*) and three years' secondary schooling (*enseignement complémentaire*).

Preprimary schooling and daycare centres: a split system

Preprimary schooling for the 4–6-year-olds is compulsory, free of charge, centrally regulated and part of the education system under the responsibility of the national Ministry of Education. The daycare centres (*foyers de jour*) for 0–4-year-old children and for school-age children are part of the welfare system regulated by the Ministry of Family Affairs. Services in this sector are generally either initiated by private organizations which sign a contract with the government in order to receive state subsidies, or by purely private agencies.

Mothers in the labour force, level of provision

The number of mothers in the labour force (with a child under the age of 10) is relatively low: 42 per cent, with only 29 per cent in full-time employment. Due to the high number of private agencies providing childcare services it is difficult to obtain reliable statistics of the overall rate of provision for the age-group 0–4-year-olds (see Table 14.1 for estimated figures). Practically 100 per cent of 4 and 5-year-olds attend compulsory preprimary schooling.

Current issues, trends

Expansion of childcare and education services

Since the early 1990s, both central and local government have worked towards expanding and improving the quality of services for children under 4 years of age. Under-resourced regions, particularly in the north of the country, have been prioritized. Further priorities are the expansion of 'open door' daycare centres and provision in areas of social disadvantage, and the integration of handicapped children into mainstream early childhood settings. The highest growth rate has been in services for the under 2s. Between 1992 and 1993 the number of places in centres under government contract (*foyers de jour conventionnés*) increased by 49 per cent for the 0–2-year-olds, by 19 per cent for the 2–4-year-olds and by 18 per cent for children aged 4 and over.

Need for further expansion

Despite recent expansion, the number of places available is still not nearly enough to satisfy the current demand, and waiting lists are long. This is a problem not only for the 0–4 age-group but also for children attending preprimary classes and primary school. School hours are from 8.30 a.m. to 11.30 a.m. six times a week and from 2.00 p.m. to 4.30 p.m. on three afternoons a week. There are therefore considerable 'gaps' in provision, and children often have to change settings two or three times a day – from the preprimary class to the daycare centre and back again, and so on. As one step towards mitigating this problem, the Ministry of Family Affairs has supported the opening of school canteens in some schools.

The following issues are currently under debate:

- More flexible working hours for parents and more flexible opening hours in daycare centres.
- Nationwide expansion of publicly funded centres.
- Regulation and support of family daycare services through state subsidies, basic training and a clearly defined job profile (Charlier, 1994).

B FORMS OF CHILDCARE AND EDUCATIONAL PROVISION

AT A GLANCE

- Compulsory attendance of preprimary schooling as from the age of 4; staff specially trained to work 4–6-year-olds.
- Educational programme of preprimary schooling a mixture of graded learning objectives and holistic, child-centred approach.
- Ethnic minority children account for 30 per cent of child population in preprimary schooling.
- Care and recreation services for school-age children predominantly private.
- Childcare centres (*foyers de jour*): an umbrella institution with provision for children of different age-groups (0–12 years) under the supervision of qualified staff.

In Luxembourg, compulsory schooling begins in effect at age 4. Preprimary schooling is part of the official education system and is centrally regulated by the state. The daycare sector for children under 4 years of age and for the out-of-school care of school-age children is both less regulated and more diverse (see Table 14.1).

Table 14.1 Childcare and education services for children aged 0–16 years

Form of provision	Age of children/coverage rate	Opening hours	Administrative responsibility
Spillschoul (preprimary schooling) Variety of terms used: Letz: *spillschoul* Fr.: *jardin d'enfants, éducation préscolaire* Ger.: *Kindergarten, Vorschule*	4–6 years (compulsory); approx. 100%	Usually open 6 mornings from 8.30 a.m. to 11.30 a.m. and 3 afternoons from 2.00 p.m. to 4.00 p.m.	Ministry of Education
Foyers de jour (childcare centres) usually with: • nursery (*crèche*) • kindergarten (*jardin d'enfants*) • children's centre (*centre d'enfants*) Figures for *foyers de jours* under government contract:* 0–1 years: 1.8% 1–2 years: 2.6% 2–3 years: 5.0% 3–4 years: 6.4% Estimated figures for all *foyers de jours:* 0–1 years: 5.4% 1–2 years: 7.8% 2–3 years: 15% 3–4 years: 19.2%	0–12 years 0–12 months 2–4 years 4–12 years	7.30 a.m. – 6.30 p.m.	Ministry of Family Affairs, private agencies
Garderies (short-term sessional care either within child-care centre or on separate premises)	2–4 years, occasionally older children	Flexible	Ministry of Family Affairs, private agencies
Foyers de jour porte ouverte ('open-door' centres): • for children (*pour enfants*) • for adolescents (*pour adolescents*)	 4–12 years 12–16 years	Flexible	Ministry of Family Affairs, private agencies

Note:
*Calculations based on figures from Ministère de la Famille et de la Solidarité, June 1996. No reliable data for the privately run *foyers de jours* (which account for over half the available provision).

Preprimary schooling (*éducation préscolaire*)

The two years' compulsory preschooling are considered on the one hand a grounding and preparation for primary school; on the other, they are seen as part of a tradition based on the 'classical' kindergarten education ideas of Froebel and Montessori. In practice, specific learning goals and developmental objectives based on defined curriculum areas and a structured approach towards progression form the basis of the educational work with children.

Staff are employed by the Ministry of Education. The local authorities are responsible for school administration and for allocating running costs. The children are grouped in mixed age-bands (4–6 years). Class size varies between 18 and 22 children, staffed by one preschool teacher with a three-year training at higher education level specializing in this age-group only. Preprimary schooling is considered to be an important integrating factor in this multicultural and multilingual country. Particular attention is paid to the transmission of Letzeburgisch; until now, there has been no official policy on bilingual or multilingual language transmission during the early years.

Daycare centres (*foyers de jour*)

Daycare centres for children under 4 and also for school-age children (see Table 14.1) come under the welfare system, and well over half of all services are run by private agencies. The Ministry of Family Affairs has supported the expansion of services. It makes contracts with and subsidizes childcare centres (*foyers de jour conventionnés*). There are also purely private agencies without such an agreement (*foyers de jour non-conventionnés*). Some of these now also receive state subsidies. Nevertheless present levels of provision are not sufficient to cover demand. In the allocation of places, priority is given to lone parents, socially and economically disadvantaged families and working parents.

In each group there are two members of staff, usually trained 'social educators' (*éducateurs*), or in groups with babies and toddlers under 18 months' sometimes a children's nurse (*infirmière en pédiatrie*). Staff/child ratios are 1/5 for children up to 18 months, 1/7 for children between 18 months and 3 years, 1/8 for children aged 4–12 years and 1/10 for older children. Centre directors may be 'graduated social educators' (*éducateurs gradués*), social pedagogues (*assistantes sociales*), preprimary teachers (*instituteurs de l'éducation préscolaire*) or also graduates in education or psychology. Small centres sometimes employ an *éducateur* as director. Private centres generally also comply with the above-mentioned staffing requirements.

The predominantly private nature of provision makes it difficult to make generalized statements about centre objectives and approaches. Compared with preprimary schooling, however, provision for the 0–4-year-olds is less structured and directed, with greater emphasis on free play and child-initiated activities. The integration of handicapped children is one of the objectives officially supported by the Ministry of Family Affairs.

Further forms of provision

Garderies

Short-term sessional care of children for parents needing provision for a few hours. Often staffed by non-qualified and voluntary personnel.

Foyers de jour porte ouverte

This 'open door' service provides different kinds of social and cultural activities and staff also supervise homework. Since the early 1990s, the Luxembourg government has placed emphasis on the development of this kind of service, particularly in underprivileged areas and in urban centres with a large immigrant population.

Assistance maternelle

Family daycare is not regulated, and there are no reliable statistics about the number of children in this type of service: a recent survey estimated approximately 4 per cent of children under 7.

C STAFF TRAINING

AT A GLANCE

- Sufficient knowledge of the three national languages – Letzeburgisch, French, German – a necessary entry requirement for all relevant training schemes.
- Preschool teachers (instituteur de l'éducation préscolaire) trained specifically for the 4–6 age-group.
- Qualified 'social educators' (éducateur and éducateur gradué) work with 0–4-year-olds and in out-of-school provision.
- 'Social educator' training at two different levels: both broad-based schemes combining a sociopedagogical with a remedial/special needs focus.

First it is necessary to distinguish between three different kinds of training and career paths in the work with children aged 0–6 and with children outside school hours:

1) The training as instituteur de l'éducation préscolaire (preschool teacher) at a non-university higher education institution (institut supérieur d'études et de recherches pédagogiques – ISERP) for work with 4–6-years-olds in preprimary education.

2) The broad-based sociopedagogical training schemes for the *éducateur* ('social educator') and *éducateur gradué* ('graduated social educator') at higher education institutions specializing in education and social work (*institut d'études éducatives et sociales – IEES*) for work with children under 4 years of age, in out-of-school care for school-age children and in diverse other fields.

3) The paramedically oriented training as *infirmière en pédiatrie* (children's nurse, formerly known as *puéricultrice*) at the National School for Paramedical Professions (École d'Etat pour Paramédicaux) for work with babies and toddlers (under 18 months) in daycare centres and in diverse other fields.

Table 14.2 summarizes the main features of these training schemes. The schemes for the *instituteur* and the *éducateur* are then described in more detail.

Table 14.2   Staff in childcare and education services

Professional title	Initial training/professional qualification	Fields of work
Instituteur de l'éducation préscolaire ('teacher, preprimary education')	*Entry requirements:* University entrance (*diplôme de fin d'études secondaires*) Proficiency in the three national languages: Letzeburgisch, French, German *Training:* Post-1983: 3 years' higher education at *institut supérieur d'études et de recherches pédagogiques* in association with the university (*centre universitaire*). One year jointly with primary schoolteachers, 2 years' specialist study for preprimary education *Award:* Certificat d'études pédagogiques, option éducation préscolaire Pre-1983: 2 years at the *institute pédagogique* (same status as training for primary schoolteachers)	*Éducation préscolaire* – obligatory preprimary education for 4–6-years-olds (see Table 14.1 for alternative terms)
Éducateur ('social educator') Pre-1990: *moniteur d'éducation différenciée* (special needs worker)	*Entry requirements:* Proficiency in Letzeburgisch, French and German. 11 years' schooling, including 5 successfully completed years at upper secondary level (*gymnasium*) *or* 5 years' vocational secondary level (social and paramedical) *or* equivalent	Broad-based qualification for work with all age-groups in a range of institutions and services, e.g.: • *crèche* (nursery) • *foyer de jour* (daycare centre) • centres for handicapped • residential care for children and adolescents

Table 14.2 continued

Professional title	Initial training/professional qualification	• boarding schools Fields of work
	Pre-1990: 11 years' schooling or completion of the former 'intermediate school' (*école moyenne*) *Training:* 3 years at a higher education college for education and social work (*institut d'études éducatives et sociales*) with integrated work placements, or 6 years' part-time training Pre-1990: 2 years' remedial/ sociopedagogic/special education training within the special education system *Award:* *Diplôme luxembourgeois d'éducateur*	• schemes to support the young unemployed • rehabilitation schemes for adolescents and handicapped • centres and services for the elderly • leisure education • *maison des jeunes* (youth centre)
Éducateur gradué ('graduated social educator') Pre-1990: *Éducateur*	*Entry requirements:* University entrance (*diplôme de fin d'études secondaires* or equivalent) *or* the Luxembourg social educator diploma (*diplôme luxembourgeois d'éducateur*) and 3 years' relevant work experience Proficiency in Letzeburgisch, French and German *Training:* 3 years at higher education institution (*institut d'études éducatives et sociales*) with integrated work placement: 2 years' general training, 1-year specialist study in two areas of choice: special education, educative work in centres (e.g. daycare centre), leisure education, health education, socioprofessional orientation, forms and treatment of social maladjustment, work with the elderly, work with the handicapped *Award:* *Diplôme d'éducateur gradué* Pre-1990: 2 years' remedial/ sociopedagogic/special education training within the special education system	Broad-based qualification for work with all age-groups in a range of institutions and services at different levels: practical work with children and adults, counselling, intervention schemes for children and adults with special needs, management role in centres, e.g.: nurseries, daycare centres, special education centres, services for the elderly, residential care, career counselling, support schemes for the young unemployed, health education, support schemes for marginalized groups, *lyceum*

Table 14.2 continued

Professional title	Initial training/professional qualification	Fields of work
Infirmier/infirmière en pédiatrie (children's nurse – formerly *puériculteur/puéricultrice*)	*Entry requirements:* • 11 years' schooling • proficiency in Letzeburgisch, French and German • qualification as medical nurse (*diplôme d'infirmière*) *Training:* 1-year specialist training at the National School for Paramedical Professions (École d'Etat de Paramédicaux)	*Crèche* (nursery); *foyer de jour* (daycare centre); children's hospital; residential care

Teacher, preprimary schooling
(*instituteur de l'éducation préscolaire*)

Initial training

Since 1983, preprimary teachers have been trained at higher education level. Candidates are selected according to the grades of their school leaving certificate (*examen de fin d'études secondaires*). This is one of the reasons why many students choose to study in Belgium instead of their home country.

Aspiring preschool teachers attend the same training institution as future primary schoolteachers (*instituteur de l'enseignement primaire*). The use of the term *éducation* in the professional title signifies the educative emphasis compared with the more instructive 'teaching' approach (*enseignement*) at primary level. Both kinds of teachers are civil servants.

The three-year training comprises a one-year foundation course together with primary students and a two-year specialist option in preprimary education. The one-year foundation course covers general studies in education, sociology, general psychology, social psychology, developmental psychology, educational psychology, clinical psychology, computer-based learning, information technology, linguistics, geography and history. The two-year option includes developmental psychology and developmental psychopathology; curriculum studies; policy; teaching styles and methods. Professional studies include: Letzeburgisch, mathematics, social studies, art education, play, sport, music. The work placements over a period of 7–9 weeks take place either in preprimary centres or primary schools.

In-service training

Most in-service courses are provided by the initial training institutions (*institut supérieur d'études et de recherches pédagogiques*). The two main objectives are to increase professional knowledge and to strengthen didactic expertise. Following completion of 90 hours of in-service courses, candidates are awarded a certificate (*Certificat de Perfectionnement*) which can influence pay, career chances and further in-service options. After 10 years' work experience preprimary teachers may change to working in primary schools if they so wish and if they pass the necessary entrance examination. The same procedure is possible for primary schoolteachers wishing to work with younger children.

'Social educator' training schemes

In Luxembourg, training for work with children outside the compulsory education system originally developed within the special education system. The profession of *éducateur*, founded in 1973, focused initially on remedial and special needs work. Since 1990, when a new training institution (Institut d'Études Éducatives et Sociales) was founded within a wider reform of the 'social and educational training schemes', the sociopedagogic branch of education has become more firmly established as an independent training and professional sector, and relevant training schemes have been upgraded (see Table 14.2). Both the training schemes as *éducateur* and *éducateur gradué* still pay particular attention to children with special needs, and 'Psychopedagogy' (*psychopédagogie*) is given considerable weight alongside the more general sociopedagogic subject areas.

Since 1990, the reformed training scheme for *éducateurs* takes place at the above-mentioned training institution and lasts three years (six years part-time). Approximately one third of the course is spent in work placements. The training prepares for work with children and adults in a wide range of sociopedagogical, remedial and special education services and settings. Professional studies include the role of the *éducateur* in nurseries, daycare centres, residential care, special education units; psychopedagogy and remedial education with children and adults; gerontology; support for children in school and supervision of homework; psychomotor, music and aesthetic education with handicapped persons; children's literature and media education; health education; accountancy; statistics; French, German, English; youth employment schemes, etc.

The approximate weighting of the various areas is as follows (pers. comm., J. Matheis, 1995):

• *Year 1*: 20% remedial and special education; 80% social pedagogy.
• *Year 2*: 33% remedial and special education; 67% social pedagogy.
• *Year 3*: 25% remedial and special education; 75% social pedagogy.

Qualified *éducateurs* with three years' work experience may decide to complete the training scheme to become an *éducateur gradué*, which in 1990 was upgraded from a two-year to a three-year training at higher education level. The course comprises two years of general studies and one-year specialist study in two areas of choice. Approximately one quarter of the course is spent in work placements. The theoretical part of training comprises education and social work (including remedial and special education), psychology (psychology of learning, clinical psychology), sociology, gerontology, biology, medical studies (biological roots of behaviour, paediatrics, social psychiatry), law (relevant legislation for work in Luxembourg), social science research methods. Professional studies include aesthetic education, music, movement, expression, sport, theatre for children and adolescents, body expression, psychomotor development, sociocultural animation with the elderly, social science research methods, audio-visual techniques in education. The options during the third year of study include the whole range of workplace settings (see Table 14.2). The option 'educative work in centres' includes the following topics (number of hours in brackets):

- Psychopedagogical approaches in nurseries and daycare centres (40).
- Play activities in daycare centres (20).
- Psychodynamic processes in groups (40).
- Planning methods in education (20).
- Psychotherapeutic approaches in education and social work (40).
- Non-directive methods in education and social work (40).
- Working with socially maladjusted and behaviourally disturbed children (40).
- Social care and rehabilitation of adolescents and young adults (20).
- Sociopedagogical work with families: levels and forms of co-operation (20).
- Professional responsibilities (20).
- Education and social work in centres (weekend introductory course).

The training scheme qualifies both for group work and management positions in all kinds of sociopedagogical, remedial and special education settings. Qualified *éducateurs gradués* are eligible for university study, and they are excepted from certain requirements on the basis of their previous studies (e.g. in education, psychology).

In-service training for *éducateurs* is optional, but both *éducateurs* and *éducateurs gradués* may be obliged by law to attend a certain course if this is considered necessary. There are no certificated in-service courses which affect either salary or promotion prospects.

NOTES

We much appreciate the help of the following people in obtaining the necessary information for this chapter:

- Jean Altmann – Representative for Luxembourg, European Childcare Network.
- Claude Janizzi – Officer-in-Charge of Daycare Centres, Ministry of Family Affairs (Ministère de la Famille et de la Solidarité).
- Jos Matheis – Director, Institute for Education and Social Work (IEES – Institut d'Études Éducatives et Sociales) – training college for *éducateurs*.

- George Wirtgen – Director, Institute for Educational Training and Research (ISERP – Institut Supérieur d'Études et de Recherches Pédagogiques) – training college for teachers.

REFERENCES AND SOURCES

Altmann, J. (1994) Luxembourg, in *Annual Report 1993, European Commission Network on Childcare*. Commission of the European Communities, Brussels.

Charlier, J. (1994) *Dossier 'Le gardiennage à domicile'*. Femmes Europe, Luxembourg.

Ministère de l'Education Nationale (1993) *Eis Spillschoul. Plan cadre pour l'éducation préscolaire au Grand-Duché de Luxembourg*. MEN, Luxembourg.

15

The Netherlands

(This chapter is based on a report submitted to the State Institute of Early Childhood Education and Research by Frea Janssen-Vos, Utrecht, and Liesbeth Pot, Castricum. See Appendix I for further details.)

[A] SOCIAL CONTEXT OF CHILDCARE AND EDUCATION SERVICES

AT A GLANCE

- A split system of provision for the 4–6-year-olds (education) and for children under 4 years of age (welfare).
- Compulsory schooling at age 5, almost all 4-years-olds in school.
- Kindergarten and primary school integrated into single educational unit (*basisschool*) for 4–12-year-olds in 1985; staff training for both sectors also amalgamated.
- Low number of working mothers compared with other EU countries.
- Government incentive scheme 1990–1995 to support expansion of childcare provision.
- Increasing market orientation and privatization in the welfare sector.

Three strands of development

From today's perspective it is possible to trace three main strands in the development of childcare and educational provision in The Netherlands. One is the expansion of 'kindergartens' (*kleuterscholen*). The first kindergartens were based on the ideas of Pestalozzi and Froebel, and later, Montessori. During the postwar years, kindergartens became a widespread form of educational provision for 4 and 5-year-old children and in 1956 they were defined by law as a free service for this age-group. Finally, in 1985, they were integrated into the compulsory school system as part of the *basisschool* – the primary school for 4–12-year-olds. The second strand of development concerns daycare centres, initially established not as an educational measure but for the care of children of working mothers in need of support. In 1956 there were only 30 such establishments – *kinderdagverblijven* – in The Netherlands, and the level of provision remained low until recently, when a targeted funding measure by the government from 1990 to 1996 furthered expansion. A third strand of development is the playgroup movement (*peuterspeelzalen*) – parent co-operatives for 2 and 3-year-old children founded in the 1960s and attended today by over half the children aged 2 and 3 years.

Preprimary education: from 'kindergarten' to 'integrated primary school'

Up until 1985, 4–6-year-olds attended *kleuterscholen* – preschool establishments under the responsibility of the Ministry of Education and Science (now called the Ministry of Education, Science and the Arts). Of 4 and 5-year-olds, 95 per cent attended this form of provision. Today – since the Education Reform Act 1985 – there is no longer a separate 'education system' for the preschool years, with its own training schemes and institutions. Education for the 4 and 5-year-olds is now integrated into the primary school system. Compulsory schooling begins at the age of 5. In practice, however, most children (*c.* 95 per cent) attend school as from the age of 4.

Primary schools are both state run and managed by private agencies. Some 70 per cent of all schools in this sector – and 60 per cent of secondary schools – are privately run (31.5 per cent by the Catholic Church, 25.2 per cent by the Protestant Church, 15.2 per cent by other denominations or non-denominational organizations).

Female employment – childcare support measures

Compared with the extent of state support for the education of children aged 4 years and older, services for young children under the welfare system have been given far less political priority, and levels of provision are low (see Table 15.1 for details on coverage rates). It is interesting to note that until recently The Netherlands has had a very low rate of female employment among women with young children – the lowest alongside Ireland. Officially, the upbringing of young children has long been considered to be a matter to be solved privately or in co-operation with employers – and here there are parallels with the situation in the UK, Ireland and Germany. Accordingly, parental responsibility and the importance of the mother–child relationship have been emphasized in public policy (Singer, 1994). During the early 1980s, however, childcare services for working parents became a political issue, both as a question of gender equality and as a result of the need for the increased participation of women in the labour market.

Government incentive scheme – expansion of services

In 1990, the government decided to support the expansion of services in the welfare system actively both for young children and for school-age children. During a five-year 'Stimulative Measure' programme, central government funds have been channelled into the setting up of a variety of services, often in conjunction with employers. Playgroups were not included in this funding strategy, since with their limited opening hours they were not considered a viable 'care alternative' for working mothers. The thrust of all measures is one closely linked to the labour market – a view that services for young children are needed to meet labour supply needs. The long-term objective is that 70 per cent of all places should be funded by employers and parents and only 30 per cent by local authorities and parents.

Current issues and trends

Decentralization, deregulation, privatization

In 1987, responsibility for the funding and management of daycare services for children under the age of 4 years was delegated to the local authorities. Only a few guidelines are still centrally regulated, and a long-term objective is that institutions should become increasingly autonomous, regulating supply and demand according to consumer needs. This competitive, market-place orientation, intended to attract employers for funding, is influencing access to services (since many are fee-paying) and quality standards. In other words, provision for very young children is not considered to be a basic right, but a factor to be adjusted according to labour market demands in negotiation with trade unions and employers.

Training for work in childcare services

The quality of training for work in services for children outside the education system has been evaluated and criticized in recent research studies. Both the level of training and course content are a focus of this criticism, as is the lack of preparation for work with children within the new broad-based training schemes.

B FORMS OF CHILDCARE AND EDUCATIONAL PROVISION

AT A GLANCE

- Provision for 4–6-year-olds integrated into the primary school system (*basisschool*).
- Long-standing debate about different models of education in the *basisschool* for the 4–6-year-olds and 4–8-year-olds respectively.
- Centres for children under 4 years of age within the welfare system, low level of provision.
- Approximately 50 per cent of 2 and 3-year-olds attend a playgroup.
- Support measures for ethnic minority children of all ages.

Table 15.1 gives an overview of the main forms of provision. Selected forms are then described in more detail.

Table 15.1 Childcare and educational provision for children aged 0–14 years

Form of provision	Age of children/coverage rate*	Opening hours	Administrative responsibility
Basisschool (primary school for 4–12-year-olds)	4–12 years; approx. 95% of 4-year-olds); compulsory schooling for 5-year-olds	At least 22 hours per week during the first 4 years; at least 25 hours per week during the last 4 years Average opening hours: Mon., Tues., Thurs., Fri. 8.30 a.m.–12.00 p.m., 1.15 p.m.–4.00 p.m., Wed. 8.30 a.m.–12.00 p.m. Mid-day supervision (financed by parents) compulsory since 1985	Ministry of Education
Peuterspeelzaal (playgroup)	2 and 3-year-olds, occasionally children under 2; approx. 50% of 2 and 3-year-olds	No attendance on a daily basis, children attend playgroups on average twice a week: • max. length of attendance per day 4 hours • min. length of attendance per day 2.5 hours	Local authorities, private agencies

Table 15.1 continued

Form of provision	Age of children/coverage rate*	Opening hours	Administrative responsibility
Kinderdagverblijf (daycare centre); if the provider is a company or a training centre this provision is entitled *bedrijfscrèches* (workplace nursery)	0–4-year-olds, occasionally attended by school children Approx. 6.1% of 0–4-year-olds, mostly children of working mothers or students	Opening hours at least 9 hours per day, mostly longer, 5 days a week. Max. daily length of attendance: 12 hours	Ministry of Social Affairs, local authorities, private agencies
Gastouderopvang (family daycare – 'care in guest families')	Mainly 0–4-year-olds (1.3% of 0–4-year-olds)	Individual agreement	Ministry of Social Affairs, private agencies
Buitenschoolse (after-school/out-of-school provision on school premises)	4–13-year-olds (0.83% of the 4–13-year-olds) 10–12-year-olds (5%)	Children are entitled to mid-day supervision Opening times flexible	Ministry of Social Affairs, local authorities, private agencies

Note:

*Coverage rate statistics: CBS (Central Statistic Office), cited in Janssen-Vos and Pot, 1994.

Early education in the primary school (*basisschool*)

The 1985 reform integrating kindergartens into a newly structured primary school for 4–12-year-olds was accompanied by a series of innovations and evaluative projects and is still today a controversial issue.

Average group size is 22 children, but many young children find themselves in larger groups. Children are mostly in same age-groups, although the 4 and 5-year-olds are often grouped together.

Research studies have shown that specific features of early childhood education as set down in the Education Act 1985 – the importance of play, an emphasis on social and emotional development and creativity, and issues of continuity, individualized learning and differentiated activities – are not being satisfactorily translated into practice. On the one hand, the integration of early childhood education into the school system has raised its visibility and status; on the other, it is proving difficult to maintain this status as a non-compulsory service within the compulsory school system. Professionals are generally concerned about the quality of education for the 4–8-year-olds. However, there is widespread appreciation of the special needs of this age-group in both government circles and within the professional training system. Different models and approaches are constantly being developed and debated (for further details, see Janssen-Vos and Pot, 1994).

Daycare centres (*kinderdagverblijf*)

Daycare centres both for children aged 2 months to 4 years and for school-age children up to around 12 years of age are considered a service for working parents, and are normally open on a full-day basis around the year. There is also part-time provision (*halvedagverblijf*) – a maximum of five hours per day – usually just for the younger children. The care aspect is paramount. According to regulations, groups should be staffed with two qualified practitioners. Workers may have a whole range of qualifications, often without any specialization in the early childhood field (see Section C for further details). The market orientation is also influencing debates on staffing. It is being asked whether personnel should be employed on a more flexible basis and whether pay should be adjusted according to individual performance.

Playgroups (*peuterspeelzaal*)

Playgroups in The Netherlands are run by private agencies and generally receive a certain amount of public funding. Since 1987 they come under the responsibility of the local authorities, like the daycare centres. Recommendations concerning group size and staffing are similar to those for daycare centres. Half (50.8 per cent) of all 2 and 3-year-olds attend this kind of provision. Playgroups are open for approximately four hours per day, whereas each child may attend for up to seven hours per week. During recent years playgroups have played an increasing role in preventive and support measures for disadvantaged groups.

Out-of-school care for school children

Since 1985 schools have been obliged to provide rooms for children to spend their mid-day break. Most children bring a packed lunch. Provision for school children after school hours is either offered by the daycare centres (*kinderdagverblijf*) or separate institutions. Some community centres also offer programmes for school children. The minimum level of qualification for work in out-of-school care services is an *MBO* award (intermediate vocational school).

Children with special needs

There are a number of government programmes aimed at supporting ethnic minority families and their children. These are community-based 'family activation' programmes in co-operation with paraprofessionals. It is assumed that mothers can significantly influence their children's success at school through specific tuition. Some of these programmes in urban areas are carried out in collaboration with playgroups. Support measures for ethnic minority children are also part of official school policy.

[C] STAFF TRAINING

AT A GLANCE

- Two separate systems of training for the care and education of 0–6-year-olds: broad-based social work orientation for work in services for children under 4, training as teacher for work in the *basisschool*.
- Different training schemes at different levels qualify for work in childcare services.
- Training as *basisschool* teacher qualifies for the age-group 4–12 years.
- Long-standing debate about the status of early childhood education within teacher training system.

Vocational education in The Netherlands takes place at three different levels: lower, intermediate and higher (*LBO*, *MBO* and *HBO* – see the glossary, Table 15.2). Vocational training schemes for work with people are described as sociopedagogical schemes. Both the training schemes at intermediate and higher level are offered as a full-time and a part-time option (van Bennekom, 1994).

Table 15.2 outlines the training requirements for preprimary/primary schoolteachers as well as the various broad-based vocational schemes which qualify – among other things – for work with young children.

Table 15.2 Staff in childcare and education provision

Professional title	Initial training/professional qualification	Fields of work
Leraar basisonderwijs (teacher)	*Entry requirements:* HAVO leaving certificate *or* VWO leaving certificate (university entrance requirement) *Training:* 4 years' HBO training (non-university higher education) at an education college (*PABO*). Training for the age-range 4–12 years	*Basisschool* (primary school for children aged 4–12 years)
LKC leidster kinder centra (care worker)	*Entry requirements:* Minimum age 18 years, work experience in a daycare centre *Training:* 2 years part time. Day-release, module system, one day per week at training centre	Daycare centres, playgroups; age-group 0–4 years
MBO training courses, including:	*Entry requirements:* MAVO or LBO *Training:* Broad training for different fields of work (educational, sociopedagogic, sociocultural), including	Sociopedagogic, sociocultural and care work in different settings (both in

Table 15.2   continued

Professional title	Initial training/professional qualification	Fields of work
• *IW (Inrich-tigswerk)* (sociopedago-gical focus)	daycare centres Part-time training courses: *IW:* 3 years, 1 day per week day-release from workplace, 18 hours' work	and outside institutions): daycare centres, residential care, etc. For workers
• *CW (Cultureel Werk)* (sociocultural focus)	*CW:* 2 years, 2 days per week day-release from workplace, 18 hours' work	with *CW* qualification – emphasis on sociocultural
• *AW (Agogisch Werk)* (educational and socio-cultural focus)	Full-time training courses: *AW:* 3 years, focus on sociopedagogic and sociocultural work	work
Post-*MBO*	*Training:* One-year, part-time training for (aspiring) centre directors	Director of daycare centre
HBO	*Entry requirements for HBO:* *HAVO* or *VWO*	Sociopedagogic work, often in leadership function
	Training: 4 years, non-university higher education qualification	
Post-*HBO*	*Training:* Part-time training for leadership posts	Leadership function in various social work placements

Note
Since 1984 there are no longer specific training schemes for work in early childhood education and care. Workers in childcare and education services outside the school system may have a variety of qualifications (mostly broad-based courses for work in the fields of education and social care) at different levels. Also, training courses vary from college to college in their content and course focus.

Glossary (in alphabetical order):
AW	*Agogisch Werk* – sociopedagogic work in institutions.
CW	*Cultureel Werk* – community cultural work.
HAVO	*Hoger Algemeen Voortgezet Onderwijs* – senior general secondary education (5 years).
HBO	*Hoger Beroepsopleiding* – higher vocational education (4 years).
IW	*Inrichtingswerk* – sociopedagogic work in institutions.
LBO	*Largere Beroepsopleiding* – basic secondary education.
MAVO	*Middelbar Algemeen Voortgezet Onderwijs* – junior secondary education (4 years).
MBO	*Middelbar Beroepsopleiding* – senior secondary vocational education (2–4 years).
PABO	*Pedagogische Academie Basis Onderwijs* – teacher training college for primary education (4–12 years).
Post-HBO	Post-higher vocational education qualification.
Post-MBO	Post-senior secondary vocational education qualification.
VWO	*Vorbereidend Wetenschappelijk Onderwijs* – preuniversity education (6 years).

Teacher, preprimary and primary education

Initial training

Until 1984–5 kindergarten educators in the *kleuterscholen* (for 4 and 5-year-olds) were trained in separate training institutions. In 1985, this training course was amalgamated with that for primary schoolteachers, and the new combined training takes place at higher education colleges for primary education (*PABO – Pedagogische Academie Basis Onderwijs*). Course content varies from college to college, but generally studies are divided into three main areas: 1) education; 2) curriculum studies in language, literature, social studies, history, geography, road safety, health education, science, music, art, sport, writing; and 3) sociocultural studies. Aspects specifically concerning early childhood education (e.g. child development studies) are generally integrated into other areas. Some colleges see this as a problem and are trying to give this area more attention. Approximately one quarter of the total course length (four years) is spent in work placements (primary schools, special education, counselling services).

In-service training

In-service training courses are generally offered by training colleges and educational institutes, and some by the Ministry of Education (e.g. on topics such as school management or intercultural education). Numerous courses focus on the 4–8 age-range in areas such as developmental education, discovery learning, play, socioemotional development, language development, Dutch as a second language, multicultural education, child observation.

Professional status

Whereas kindergarten educators formerly received less pay, they are now on a par with primary schoolteachers in terms of salary and professional status. Teachers in state-run schools (approximately 30 per cent of all primary schools) are public service employees. Those employed in private schools have more or less the same status concerning pay, pensions rights, etc.

A long-standing controversy: the early education element of teacher training

Evaluation studies have indicated that early childhood education is not given sufficient attention within the combined training scheme. On the one hand, time allocated for this focus has been reduced considerably. Whereas kindergarten educators were formerly trained for three years with a specific early education focus, there now remains only approximately one year for considering the developmental needs of the youngest children in school. Another problem lies in the fact that many former college tutors in early childhood education lost their jobs during the process of amalgamation, and there are often not enough early childhood experts on the staff.

Professionals have long discussed the advantages and disadvantages of the amalgamation move. Raising the status of early childhood education is considered to be one of the positive aspects – through the upgrading of training to higher education level and integration into the public school system. A further positive aspect, so it is argued, is the improved chance for teamwork during the early years of schooling (whereas in the past, kindergarten educators and primary teachers co-operated only rarely, and if so, then not on the basis of equal status).

This long-standing debate about the status of the early years element of training has led to the introduction of a one-year specialization following the first three years of training: either on the early years (4–8-year-olds) or on the later years of primary schooling (8–12-year-olds).

Training schemes for work in childcare services outside the education system

Numerous broad-based vocational training schemes prepare for work in all kinds of sociopedagogic and social care settings. Only one scheme focuses specifically on work with children in daycare centres: the apprenticeship scheme for 'childcare workers in centres' (*leidster kinder centra*).

Childcare worker (LKC – leidster kinder centra)

This two-year post-18 training scheme is part of the apprenticeship system. At least 16 hours per week are spent in a daycare centre or a playgroup and one day per week in college. Initially this scheme was introduced as part of a pilot project for the training and employment of ethnic minorities, in particular those originating from Morocco and Turkey. The number of candidates for this scheme has increased considerably – from 271 in 1988 to 2,754 in 1993, and today this is just as much a qualification route for Dutch candidates as for those from ethnic minority backgrounds. Experts have criticized several aspects of this training scheme, e.g. the low professional level of the qualification, the lack of theory-based knowledge of students, the lack of effective co-operation between the training institutes and workplace settings, and the limited age-group (0–4 years) for which students are trained.

MBO training schemes (senior secondary vocational education)

There are a number of broad-based social work training schemes at the intermediate level (see Table 15.2). The idea behind these schemes is that it gives students who have completed a course the chance to work in a variety of settings. There are eight different training schemes at MBO level, about half of which qualify – among other things – for work in childcare services. Two part-time programmes also prepare for work in this area: the *IW* (*Inrichtungswerk*) scheme, which focuses on work in centres, and the *CW*

(*Cultureel Werk*) scheme for all kinds of social and cultural community work. Among the full-time options the training scheme AW (*Agogisch Werk*) prepares most specifically for work in childcare services. This is a three-year course, the second year of which is spent in a work placement.

HBO training schemes (higher vocational education)

Two training schemes among the various options at higher education level prepare for work in childcare and education services: 'Social work' and 'cultural and social education'. Both are four-year schemes which can also be completed on a part-time basis. Staff in management positions need this type of qualification, and it is common among workers in services for school-age children.

Management posts in childcare services

Qualification requirements for management posts depend on the size of the centre. Two post-*MBO* training schemes qualify for headships in smaller centres. For larger centres, a *HBO* qualification is necessary (see above). A number of post-*HBO* courses focus specifically on management studies.

In-service training

In-service seminars and centre-based training are one of the tasks of the so-called support organizations for daycare centres and playgroups – organizations founded in the 1970s on the initiative of various childcare services. Because of the general reform of social work structures, these organizations now support a range of services in the social sector. Most in-service seminars are arranged on a regional basis, and the in-service providers have regular contact with services. There are also a number of courses offered by recognized private agencies; a growing market orientation also applies to the whole area of in-service training.

REFERENCES AND SOURCES

Alberts, E. (1993) PABO Dordrecht. Gleiche Ausbildung für Kindergarten und Grundschule: Verbesserung oder Bedrohung? Paper given at the Congress 'Europa 1993. Blickpunkt Kindergarten', Bern, 26–7 November.

Bennekom van, J. (1994) *Opleidingen Kinderopvang in Nederland. Kinderen opvangen dat kan je leren!* Vormingscentrum voor de Begeleiding van het Jonge Kind, Gent.

Centraal Bureau voor de Statistiek (1994) *Kindercentra 1993.* CBS, Voorburg.

Heijnen, J. (1993) Algemeen Pedagogisch Studiecentrum. Kindergarten und Schule. Eine Annäherung. Paper given at the Congress 'Europa 1993. Blickpunkt Kindergarten', Bern, 26–7 November.

Janssen-Vos, F. (1994) From narrator to writer. Promoting cultural learning in early childhood. Paper given at the 4th European Conference on the Quality of Early

Childhood Education, Gotheborg, September.

Janssen-Vos, F. and Pot, L. (1994) *Early Childhood Provision in The Netherlands. Personnel in Early Childhood and Out-of-School Provision.* Report commissioned by the State Institute of Early Childhood Education and Research, Munich. Utrecht and Castricum.

Lutz, H. (1995) Die multikulturelle Gesellschaft. Das Beispiel Niederlande. Migrations- und Asylpolitik in Europa, *IZA Informationsdienst zur Ausländerarbeit*, Vol. 1, pp. 32–7.

Meijvogel, R. (1993) *Voorstudie kinderopvang.* Rijksuniversiteit, Groningen.

Pot, L. (1993) Netherlands, in *Annual Report 1992, European Commission Network on Childcare.* Commission of the European Communities, Brussels.

Pot, L. (1994) Netherlands, in *Annual Report 1993, European Commission Network of Childcare.* Commission of the European Communities, Brussels.

Singer, E. (1992) Family policy and preschool programs in The Netherlands, in G. A. Wardill and B. L. Prochner (eds.) *International Handbook of Early Childhood Education.* Garland, New York.

Singer, E. (1993) Shared care for children, *Theory and Psychology*, Vol. 3, no. 4, pp. 429–49.

Singer, E. (1994) Family upbringing and child care facilities in The Netherlands, *Tijdschrift voor Ontwikkelingspsychologie*, Vol. 21, no. 4, pp. 1–7.

16

Portugal

SOCIAL CONTEXT OF CHILDCARE AND
EDUCATION SERVICES

AT A GLANCE

- Non-statutory early childhood services not significantly established until the onset of democracy around 1970 – rapid expansion since this time.
- High rate of working mothers in comparison with other EU countries, and a relatively low rate of coverage in the institutional care and education of 3–6-year-olds.
- Diverse organizational forms, structures and programmes for the education and care of 3–6-year-olds.

Historical background of early childhood education

The first official kindergarten in Portugal (*jardim de infância*) was opened in 1882, to celebrate Friedrich Froebel's centenary. Alongside the Froebelian kindergartens, a national tradition of institutions for young children also developed. This was based on the initiative and ideas of the Portuguese poet and educational reformer João de Deus – famous among other things for his new methods of learning to read published in 1878. The first two João de Deus kindergartens were officially opened in republican Portugal in 1911. Although the importance of early childhood education was included in official declarations of both the First Republic (1910–26) and the Second Republic (1926–37), the plans to establish it were thwarted by continuing financial setbacks and political instability (46 governments in 16 years). The rate of coverage remained at under 1 per cent. In the mean time, a specific course of training for early childhood educators had been established within the training colleges for teachers.

Under the regime of President Salazar which followed – from 1937 over the next 30 years – preschool education had no priority in official policy and the Ministry of Education was stripped of its responsibilities in this area. With the onset of increasing maternal employment, diverse forms of early childhood institutions were in fact set up, but under the responsibility of other ministries (Ministry of the Interior, Ministry of Social Security). In most of these establishments the social welfare role was predominant, although some did have an explicit eductional programme, and in the majority the staff employed were not professionally trained.

Democratization and childcare services after 1970

The onset of democracy at the beginning of the 1970s had a strong influence on educational policies. Legislation in 1973 reinstated preschool education as a responsibility of the state and as part of the official education system. With the revolution of 25 April 1974 there followed a new phase of development. Provision of all kinds (day nurseries, kindergartens, projects for school children, etc.) mushroomed at the level of local initiatives, partly without the necessary funding to ensure adequate standards of quality. This strong grass-roots movement gradually lost its driving force during the following years (partly through the lack of adequate funding), and forms of centralized state support, planning and supervision gained in importance. Today the expansion and development of preschool education has a very high priority in government policy.

General objectives of early childhood education

The state is responsible for creating a network of childcare and educational provision in co-operation with the local authorities and social partners. The state can also take the initiative in setting up kindergartens. Preschool education is defined as the first step in the educational system (Law for Pre-School Education 1996). Some of the official objectives of early childhood education are: to create in the child the feeling that kindergarten is a chance for diverse learning experiences; to encourage the development of social competence – including the respect for cultural plurality, a sense of responsibility and education for citizenship; to promote cognitive development and active learning habits; to support the development of emotional stability; to improve guidance and referral for children with problems; and to ensure the participation of families in the educational process (Ministério da Educação, 1996).

Administrative responsibility, funding, forms of organization

The Portuguese system of non-statutory childcare provision for both preschool and school-age children has diverse organizational forms. Two ministries are responsible for this area: the Ministry of Education (Ministério da Educação) and the Ministry of Employment and Social Security (Ministério do Emprego e da Segurança Social). The Ministry of Social Security is – apart from a few exceptions – responsible for the care of children under 3 years of age, whereas the preschool education of 3–6-year-olds comes under the auspices of both ministries, expressed through different programme emphases and different kinds of centres. Within this framework there are public, private (both non-profitmaking and for-profit) and co-operative organizing bodies and institutions.

Private, non-profitmaking associations – in particular the IPSS (Institução Particular de Solidaridade Social = social solidarity private organizations) – play an important role in the establishment of various forms of daycare provision. The IPSS forms of provision have a special status based on contracts between the IPSS and the Ministry of Employment and Social Affairs. These contracts and the specific regulations for non-statutory childcare and education provision vary considerably from region to region – as does the quality and programme content of the different centres. This special status also applies to the staff employed in IPSS centres. They have different conditions of work from personnel in other institutions, whether public or private.

Mothers in the labour force, levels of provision

Compared with central and northern European countries, industrialization and urbanization developed relatively late in Portugal, and the work of mothers in rural, agricultural areas was not generally associated with the need for support in terms of childcare provision. The 1960s witnessed a drastic change in the situation of women and mothers, brought about by an exodus of men from rural areas into the cities, emigration and colonial wars. The number of single and employed mothers rose significantly, and with it the need for childcare services. The Health and Social Security Ministry of the time declared intervention measures as a state priority. This represented a move away from the pervading idea that voluntary organizations should be responsible for this kind of provision. The 1974 revolution subsequently sparked off a debate which firmly placed the issue of childcare within the context of women's rights.

In Portugal there is a noticeable discrepancy between the number of mothers working outside the home and the availability of childcare provision. Of mothers with children under 10 years of age, 70 per cent work, the majority (63 per cent) in full-time employment (European Commission Network on Childcare, 1996). In contrast, the number of places available for children of preschool age (3–6 years) is relatively low compared with other EU countries: the Ministry of Education (1996) quotes a national average for 1994–5 of 54 per cent; there are other sources quoting a lower level of provision. With the diversity of services it is difficult to get reliable statistics. There are considerable regional differences in the availability of places: densely populated industrial zones have the lowest level of provision (Ministério da Educação, 1996). Despite the current lack of places it is nevertheless important to point out that today's coverage rate is relatively high if one considers that there were hardly any kindergartens at all before 1970. In 1970 the official coverage rate for the 3–6-year-olds was a mere 3 per cent. This had risen to 17 per cent by the early 1980s, and to 40 per cent in 1995 (Leal *et al.*, 1997).

Current trends and issues

Administrative structure

Current debate is centred around the relationship between central, local and private responsibility for childcare and education services. On the one hand, it is argued, economic constraints combined with a much-needed expansion of services call for a more far-reaching privatization of provision; others argue that this would result in a strong market orientation and a consequent lowering of quality standards.

There is general agreement that co-ordination between central government, local authorities and grass-roots initiatives needs to be improved. Some experts favour a more stringent state appraisal system concerning quality standards, and a more systematic integration of the diverse forms of provision. At the same time, local activists tend to reject state regimentation as centralistic and bureaucratic and see it as unnecessary interference in relatively autonomous, community-based democratic structures.

Integration and expansion of services

Both ministries have been critized: the Ministry of Education has been called upon to introduce a kindergarten policy more matched to family needs (e.g. longer opening hours, integration of different forms of provision for different age-groups and target groups), whereas the Ministry of Employment and Social Security has been asked to pay more attention to the educational objectives of provision, to ensure better working conditions for staff and to introduce more stringent quality-control measures. It is argued that only an integrated form of provision which combines education and care with a preventive approach for risk populations can truly offer what both parents and children really need. In 1996 the Ministry of Education laid down an official 'Programme for the expansion and development of preschool education' (Ministério da Educação, 1996).

The transition from kindergarten to school

As in most other European countries, the transition between kindergarten and school and the education of 5-year-olds is a focus of discussion in Portugal – in particular because of the large number of children from immigrant families from former colonies who have difficulties within the school system. In this connection one of the key questions is: would a lowering of compulsory school-entry age or a stronger integration of the two systems 'kindergarten' and 'school' help to improve equality of opportunity?

Should early childhood educators be trained at university?

Proponents of a four-year university-level training for educators argue as follows:

- Early childhood educators should have the same level of training as schoolteachers.
- Educational professions demand a high degree of reflective judgement and self-evaluation and the necessary analytical skills.
- Educators should be given a clear training and supervisory function with regard to the mostly untrained assistants.
- Educators should be able to change professions more easily.

B FORMS OF CHILDCARE AND EDUCATIONAL PROVISION

AT A GLANCE

- Different administrative systems and conditions for the care and education of 3–6-year-olds.
- Different approaches towards kindergarten education: preparation for school, support for families and children, Freinet model of emancipation, equality of opportunity and compensatory education.
- Regulated, state-funded family daycare system (alongside private family daycarers).

Diversity is the key word to describe Portugal's system of non-statutory childhood education and care – in educational, legislative and organizational terms. The most common form of provision is the kindergarten for 3–6-year-olds, and here again there are different approaches and organizational structures. Table 16.1 illustrates key data concerning the main forms of provision, which are subsequently described in more detail.

Kindergarten – daycare centre (*jardim de infância*)

Kindergartens (*jardims de infância*) are for children from the age of 3 up to compulsory school age (6 years). They are sometimes called *centros do dia* ('day centres') or *escola infantil* ('preschool'), but the common umbrella term is *jardim infantil* ('kindergarten').

under the Ministry of Employment and Social Security are targeted primarily towards families and their needs, the Ministry of Education kindergartens focus primarily on providing educational experiences for the child. This division is the focus of controversial debate among experts.

Children in Portugal are grouped both in same-age and in mixed age-groups. Maximum size for a group of 3-year-olds is 15, for a mixed age-group of 3–6-year-olds, 25. In many rural areas groups are smaller, whereas in some private centres in urban areas they are considerably larger. A fully qualified educator (*educadora de infância*) works in each group, and is supported by a generally non-qualified assistant. Large centres (integrating different kinds of services) are usually run under the supervision of a professional with a social work qualification (*assistente social*).

Day nurseries and family daycare

Day nurseries (*creche* or *infantário*) are the responsibility of the Ministry of Employment and Social Security and provide for children from 3 months to 3 years. A qualified professional (usually an educator, sometimes a nurse) is responsible for up to 10 children. Day nurseries are usually financed jointly by public and private funds. Parents cover approximately 30 per cent of the costs; parental fees are income related.

Family daycare is also the responsibility of the Ministry of Employment and Social Security and is managed locally by the 'Regional Social Solidarity Centres' (CRSS – Centros Regionais de Solidaridade Social). State-regulated childminders (*amas*) are generally grouped together in units of 12–20 providers – known as *creche familiar* – who receive training and supervision from the organizing body. Following introductory, on-site training, childminders are granted a provisional licence for five months. They are then assessed and receive their first official licence. The organizing bodies are responsible for the allocation of children, payment of service, in-service training and monitoring the children's progress. Childminders may take up to four children.

Professional supervision is normally carried out by a qualified educator (*educadora de infância*), occasionally by a qualified nurse. Each supervisor is responsible for up to 10 childminders. Organized family daycare providers are entitled to social benefits and insurance. Privately arranged childminding is not regulated, and providers work without social benefits.

Care and leisure facilities for school-age children

Out-of-school provision for school children falls under the umbrella term of 'leisure time activities' (*ATL – actividade de tempos livres*), even when it includes centre-based facilities with a fixed intake. This area of childcare provision is the responsibility of the Ministry of Employment and Social Security, and the individual services are often organized by voluntary associations attached to IPSS. As in other countries, provision is diverse: holiday playschemes, cultural activities, intervention projects for at-risk groups, homework supervision, etc. In the centre-based activities 20 children are allocated to a qualified member of staff (usually an educator, sometimes a teacher).

[C] STAFF TRAINING

AT A GLANCE

- Initial training of educators at higher education institution (non-university) since the 1980s.
- Conditions of work for educators vary according to the ministry responsible for provision.

Table 16.3 outlines the various forms of training for work in the early childhood and out-of-school sectors. Educators (*educadora de infância*) are the professionals who most commonly work with children in this non-statutory provision.

Table 16.3 Staff in childcare and education services

Professional title	Initial training/professional qualification	Fields of work
Educadora de infância (early childhood educator)	*Preliminary remarks:* From 1977 onwards the 'colleges for early childhood educators' (*escolas para educadoras de infância*) were gradually upgraded into 'higher training institutions' (*escolas superiores de educação/de educadores de infância*) and are now non-university higher education institutions. The transformation was completed when the Education Act 1986 came into force *Entry requirements:* Pre-1977–86: 9 years' compulsory schooling, certificate of secondary education Post-1986: 12 years' schooling, university entrance qualification, entrance examination *Initial training:* Pre-1977–86: 3 years at a college of education Post-1986: 3 years at a non-university higher education institution or at a training centre attached to a university *Award:* Pre-1977–86: *Diploma de Educadora de Infância* Post-1986: *Bacherelato em Educação de Infância* The former diploma qualification is fully recognized as far as employment is concerned, but it is not recognized as being at the same	Main field of work: *jardim de infância* (kindergarten, 3–6-year-olds) Less frequent fields of work: *creche/infantário* (day nursery) *Educação de infância itinerante* (mobile services in sparsely populated rural areas) *Centros de actividades de tempos livres (ATL)* (leisure centres – sometimes with after-school provision) *Ludoteca* (toy library – often combined with library) *Colónias de férias* (holiday camps) *Centro de pediatria* (hospital childcare) *Projectos de intervenção*

Table 16.3   continued

Professional title	Initial training/professional qualification	Fields of work
	academic level as the *Bacharelato*. Educators with the former qualification can update it by means of a qualifying course	*comunitária* and *projectos de animação infantil e comunitária* (community projects, in particular in social priority areas)
Enfermeira (nurse)	*Entry qualifications:* Since 1990: 12 years' schooling Leaving certificate, upper secondary education Entrance examinations	Hospital Care of sick children and adults Day nursery/crèche
	Initial training: Until 1988: 3 years, intermediate level, nursing college Since 1988: upgrading of nursing colleges to tertiary level (*escolas superiores de enfermagem*)	
Assistente social (social worker)	*Entry qualifications:* 12 years' schooling Leaving certificate, upper secondary education Entrance examinations	Socioeducational work placements, usually as director
	Initial training: Until 1990: 4 years' tertiary-level training Since 1990: 5 years' university-type institute	
	Award: Until 1990: *Bacharelato* Since 1990: *Licenciatura*	

Educator (*educadora de infância*)

Initial training

Until 1977 the initial training of personnel for work in early childhood and out-of-school provision was at an intermediate level. Training was for a period of three years at colleges specifically for this purpose. As from 1977 these colleges were gradually upgraded to tertiary-level institutions and the training consequently to higher education level, a process which was finally completed in 1986 (see Table 16.3). Some universities also offer courses of training for educators. Training still takes three years and is completed with the award of the *Bacharelato*. A further upgrading of training to a four-year university degree is currently under debate (see Section A).

Over half the training institutions are private, but all come under the responsibility of the Ministry of Education. Courses of study are not identical, but usually include the following subjects: developmental psychology, psychology of learning, education, sociology of education, teaching methods, language and literature, mathematics, expressive arts (drama, music, fine arts, movement), health education, leisure education, leadership and management, research and intervention approaches, options. Education and psychology account for between 20 and 25 per cent of instruction. Between 22 and 28 per cent of the three years are spent in work placements, primarily in kindergartens, sometimes also in day nurseries or community-based intervention projects.

In-service training

Since the Education Act 1986 came into force both educators and schoolteachers are entitled to in-service training. An EU-project, FOCO, which was piloted in the early 1990s, provided an important impetus, both politically and professionally. There is now a system of official accreditation for certain in-service courses which can result in promotion. Courses are offered by a variety of providers: training institutions, universities, professional organizations, trade unions, municipal authorities and private institutions. At present this system is the focus of critical debate. It has been suggested that the universities should take the lead in offering in-service courses, and that trainers should have a profession-linked degree. The remaining providers are, understandably, against this suggestion. One of the controversial issues is the centralization and monitoring of in-service courses, and the accompanying evaluation and accreditation measures.

Since training was raised to tertiary level, educators now have no problem if they want to pursue further studies and qualifications such as a university degree, masters, etc. Some training institutions offer specific two-year courses for trained educators on topics such as research and intervention, leadership or supervision, which qualify for a university degree.

Conditions of work, status

Even though the initial training of educators has been upgraded to tertiary level, it nevertheless has a lower social status compared to that of a schoolteacher. However, career chances have improved generally, not only through the higher academic status but also through the new accreditation system for in-service courses.

There are no recruitment problems in this area, and training institutions have to turn applicants away. A current problem, however, is the stagnation concerning the creation of new posts.

In the report of the National Advisory Board of Education (Conselho Nacional de Educação) (1994) attention is drawn to problems of isolation and the lack of networking within the profession. One of the urgent issues to tackle is the discrepancy between the status and conditions of work of educators in IPSS establishments and those in other forms of provision. Whereas educators generally have the same conditions of service as schoolteachers, the IPSS educators are aligned to the general conditions of work for employees. This means that they are subject to less favourable conditions with regard to pay, hours of work and in-service regulations.

Fluctuation is consequently high among IPSS workers, and this in turn affects the quality of the work with children and families. This is all the more a problem since IPSS centres have the potential to be particularly family-friendly, client-oriented and community-based establishments, with long opening hours and integration of services. The National Commission report puts it this way: 'The current situation is counter-productive: those who work longest are paid lowest'.

Childcare assistants

In kindergartens and day nurseries educators are assisted by staff who have no formal qualification apart from the completion of compulsory schooling and possibly a short induction course. In practice, however, these assistants often also fulfil an educational function, since in the everyday work with children it is difficult to delineate tasks and roles clearly. It is argued on the one hand that assistants should receive a relevant course of training; on the other, educators fear that their jobs could be eroded if less well qualified, i.e. cheaper, staff compete with them – particularly in times of economic restraint.

Nurse (*enfermeira*)

Until 1988 nurses received a three-year training at intermediate level. Between 1988 and 1990 the nursing colleges were gradually upgraded to become higher education institutions (*escolas superiores de enfermagem*) which also – like the training institutions for educators – now award the *Bacharelato* for a successfully completed course of study. For work in day nurseries, employers prefer nurses with a social care qualification (*enfermeira social*) to those with a general nursing qualification.

Further training courses in the sociopedagogical field

Alongside the general course for the training of educators, a number of private training institutions also train 'social educators' (*educadora social*). Entry requirements are the same, and the course also lasts three years. However, the areas of focus are broader – alongside work in kindergartens and day nurseries they include working with the aged and with children with special needs, including handicapped children. Work placements tend to be in the fields outside regular childcare provision. The award is not at present recognized as an official professional qualification.

The qualifications of 'leisure-time workers' (*animador cultural, animador social*) have also not yet gained official recognition. The three-year training takes place in the vocational branch of the upper secondary school. Leisure-time workers are not allowed responsibility for a group, they may only work as assistants.

Until 1990, social workers (*assistente social*) received a four-year training in the higher training institutions and were awarded a *Bacharelato*. Since 1990 the length of training has been extended from four to five years and graduates are awarded a university degree (*licenciatura*). Social workers are normally employed as director of large social institutions, including early childhood centres.

NOTE

Our thanks go to João Formosinho (Conselho Nacional de Educação, 1994) for giving us his unpublished manuscript on preschool education in Portugal which was a great help for compiling this chapter.

REFERENCES AND SOURCES

Bairrão, J., Barbosa, M., Borges, I., Cruz, O. and Macedo-Pinto, I. (1990) *Perfil nacional dos cuidados prestados às crianças com idade inferior a seis anos*. Fundação Calouste Gulbenkian, Lisbon.

Bairrão, J., Marques, T. N. and de Abreu, G. (1986a) Educação pré-escolar: perspectiva atitudinal de educadoras de infância, *Revista de Psicologia e de Ciências da Educação*, Vol. 1, pp. 143–63.

Bairrão, J., Marques, T. N. and de Abreu, G. (1986b) Atitudes e representações em educação pré-escolar, *Análise Psicológica*, Vol. 1, no. 5, pp. 91–103.

Barbosa, M., Cruz, O., Abreu-Lima, I., Henrique, M. R., Bairrão, J. and Borges, M. I. (1992) Situação dos cuidados prestados a crianças de quatro anos de idade em Portugal: Alguns resultados de uma sondagem nacional, *Inovação*, Vol. 5, no. 1, pp. 57–80.

Conselho Nacional de Educação (ed.) (1994) A educação pré-escolar em Portugal. Report no. 1/94 by J. Formosinho. Unpublished MS, Lisbon.

Leal, T. *et al.* (forthcoming, 1997) Kinderbetreuung in Portugal, in W. E. Fthenakis and M. R. Textor (eds.) *Qualität der Kinderbetreuung. Deutsche und internationale Perspektiven*. Beltz, Weinheim and Basel.

Ministério da Educação, Departamento da Educação Básica (1996) *Educação Pré-Escolar em Portugal (Preschool Education in Portugal)*. Ministério da Educação, Lisbon.

Nabuco, M. and Sylva, K. (1995) Comparisons between ECERS ratings of individual pre-school centres and the results of target child observations: do they match or do they differ? Paper given at the 5th European Conference on the Quality of Early Childhood Education, La Sorbonne, Paris, 7–9 September.

Niza, S. (1987) O movimento da escola moderna, *Cadernos de Educação de Infância*, Vol. 1, pp. 8–10.

Santiago Rodrigues, M. E. C. (1994) Por onde passa a infância e a edução pré-escolar? Unpublished MS, University of Porto.

17

Spain

[This chapter is based on commissioned reports submitted to the State Institute of Early Childhood Education and Research (IFP) by Jesús Palacios et al., Paloma Sainz de Vicuña, Irene Balaguer, Lurdes Molina and Elena Lobo Aleu. See Appendix I for further details.]

A SOCIAL CONTEXT OF CHILDCARE AND EDUCATION SERVICES

AT A GLANCE

- Compulsory school entry age: 6 years.
- Expansion of early childhood provision in the 1960s, increase in number of state-run centres (in particular for the 3–6-year-olds) from the mid-1970s onwards.
- Since 1975: decentralization policies.
- 17 autonomous communities, six with full responsibility for education services.
- Education Reform Act 1990 (LOGSE): restructuring of national education system, including the education of 0–6-year-olds.

Decentralization – administrative responsibility for early childhood education

Spain is one of Europe's oldest nation-states. The end of the fascist regime with the death of Franco in 1975 witnessed the rise of autonomy movements and a long process of decentralization still not completely finished today. In the mean time Spain has 17 autonomous communities (*comunidades autónomas*), each with its own constitution. Six of these communities have full responsibility for public education in the region. This means that, since comprehensive educational reform in 1990, both the national Ministry of Education and the education departments of these six autonomous communities are responsible for early childhood education for children from birth up to compulsory school age (6 years). Responsibility for the management of publicly funded early childhood services may be delegated to local authority organizations or private, non-profit-making agencies which sign an agreement with the education authorities; recently there has been a tendency to delegate social services to private agencies (Schilling, 1995, p. 452).

Mothers' employment and levels of provision

Compared with other EU countries, Spain has a low-level employment rate among mothers with children below 10 years: 35 per cent are in the labour force, 29 per cent in full-time employment (European Commission Network on Childcare, 1996).

The number of places in publicly funded centres expanded rapidly during the last decade. Today, over 90 per cent of 4 and 5-year-olds, almost 100 per cent of 5-year-olds and approximately 55 per cent of 3-year-olds are in publicly funded provision (Palacios et al., 1995). Expansion of places for 3-year-olds is a political priority. There are no reliable figures on the extent of provision for children under 3 years of age.

Important education reform Acts: 1970 and 1990

Preschool education was officially defined as part of the education system for the first time in the Education Reform Act 1970 (Ley General de Educación y Financiamiento de la Reforma Educativa = LGE). This first stage was at that time divided into 'kindergartens' (for 2–3-year-olds) and 'preprimary' (for 4–6-year-olds), and only the latter had a clear educative function. The Education Reform Act 1990 (Ley de Ordenación General del Sistema Educativo = LOGSE) now defines provision for the age-group 0–6 years as the first stage of the Spanish education system. This is a completely new departure – also compared with other EU countries. Those with an integrated system of services for this age-group have generally located them not within the education system but within the welfare system.

The first stage of education in Spain is now divided into two cycles: from birth to 3 years, and from 3 to 6 years. The educational objectives in LOGSE emphasize a holistic, developmental approach for both phases. 'School readiness' or specific subject areas are not mentioned in the official aims and guidelines. The term *educación preescolar* ('preschool education') has now been replaced by the broader term *educación infantil* ('early childhood education').

The Education Reform Act 1990 also makes provision for the upgrading of training. All publicly funded centres for children aged 0–6 years (and also existing private centres) are supposed to meet the legal requirements concerning staff qualifications, staff/child ratio and space allocation by the year 2000.

Current issues and trends

Public education for children under 3 years of age

Spain was the first EU country to officially designate publicly funded centres for children under 3 years of age as part of the public education system (LOGSE, 1990). The aim is to abolish the traditional divide between 'care' services for children under 3 years of age and 'education' services for the 3–6-year-olds and to raise the status of work with young children. The fact that this objective has not yet been translated satisfactorily into practice is due to reasons of finance and staffing, and is not a matter of ideology. As already noted, a clear political stance concerning the education of children under 3 years of age is most unusual (Finland and Sweden are the only countries with a similar nationwide pledge). In many countries the low level of provision for this age-group suggests that childcare is a purely private matter, and that provision is only to be seen in relation to issues of female labour market participation. However, this line of argument is seldom heard in Spain – neither in official policy documents, nor in general public attitudes towards the education of very young children.

A new era of reform – and some problems

The reform heralded by the Education Reform Act 1990 (LOGSE) had long been the subject of pilot projects and debate between practitioners, researchers and the Ministry of Education. The question now is how effectively these ideas can be translated into practice. Growing economic restrictions are one of the main obstacles. This is the reason why the 3-year-olds are next on the priority list, and not the 0–2-year-olds. Another open issue is to what extent a new government will support the reform plans. Yet another hindrance lies within the profession itself, which has traditionally conceptualized preschool education as 'preparation for school' – a view at odds with the holistic objectives and developmental goals of LOGSE. This will be one of the most significant challenges for in-service training measures and the newly reformed teacher training courses.

B FORMS OF CHILDCARE AND EDUCATIONAL PROVISION

AT A GLANCE

- Different systems of childcare and education services before and after the Education Reform Act 1990.
- Objectives of reform: early childhood education for 0–6-year-olds in two cycles (0–3 years and 3–6 years) as part of the public education system; revised educational guidelines; higher-level training for both cycles.
- Family daycare and out-of-school provision for school children – uncommon forms of provision and not regulated.

In order to describe the various types of provision it is first necessary to differentiate between the terms used before the 1990 reform and those used afterwards. These are summarized in Table 17.1, after which salient features of the various forms of provision will be described in more detail.

Table 17.1 uses the official terminology for early childhood centres. However, there are a number of features which differ from centre to centre. First of all, it is necessary to distinguish between state-regulated centres (the norm for 3–6-year-olds) and those run by private agencies (as is usually the case for children under 3 years of age). The term *guardería* is an umbrella term for 'care' establishments which have traditionally emphasized the custodial function – not only for younger children but also for the 4 and 5-year-olds. *Guarderías* are normally privately organized and before the 1990 legislation they were seldom officially inspected. Staffing, the programme of activities and space regulations all tended to be of a lower standard than in publicly funded centres.

State-run centres for 3–6-year-olds are often attached to primary schools. Some centres cater for the whole age-range (0–6 years), some only provide for the 3–6-year-olds. Opening times also vary. *Guarderías* are generally open from 7.30 a.m. until around 3.30 p.m., and full-day centres until 6.00 p.m. The opening hours of the state-run and local authority centres vary according to the aims of the centre and to local needs. State-run centres attached to schools are open during school hours (9.30 a.m.–1.00 p.m. and 3.00 p.m.–4.30 p.m.). A distinction is usually made between main sessions (*horario lectivo*) and complementary sessions (*horario complementar*). The main sessions cover approximately five hours a day; complementary sessions include breakfast, a mid-day meal and other 'non-educative' activities, for which there is normally a small charge.

In the case of state-run and state-subsidized centres admission criteria such as family income, vicinity of home, sibling attendance or children with

Table 17.1   Childcare and education services for children aged 0–6 years

Form of provision	Age of children/coverage rate	Administrative responsibility
Pre-1990 Education Reform Act (LOGSE)		
Guardería (day nursery/daycare centre)	0–6 years (mostly 0–3 years)	Private and local authority organizations; no set guidelines for educational work; few state inspections
Educación preescolar ('preschool education')	2–6 years	Ministry of Education; local authorities and private providers
• *jardín de infancia* ('kindergarten')	2–3 years	
• *parvulario* ('preprimary schooling')	4–6 years	
Post-1990 Education Reform Act (LOGSE)		
Educación infantil ('early childhood education') *Escuela de educación infantil* ('school for early childhood) education'	0–6 years	Ministry of Education, local authorities
1er ciclo (1st cycle)	0–3 years	
2er ciclo (2nd cycle)	3–6 years (3-year-olds: 55%; 4 and 5-year-olds: 90–100%*)	

Notes:
Table adapted from Schilling, 1994, p. 18.
*Figures for coverage rate in Palacios *et al.*, 1995.

handicaps are applied in the case of oversubscription. In the case of children under 3 years of age places are allocated first to families with special needs, such as one-parent families.

The 1990 legislation stipulates that only trained staff are to work with 0–6-year-olds. Minimum qualification for work with the under 3s is that of 'early childhood education teacher' (*maestro*) or 'senior early childhood worker' (*técnico superior*) (see Table 17.2). All groups of children in the 3–6 age-range must now be supervised by an 'early childhood education teacher'.

Educational approach

In the *guarderías* the custodial function tends to dominate, even today. The fact that they were often staffed with low-qualified and partly unqualified personnel and that they were not subject to any form of inspection was a major point of criticism before LOGSE (Schilling, 1995, p. 445). They now have to meet the basic requirements set down in LOGSE by the year 2000, and in the mean time many have significantly improved quality standards. The former preschool centres, unlike the *guarderías*, placed emphasis on school readiness, in particular from a compensatory perspective. As we have heard, the 1990 Act rejects this idea and has also broadened the general educational objectives to include children under 3 years of age. To what extent are these aims reflected in the work in centres across the country?

First it is important to know that apart from a few exceptions, e.g. in Catalonia, Spain does not have a strong 'kindergarten' tradition. Preschool education developed as an extension of schooling in general, an emphasis still prevalent today. Empirical studies in Andalusian centres (Lera, 1994) have shown that in the early 1990s most of the time in centres was spent on structured activities, in particular on 'pen and paper' tasks. However, it is feasible to expect that the reformed training approach will step by step transform current practice for all age-groups before compulsory schooling.

C STAFF TRAINING

AT A GLANCE

- Level of training and entry requirements for work with 0–6-year-olds upgraded within the Education Reform Act 1990 (LOGSE): transition regulations for staff up to the year 2000.
- Three-year university-level training as 'early childhood education teacher' for work in the first two cycles of the education system (0–3 years, 3–6 years).
- New training scheme (higher vocational education level) for work with children under 3 years of age.
- Expansion of in-service provision and supplementary training for staff; certificated courses combined with salary increments.

The Education Reform Act 1990 (LOGSE) not only made provision for a complete restructuring of the education system for children aged 0–6 years but also for a reform and upgrading of the training qualifications needed to work in this field.

Before 1990 there were three main training schemes:

- *Profesor de EGB, especialista en preescolar* – 'preschool teacher'.
- *Técnico especialista en jardín de infancia* – 'kindergarten educator'.
- *Técnico auxiliar de jardín de infancia* – 'kindergarten auxiliary worker'.

Since 1990 two schemes of training focus on the early years:

- *Maestro especialista en educación infantil* – 'early childhood education teacher'.
- *Técnico superior en educación infantil* – 'senior early childhood worker'.

A number of transition regulations apply up to the year 2000, in particular for those who had a job before the legislation came into force.

Table 17.2 summarizes the main features of the various training schemes. Both the 'old' and 'new' schemes are then described in more detail.

Table 17.2 Staff in childcare and education services

Professional title	Initial training/ professional qualification	Fields of work
Pre-1990 Education Reform Act (LOGSE)		
Profesor de EGB especialista en preescolar ('teacher, preschool education')	*Entry requirements:* 12 years of schooling, school leaving certificate *Training:* 3 years at a teacher training college (*escuela de magisterio*)	*Parvulario educación preescolar* ('preprimary schooling' mainly for 3–6-year-olds, occasionally for children under 3 years of age)
Post-1990 Education Reform Act (LOGSE)		
Maestro de EGB especialista en educación infantil ('early childhood education teacher')	*Entry requirements:* 12 years of schooling, school leaving certificate plus 1 pre-university foundation year (COU) *Training:* 3 years at a university college for teacher training (*escuela universitaria de formación de profesorado*) *Award:* Diplomado Maestro Especialidad en Educación Infantil (university degree)	*Escuelas de educación infantil* ('schools of early childhood education' for 0–3-year-olds (1st cycle) and 3–6-year-olds (2nd cycle))
Pre-1990 Education Reform Act (LOGSE)		
Técnico auxiliar de jardín de infancia ('auxiliary worker, kindergarten')	*Entry requirements:* 8 years' schooling (*ensino general basico*) – leaving certificate not compulsory *Training:* 2 years' basic vocational training (*instituto de formación profesional*). This training scheme no longer exists. Personnel with this qualification can not be employed in recognized day nurseries, only in privately run centres. The award counts towards the necessary entry requirements for the training scheme *técnico especialista* (see below), but only	*Guardería* and *jardín de infancia* as auxiliary worker, in particular with younger children (0–3/4 years)

Table 17.2   Continued

Professional title	Initial training/ professional qualification	Fields of work
	in conjunction with additional general education studies	
Técnico especialista en jardín de infancia ('kindergarten worker')	*Entry requirements:* 12 years' schooling, leaving certificate (*BUP – Bachillerato Unificado Polyvalente*) *or técnico auxiliar* plus additional general education studies	*Guardería* and *jardín de infancia* • as group leader with 0–3-year-olds • as auxiliary worker with 3–6-year-olds
	Training: 3 years at a vocational training college	

Post-1990 Education Reform Act (LOGSE)

Técnico superior en educación infantil – also called *educador infantil* ('senior worker, early childhood education')	*Entry requirements:* Minimum entry age 18 years 12 years schooling, leaving certificate (*BUP*) + 1 pre-university foundation year (*COU*) or *bachillerato experimental* (new A-level type qualification) *or FP2 (formación Profesional, Módulo 2)* N.B.: These entry requirements can be replaced by a qualifying examination held by the training college (minimum age 20 years).	*Escuela infantil* 1st cycle (0–3 years) – as group leader 2nd cycle (3–6 years) – as auxiliary worker Leisure centres Youth clubs Residential care Special needs centres Family centres
	Training: Approx. 1 year (900 hours) at a higher vocational education institution + 3 months (400 hours) in a work placement. Focus on age-group 0 to 3 years.	

From 'preschool teacher' to 'early childhood education teacher'

The former course of training for work in the preschool field took place at a teaching training college and lasted three years. While training focused on work with 3–6-year-olds (in *parvulário* and *educación preescolar*, see Table 17.1), content-wise the orientation was that of the school curriculum and subject-based teaching.

Today's training as 'early childhood education teacher' demands higher entry requirements, takes place at university-based teaching training institutes and qualifies for the age-group 0–6 years. The following subject areas account for 55–65 per cent of the timetable and are compulsory for all university courses: educational psychology, developmental psychology, sociology of education, theories of education, early childhood institutions, centre management, new technologies and media, teaching methods, work with handicapped children, environmental studies, language development, mathematical thinking, music, art, children's literature. Approximately 20 per cent of the timetable is structured according to local needs. In Catalania, for example, Catalan children's literature is part of the course of studies. Beyond this, between 10 and 15 per cent of the allocated hours may be spent on options chosen by the students.

Work placements are integrated into the three-year period of study and are organized by the university institutes.

Early childhood education teachers are on the same salary scale as primary schoolteachers.

Training schemes at intermediate vocational and higher vocational level

The former training scheme for auxiliary workers in kindergartens (*técnico auxiliar de jardín de infancia*) was criticized for its low entry requirements (completion of compulsory schooling, but not necessarily with leaving certificate). Former kindergarten educators (*técnico especialista en jardín de infancia*) worked either as group leaders in *guarderías* or in conjunction with preschool teachers with the 4–6-year-olds. Today, these workers may only be employed in the first cycle of early childhood education (0–3 years).

Following the Education Reform Act 1990, the auxiliary worker training scheme was abolished and minimum entry requirements for other personnel in the early childhood field were upgraded considerably. Staff with appropriate work experience may take a qualifying examination instead. The new 'senior early childhood worker' (*técnico superior en educación infantil*) may work with the 0–3-year-olds, although at least one early childhood education teacher must also be employed in the institution. The training scheme is fairly short and emphasizes the 0–3 years age phase, whereas the early childhood education teacher course has been criticized for its lack of focus on work with children from birth to 3 years of age.

Work placements for *técnico superior* account for 400 hours and take place in early childhood centres, hospitals and other childcare and social institutions.

This training scheme is still in its early stages and is under constant review. According to experts, the higher entry requirements and general education of candidates and the specialization on the 0–3 age-group are considered to be positive aspects of the new scheme. Critical points are the short length of study and the lack of theory–practice integration through the placement of the practical part of the training scheme at the end of the college course (Sainz de Vicuña, 1994).

In-service training, further studies

Following the 1990 reform, the system of in-service training was expanded considerably, partly as a measure for personnel trained under the pre-1990 system, i.e. the majority of staff in early childhood centres, who have until the year 2000 to 'top up' their qualifications. In-service provision is also seen as an innovatory measure to help introduce new educational ideas and methods. Employers and training institutes are to ensure that staff are given the appropriate opportunities for further studies.

In-service courses for early childhood education teachers are a matter for the education authorities and are held by training institutes or private providers recognized by the authorities. Course topics are generally planned by the local education authorities on an annual basis, and most focus on goals of the education reform.

In-service courses are not compulsory and generally take place outside working hours, apart from some centre-based courses. Each course is certificated, and successful participation affects salary and career chances (pay increments every six years following 100 certificated in-service units). Early childhood education teachers are permitted one or two years' secondment for further university studies (Lobo Aleu, 1995; Palacios *et al.*, 1995).

In-service provision for staff working with children under 3 years of age is generally less regulated and is more directed to regional needs. Implementation of the aims of the Reform Act 1990 are also a priority for this group, with an emphasis on educational aspects of the work compared to the traditional custodial focus.

REFERENCES AND SOURCES

Balaguer, I. and Molina, L. (1995) *La Formación de Maestros Especialistas en Educación Infantil en España*. Report commissioned by the State Institute of Early Childhood Education and Research, Munich. Barcelona.

Lera, M. J. (1994) Ideas de los profesores y su práctica educativa. Un estudio en preescolar. Unpublished thesis, University of Seville.

Lobo Aleu, E. (1995) *Formación Permanente de Educadores en España*. Report commissioned by the State Institute of Early Childhood Education and Research, Munich. Escuela de Educadores, Madrid.

Oliva, A. (1992) Madres y educadores: diferentes concepciones del desarrollo y la educación infantil. Unpublished thesis, University of Seville.

Palacios, J. (1989) Child care and early education in Spain, in D. P. Weikart and P. P. Olmsted (eds.) *Child Care and Early Education in Fifteen Countries*. High Scope, Ypsilanti, Mich.

Palacios, J., Lera, M.- J. and Oliva, A. (forthcoming) Die Qualität der Kinderbetreuung in Spanien, in W. E. Fthenakis and M. R. Textor (eds.) *Qualität von Kinderbetreuung: Deutsche und internationale Perspektiven*. Beltz, Weinheim and Basel.

Palacios, J., Rincón, E., de Prada, M. J. and de Francisco, M. J. (1995) *Educación Infantil en España. Algunos Rasgos Característicos*. Report commissioned by the

State Institute of Early Childhood Education and Research, Munich. Ministerio de Educación y Ciencia, Madrid.

Sainz de Vicuña, P. (1994) *La Formación de Educadores Infantiles Antes y Después de la LOGSE*. Report commissioned by the State Institute of Early Childhood Education and Research, Munich. Instituto de Formación Profesional, Madrid.

Schilling, M. (1994) *Soziale Berufe in Spanien. Ausbildungen, Arbeitsmarkt und Arbeitsfelder im Bereich der Sozialerziehung und Kleinkinderziehung in Spanien aus bundesdeutscher Sicht*. Deutscher Verein für öffentliche und private Fürsorge, Frankfurt.

Schilling, M. (1995) Erzieherinnen in Spanien, in T. Rauschenbach, K. Beher and D. Knauer *Die Erzieherin. Ausbildung und Arbeitsmarkt*. Juventa, Weinheim and Munich.

Schilling, M. (1996) ErzieherInnen in Spanien. SchulpädagogInnen oder SozialpädagogInnen? Paper given at Didacta Conference, Berlin, 17 April.

18

Sweden

SOCIAL CONTEXT OF CHILDCARE AND
EDUCATION SERVICES

AT A GLANCE

- School starting age: 7 years (trend to lower school age to 6).
- Childcare and education services a clear social policy issue and part of public sector spending.
- High employment rate of mothers with children below compulsory school age.
- Comprehensive family support measures.
- Decentralized organization structures.
- Children aged 1–12 years whose parents work or study entitled to a place in a publicly funded centre for children.
- Children's needs and rights a considered focus of different policy areas.
- As from 1997: all publicly funded services for children outside the compulsory school system to be transferred from the Ministry of Social Welfare to the Ministry of Education.

In Sweden, the education and care of children outside the compulsory school system are embedded in a comprehensive social policy closely linked with other policy areas affecting children and families: the economy, the labour market, environment and health, family support measures, gender equality and so on. Today, Sweden not only has one of the highest rates of employment among mothers with children of preschool age but also one of the highest birth rates. One of the explanations often given for this unusual situation is that the decision to have children is positively influenced by the extensive support measures offered by the state. These include a well designed network of publicly funded early childhood centres and family daycare. Since 1995 the municipalities are obliged to provide a place in a daycare centre or family daycare provision for children between 1 and 12 years if their parents are employed or studying (Social Services Law, 1995 amendment). Since 1982 they have been committed to providing a free-of-charge, half-day place for 6-year-olds. The starting age for compulsory schooling is (still) 7 years.

As from 1997, all publicly funded services outside the compulsory education system were transferred from the responsibility of the Ministry of Social Welfare to the Ministry of Education.

Development and expansion of early childhood centres

Today's early childhood centres can be traced back to three different kinds of provision: infant schools, day nurseries and kindergartens (cf. Hwang and Broberg, 1992). The first infant school (*smábarnsskola*) was opened in 1836 with the aim of providing children from underprivileged families with basic mastery competences. This kind of establishment existed right up until the 1950s. The first day nursery (*barnkrubba*) for very young children was opened in 1854, but it was not until the Second World War (in 1943) that state subsidies for nurseries were first granted. Up until the 1960s, social criteria (e.g. support for single mothers) were the main justification for these establishments (Gunnarsson, 1993). Kindergartens (*deltidsförskolan*) based on Froebel's ideas were founded at the turn of the century. In their present-day form (*deltidsgrupper*), they offer part-time provision mainly for 6-year-old children during the year preceding compulsory schooling. The onset of increasing maternal employment in the mid-1960s was the starting point for the systematic expansion of early childhood services.

Daycare centres and family daycare are normally the responsibility of the municipal authorities. However, since 1991 the number of private centres has increased – both as a result of the necessary expansion of services and of government policy aimed to increase parental choice. In fact, the number of children in private provision tripled over the following four years. Both municipal centres and private institutions are funded according to the same regulations.

Maternal employment, family support measures, levels of provision

During the past 25 years the number of women aged 16–64 in gainful employment has risen steadily, reaching a peak of 90 per cent during 1985–90 – a record among industrialized nations. In 1993, 75 per cent of mothers with children under 10 years of age were employed, 40 per cent on a part-time basis (European Commission Network on Childcare, 1996).

Following the birth of a child, either the mother or the father is entitled to 360 days' parental leave. During this time he or she receives 80 per cent of his or her current salary. These days can be taken at any time before the child's eighth birthday. In 1992, 44 per cent of fathers took an average of 45 days of parental leave during the child's first year of life. Since 1995 a month of parental leave is reserved especially for fathers. If a child is ill, one or other of the parents is entitled to 120 days a year and 80 per cent of current income in order to stay at home with the child. This applies for children up to the age of 12, and for handicapped children up to the age of 21. Parents with a child aged 4–12 years are entitled to two days off a year in order to visit the child's daycare centre or school.

In December 1994, 33 per cent of children aged 0–3 years attended publicly funded services (79 per cent centre based, 22 per cent in family daycare), and 72 per cent of 3–6-year-olds (European Commission Network on Childcare, 1996).

Children's rights and lobby organizations for children

Children's rights are anchored in legislation to a greater extent in Sweden than in many other countries. In the case of divorce, children are entitled access to both parents, and there is a move towards introducing joint custody. Although the divorce rate in Sweden is high (45 per cent of all marriages end in divorce), 80 per cent of preschool children live with both parents. Corporal punishment is forbidden by law. In 1993 a Children's Ombudsman was appointed. A major task of the Ombudsman is to ensure the implementation of the UN Convention on the Rights of the Child in Sweden.

Current issues and trends

The move from a centralized to a decentralized system

During the phase of expansion in the 1970s and 1980s daycare centres were part of centralized government funding and regulation. Guidelines issued by the National Board for Health and Social Welfare established high-quality standards concerning space requirements, staff training, group size and staff/child ratios. During recent years there has been a delegation of responsibility to the 286 municipalities in Sweden. Through increased privatization, the standardized, national framework is gradually being replaced by a host of local variants. Decentralization measures have coincided with economic recession, and experts fear a lowering of standards (Lidholt and Norrman, 1994). However, despite recent cuts, most early childhood centres in Sweden are still very well resourced in terms of staff, rooms and equipment compared with many other European countries.

Most municipalities have set up local committees to deal with issues concerning children and adolescents on a regional basis. Among the members are the heads of local schools (the management of schools has also been transferred to the municipal level) and the directors of early childhood centres and out-of-school provision for school children.

Lowering school entry age from 7 to 6 years

For some years now the issue of lowering school entry age from 7 to 6 years has been a matter for controversial debate. Pilot projects have given parents the chance to send their child to school at age 6 if they so wish. However, many parents have not taken up this option since they are apparently not convinced that schools in their present form can offer their children better opportunities than the daycare centres. Nevertheless, it is expected that ten-year compulsory schooling will be introduced very soon and that in this connection the school starting age will be lowered to 6 years. Stockholm has already introduced compulsory pilot classes for 6-year-olds in all primary schools in the city.

International training course in early childhood education

The Stockholm Institute of Education, the largest training institution for teaching staff in Sweden, introduced a new four-year course in early childhood education in 1995–6: the International Programme in Early Childhood Education. One year of the course, which hopes to attract both Swedish students and students from abroad, is spent in another European country (as part of EU exchange programmes). The novelty of this course of study is its commitment to an international approach: a year abroad, English as the language of instruction, 20 weeks' practical experience in a further country and 10 weeks of instruction on 'Early childhood education in an international perspective'. A further innovative aspect is the inclusion of management studies in the course syllabus.

B FORMS OF CHILDCARE AND EDUCATIONAL PROVISION

AT A GLANCE

- A co-ordinated approach towards the education, care and development of children.
- High-quality standards in childcare provision, in particular through a high ratio of staff to children.
- Decentralized structures, centres have a good deal of autonomy.
- Gradual transfer of out-of-school provision for school children from separate centres to the primary school.

Publicly funded centres for children from birth to 12 years include (see Table 18.1) full-day centres (*daghem*), half-day kindergartens or preschool groups (*deltidsgrupper*), drop-in centres for children and parents (*öppen förskola*), out-of-school centres (*fritidshem*) and out-of-school provision in schools. A well funded system of family daycare (*familjedaghem*) complements the centre-based provision. Altogether, 72 per cent of children aged 3–6 years attend some form of state-subsidized provision (European Commission Network on Childcare, 1996). Nearly all 6-year-olds attend either a kindergarten or one of the pilot classes for 6-year-olds in the primary schools.

Table 18.1 Childcare and education services for children aged 0–12 years

Form of provision	Age of children/ coverage rate*	Opening hours	Administrative responsibility
Daghem (early childhood centre)	0–6 years (39%)	6.30 a.m. – 6.00 p.m.	Ministry of Social Welfare/as from 1997: Ministry of Education/local authorities
Deltidsgrupper (pre-school class)	mainly 6-year-olds, some 4, 5 and 7-year-olds (approx. 98% of 6-year-olds in *deltidsgrupper* or pilot classes in primary schools)	3 hours, usually mornings	Ministry of Social Welfare/as from 1997: Ministry of Education/local authorities
Öppen förskola (drop-in centres for children and parents)	1–6 years (no figures available)	A few hours daily	Ministry of Social Welfare/as from 1997: Ministry of Education/local authorities
Familjedaghem (family daycare)	0–6 years (12%) 7–9 years (8%)	Individual arrangements with parents	Ministry of Social Welfare/as from 1997: Ministry of Education/local authorities
Fritidshem (after-school centre/out-of-school provision on school premises)	7–9 years (44%) 10–12 years (5%**)	Before school, afternoons, school holidays	Ministry of Social Welfare/as from 1997: Ministry of Education/local authorities
Youth club	10–12 years (no figures available)	At least 4 hours daily, also in school holidays	Ministry of Social Welfare/as from 1997: Ministry of Education/local authorities

Notes:
*Figures from Swedish Ministry of Social Affairs, 1994.
**After-school centres *and* family daycare.

Guidelines for activities in daycare centres

General aims for work in childcare and education services for children aged 0–12 years are anchored in the Social Services Law and have been elaborated in a number of official documents (Lidholt and Norrman, 1994). Sweden has adopted a co-ordinated approach towards the education, care and development of children within a set of sociopolitical objectives. Key concepts are democracy, solidarity, gender equality and social responsibility. In the case of children from other cultural backgrounds, daycare centres are expected to lay the foundation for developing active bilingualism and a bicultural identity.

Daycare centres (*daghem*)

Full-day centres in Sweden are primarily for children whose parents work or study, or for children who need special support. Daycare centres are open throughout the year from 6.30 a.m. to 6.00 p.m., Mondays to Fridays. A warm meal is generally prepared on the premises by kitchen staff.

The centres cater for children from 1 year to the age of 5 or 6. In 1994 there were only 155 children under 1 year in a centre – almost certainly due to the fact that the conditions for parental leave are so favourable. The children are normally grouped in two mixed age-groupings for children under 3 years and over 3 years. Most centres have three groups; a few have only two groups, a few six to seven groups.

Parents pay a fee according to their income, the number of siblings and the length of time the child attends. Surprisingly, there is no official form of parent participation in Sweden, such as parent boards or parent committees. Despite cuts in recent years, the number of qualified staff per child is still favourable compared to the situation in other countries. Three qualified members of staff work in a group of 15 children under 3 years of age or in a group of 20 3–5-year-old children – usually two early childhood educators (*förskollärare*) and one nursery worker (*barnskötare*). About half the staff in early childhood centres are educators and about 40 per cent are trained nursery workers. The favourable adult/child ratio is considered essential in order to build up stable and close relationships and to support the development of democratic attitudes and group processes.

Preschool classes (*deltidsgrupper*)

The preschool classes are a form of part-time provision mainly for 6-year-olds. Since 1982 all 6-year-olds are entitled to attend a preschool group free of charge. They are sometimes located within the daycare centres, but more often they are independent institutions with their own director. In terms of room arrangement and basic objectives they do not differ significantly from the early childhood centres. They do not specifically aim to 'prepare' children for school. Two qualified staff – an early childhood educator and a nursery assistant – work with a group of 20 children. Until some years ago, two different groups of children used to attend the preschool classes mornings and afternoons; now they are usually opened mornings only. In line with the expansion of the full-day centres (from 33,800 in 1970 to 331,800 in 1994), the number of children in preschool groups has decreased accordingly: whereas in 1975 there were 112,030 children on roll, in 1994 this number had fallen to 66,373.

Drop-in centres for children and parents (*öppen förskola*)

Another kind of early childhood provision exists alongside the daycare centres and preschool groups: the so-called 'open preschools' or drop-in centres. These are community contact groups and advisory centres for parents whose child is not enrolled in another form of daycare provision. They also provide a base and meeting place for family daycare providers and the children in their charge. The drop-in centres receive state funding and are directed by a qualified early childhood educator. They are usually founded on the initiative of parents and not as a result of official planning decisions (Berg, 1993). Since the first centre was opened in 1972 the number has steadily increased, and in 1992 there were 1,500 centres around the country. Officially they are open for children from the age of 1 to school entry age. In practice, however, there is no age limit. The centres organize activities not just for children but also joint activities for parents and children. There is plenty of opportunity for informal contacts and also for professional advice on all kinds of issues connected with children and families. A toy library is often located on the premises, i.e. families can borrow play materials to use at home.

Family daycare (*familjedaghem*)

Family daycare provision first received state funding in 1967. Central government covers 50 per cent of the costs, the local authorities 35 per cent and parents 15 per cent. Family daycare is regulated by the Social Services Act 1980 and the Child Care Act 1994. Until recently, all providers of family daycare were employees of the municipal authorities. It is now also possible for freelance providers to receive state subsidies (Karlsson, 1995).

Family daycare providers have no formal training, but the municipalities generally organize an induction course of 100 hours. The National Board for Health and Social Welfare recommends that providers have a nursery worker training (*barnskötare*), but this is not binding. A recently developed form of family daycare is the so-called 'three family system': a qualified nursery worker is in charge of three or four children in the home of one of the three participating families (Gunnarsson, 1993). According to National Board recommendations, not more than four children should be supervised at any one time. The majority of children in family daycare provision are of preschool age, in particular under 3 years of age. School children up to the age of 12 can also be registered, but the number of school-age children has decreased noticeably in recent years. Altogether, the number of children in this form of provision has decreased in line with the expansion of full-day centres. Whereas in 1980, 43 per cent of children under 7 in municipal childcare provision were in family daycare, this percentage was down to 24 per cent in 1994 (Karlsson, 1995). In 1994, 12 per cent of children aged 0–6 years were in family daycare, whereas 39 per cent of the same age-group were enrolled at a daycare centre.

Municipal daycare providers are paid roughly the same as unqualified staff in daycare centres. They are entitled to the same social benefits as other employees.

Out-of-school provision for school children (*skolbarnsomsorg*)

The number of centres for school-age children expanded considerably during the 1970s, although not to the same extent as the early childhood centres. Just recently the number of places has increased substantially. Between 1993 and 1994 the number of places rose by 36,000 to over 178,000, a coverage rate of 27 per cent of the age-group, whereby the number of 6–7-year-olds in this kind of provision has increased most (Johansson, 1995b).

Until the mid-1980s the most common form of provision for school children was the 'leisure centre' (*fritidshem*). These centres for 7–12-year-olds whose parents work or study are open both before and after official school hours (8 a.m. to 1.30 p.m., including a warm mid-day meal) and also during school holidays. In recent years, in the context of recession and decentralization, this form of provision has become more and more attached directly to the schools and located within the school premises. Improved collaboration between school and after-school care is the official explanation, whereas critics assert that economic considerations are the guiding force. This is because the changes have also led to a reduction of the standards previously established for group size and adult/child ratios. In 1994 there were approximately 23 children per group, nearly two more than in the previous year. Because of the lack of available places in many municipalities, the 7–9-year-olds are given priority. Only a few 10–12-year-olds have a place, although they are entitled to one. There are substantial regional differences in the availability of provision. In Stockholm, nearly all school-age childcare provision is now attached to schools and comes under the responsibility of the head of the school (Johansson, 1995b).

Municipal provision for school-age children has the same holistic approach towards education and care as the early childhood centres. Guidelines for educational activities were issued in 1988 by the Ministry of Social Affairs. In partnership with the parents and with the children themselves, school-age childcare aims to support the overall development of children, to inform children about their local environment and to encourage them to take an active part in community life.

Sweden is the only country in the European Union which has, since 1977, a university-level training for out-of-school care and education (*fritidspedagoger*). Nursery workers – who now have a broader training which includes school-age children (see Section C) – assist the 'leisure-time pedagogues'. Because of the increasing integration into the school system, the job profile of leisure-time pedagogues is changing in focus. This change in workplace setting will inevitably lead to a redefinition of professional identity for this relatively 'new' professional group in the childcare field (Johansson, 1995b).

Afternoon clubs

Afternoon leisure-time clubs have been set up in recent years to provide for the 10–12-year-olds who are not able to find a place in regular out-of-school provision. Parental fees are substantially lower than for a place in a centre (approximately Kr200 compared with Kr1,400). In some municipalities there are also drop-in centres where a fee is paid per visit. The clubs are normally run by the municipal authorities, but sometimes they are organized by parents or by a welfare organization. They are generally staffed by two qualified, part-time staff if more than 45 children are on the roll. Afternoon clubs are open for at least four hours daily.

[C] STAFF TRAINING

AT A GLANCE

- University-level training (three years) for work in publicly funded provision for young children (early childhood educator).
- Unique among the EU countries for university-level training (three years) for work in public childcare and educational provision for school children (leisure-time pedagogue).
- Pay for both professions lower than that for the teaching profession.
- Qualified assistants in all publicly funded services: since 1992 a broad-based, three-year training for all age-groups.

Table 18.2 gives a detailed overview of the different professional groups, their training and their fields of work.

Early childhood educator (*förskollärare*) and leisure-time educator (*fritidspedagog*)

Initial training

Staff in early childhood and out-of-school provision – early childhood

In-service training

The municipalities are responsible for providing in-service courses for both early childhood and leisure-time educators. Until 1993 it was recommended that educators be released for 30 hours a year for in-service purposes. However, this recommendation has been withdrawn and it is now up to the local authorities to make a decision on each individual application. This inevitably means that the chances of in-service training vary from municipality to municipality.

Universities offer a number of long-term courses for early childhood and leisure-time educators which may last anything from six weeks up to a year or longer. Topics include children with special needs, intercultural education, educational administration.

Both professional groups have their own journal, each with a relatively high circulation. *Förskolan* is the early years journal, which sells 50,000 copies per issue, and *Fritidspedagogen* (circulation 14,000) is for professionals working in after-school and leisure-time facilities.

Conditions of work – status

Early childhood and leisure-time educators both work a 40-hour week. Both are paid less than primary schoolteachers. Their salary is comparable to that of a nurse. The teachers' union is working towards reducing this difference. On the other hand, early childhood educators have an unusual chance of promotion: because of the management studies and organizational theory elements in their training they can also take over the headship of a primary school.

Nursery/childcare assistant (*barnskötare*)

Initial training

Within the context of general school reform measures the initial training for nursery assistants was extended from two to three years in 1994. The training takes place at upper secondary level in the comprehensive schools (see Table 18.2). After nine years' compulsory schooling pupils choose one of 16 optional courses leading to a vocational qualification. One of these options is 'Childcare and leisure-time studies'. All vocational courses include

- common core subjects (English, aesthetic education, sport and health education, mathematics, ecology, religion, sociology, Swedish, language development, language–literature–society);
- person-oriented studies;
- professional studies; and
- topics of local interest (these are chosen after consultation with the local council).

The initial training in 'Childcare and leisure-time studies' aims to provide the trainees with basic skills and attitudes for working with human beings of all ages. (The former two-year course of training focused exclusively on childcare, particular in the early years.) Compulsory professional studies are (number of hours in brackets):

- knowledge of workplace (30);
- childcare and leisure studies (200);
- childcare as a profession (120);
- leisure time as a social phenomenon (120);
- development, social context, socialization (120);
- professional work and life-long learning (50); and
- early childhood and leisure-time education (health education (80); media studies (85); educational leadership (80); computer science (30); management (30)).

Pupils can also study an optional subject in depth. At least 15 per cent of the three-year training is spent in different work placements (approximately 15 weeks), which are allocated by the schools. Trainees are not paid during these work placements.

In-service training

In-service courses for childcare workers are provided by the municipalities. Content varies according to the current aims of the local authorities, the economic situation and staff needs. Until recently it was possible for nursery assistants to complete a 50-week course in order to gain the status of early childhood educator. The municipalities which organized the courses encouraged nursery assistants to take advantage of them. However, following the introduction of the new training course of 120 weeks per semester, this option for nursery assistants was dropped.

Conditions of work – status

In the light of the present trend to lower the school entry age, the number of jobs in early childhood centres is falling, and this situation is having a negative effect on the employment chances of staff, particularly on those of childcare assistants.

NOTE

We should like to thank Gunilla Kalderin (International Office, Stockholm Institute of Education) for her networking arrangements and support.

REFERENCES AND SOURCES

Andersson, B.-E. (1994) Public policies and early childhood education, *European Early Childhood Education Research Journal*, Vol. 2, no. 2, pp. 19–32.

Berg, L.-E. (1993) Der offene Kindergarten in Schweden, in P. Oberhuemer (ed.) *Blick auf Europa: Tageseinrichtungren für Kinder, Sonderheft der Zeitschrift Theorie und Praxis der Sozialpädagogik*, TPS extra 13, pp. 2–4.

Gunnarsson, L. (1993) Sweden, in M. Cochran (ed.) *International Handbook of Child Care Policies and Programs*. Greenwood Press, Westport, Conn. and London.

Haddad, L. and Johansson, J. E. (1994) The Swedish pre-school – the history of an integrated system for care and education. Paper given at the 4th EECERA Conference on the Quality of Early Childhood Education, Göteborg, 1–3 September.

Hallendorf, I. (1995) Fachberatung für Kindertageseinrichtungen in Schweden. Paper given at the Bundeskongreß Fachberatung, Berlin, 11–13 October.

Hwang, C.-P. and Broberg, A. G. (1992) The historical and social context of child care in Sweden, in M. E. Lamb, K. J. Sternberg, C.-P. Hwang and A. G. Broberg (eds.) *Child Care in Context. Cross-Cultural Perspectives*. Lawrence Erlbaum Associates, Hillsdale, NJ, Hove and London.

Johansson, I. (1995a) The interplay between organization and pedagogic content. Results from a study reflecting the changes within 12 preschools in Stockholm during a three-year period. Paper given at the 5th EECERA Conference on the Quality of Early Childhood Education, Paris, 7–9 September.

Johansson, I. (1995b) The link between school and after-school day care in Sweden. Ideology and reality. What is happening? Some experiences from Stockholm. Keynote paper, ENSAC Conference, Maastricht, October.

Landgren, S. H. (1990) School-age child care in Sweden with special reference to the integrated school day in Lund. Unpublished MS, Lund.

Lidholt, B. and Norrman, M. (1994) Changes in society – changes in day-care settings in Gothenburg and Uppsala. Paper given at the 4th EECERA Conference on the Quality of Early Childhood Education, Göteborg, 1–3 September.

Näsman, E. (1993) National report Sweden, in *Childhood as a Social Phenomenon, EUROSOCIAL Reports*, Vol. 36. European Centre for Social Welfare Policy and Research, Vienna.

Pramling, I. (forthcoming) Die Qualität der Kinderbetreuung aus schwedischer Sicht, in W. E. Fthenakis and M. R. Textor (eds.) *Qualität von Kinderbetreuung: deutsche und internationale Perspektiven*. Beltz, Weinheim and Basel.

Socialstyrelsen (Swedish Ministry of Social Affairs) (1988) *Educational Programme for Leisure Centres*. Socialstyrelsen, Stockholm.

Sundin, B. (1992) Preparation of early childhood teachers in Sweden, *Early Child Development and Care*, Vol. 78, pp. 183–92.

Swedish Institute (1994) *Childcare in Sweden* (Series: *Facts on Sweden*). Swedish Institute, Stockholm.

Weyler, K. (1993) *Big Changes in Swedish Education* (Series: *Current Sweden*). Swedish Institute, Stockholm.

The United Kingdom

A SOCIAL CONTEXT OF CHILDCARE AND EDUCATION SERVICES

AT A GLANCE

- A diverse and fragmented system of childcare and education services.
- Split administrative responsibility (education, health/social services) both at a national and local level (although some co-ordinated local initiatives).
- Statutory school age 5 years (in Northern Ireland 4 years), many 4-year-olds in school.
- No statutory parental leave.

Diversity of services, providers and regulatory bodies

Diversity is the key term when trying to describe the UK childcare and education services outside the compulsory school system: diversity concerning forms of provision, types of providers (public, voluntary, private) and administrative responsibility.

Compulsory schooling begins in England, Scotland and Wales at age 5 and in Northern Ireland at age 4. At a national level, services for children before statutory school age in England fall under the responsibility of three ministries: the Department for Education and Employment, the Department of Health and the Department of Social Services. Likewise, in the Northern Ireland, Scottish and Welsh Offices they come under the education or welfare sections. At a local level (except in Northern Ireland) responsibility is divided between

- local authority education departments for nursery schools and nursery classes for 3 and 4-year-olds and the growing number of children who enter schools before statutory school age;
- social services departments or health authorities for day nurseries for 0–5-

year-olds, family centres and playgroups; and
- leisure departments for community services such as open-door parent–toddler groups (known as 'one o'clock clubs'), toy libraries, play centres, after-school clubs and mobile services in rural areas.

These different departments all have their own goals and priorities, and decisions concerning the allocation of funds are made accordingly. Although there is often overlap in the areas of influence, this has tended to lead to territorial competition rather than co-operation, resulting in the lack of co-ordination between services which is so often the target of critical debate. There are examples of well co-ordinated services at a regional level due to local initiatives (e.g. in Strathclyde in Scotland), but these are still an exception.

There are three main sector providers: the public sector, the voluntary sector and the private sector. Provision within the public sector is maintained, i.e. government funded, but non-statutory (non-compulsory). It is funded either separately or jointly across the three government departments. Types of provision include nursery schools and classes, portage schemes, day nurseries, family centres, combined nursery centres, 'one o'clock clubs'. Attendance is free of charge. Voluntary sector services are provided by voluntary groups, childcare organizations and charities. Types of provision include playgroups, family centres, toy libraries, after-school clubs, and parent and toddler groups. All these receive government subsidies but are usually fee-paying. Private sector services are fee-paying and privately arranged between the family and the service provider, e.g. family daycarers, nannies, private day nurseries, workplace nurseries, independent nursery schools. The overall number of places in private provision is rapidly growing, and has shown a 500 per cent increase in the last ten years (Penn, 1995, p. 30).

New legislation – the Children Act 1989 which came into force in England, Scotland and Wales in 1991 – places a duty on local authorities to provide services for children 'in need', and to review the full range of services for children outside the education system in their region every three years. The Children Act has also led to improvements in the regulation of private sector provision for children aged 0–8 years.

Despite the apparent diversity, families often have little real choice when seeking provision suited to their needs. Regional disparaties are considerable, opening hours are often not long enough for working parents, fees may be too high and so on, not to mention differences in the quality of provision. For years now, experts have complained about the lack of political commitment towards creating a coherent and just system out of this fragmented 'muddle' (e.g. Blackstone, 1971; Pugh, 1988; David, 1990; Penn and Riley, 1992; Moss and Penn, 1996).

Mothers in the labour force – family support measures

The rate of mothers' employment in the UK increased significantly between 1985 and 1993 (from 38 per cent to 53 per cent for mothers with children aged 0–10 years). The great majority of these jobs were part time (European Commission Network on Childcare, 1996). Alongside Austria, Denmark and Sweden, the UK has a high rate of lone-parent families compared with other EU countries. Maternal leave arrangements last for a period of 40 weeks, with payment at 90 per cent of earnings for six weeks and a flat-rate payment for a further 12 weeks. However, there is no statutory parental leave in the UK, and no leave to care for sick children. Estimates of the level of provision quote 1–2 per cent of 0–3-year-olds, and 53 per cent of 3–5-year-olds attending a publicly funded place (European Commission Network on Childcare, 1996).

Current trends and issues

4-year-olds in primary school

The lack of places in publicly funded provision for children under statutory school age, combined with growing expectations and demands from parents concerning the availability of provision, has led to the practice of admitting 4-year-olds into primary schools on a voluntary basis. Experts estimate that around three quarters of children admitted to school are not yet of compulsory school age (Pound, 1995), and this solution has been criticized for some time now. Four-year-olds are sometimes placed in classes of 30–35 children supervised by one trained teacher, and sometimes without any form of continual assistance. Another problem is the 'discrete pressure' stemming from the introduction in 1988 of a National Curriculum into schools. This subject-based framework means that child-centered, holistic forms of learning based on discovery and project methods which had been a common form of practice in early years education are being swept aside.

National reports – a stepping-stone towards reform?

Recent national reports supporting the case for high-quality early childhood provision have contributed towards political prioritization of this area. These include a government-commissioned report – *Starting with Quality*, known as the Rumbold Report – which appeared in 1990 (DES, 1990), and two reports from independent organizations: *Learning to Succeed*, commissioned by the National Commission on Education (1993), and *Start Right*, commissioned by the Royal Society of Arts (Ball, 1994). While it is considered positive that early childhood education and care are now so high on the political agenda, many of the reform suggestions made by the government have been highly controversial. One is the voucher system.

Voucher system for nursery education

The government has introduced a voucher system which is currently being piloted in a small number of local authorities and expected to become government policy. All parents with 4-year-old children are to receive a voucher worth £1,200 with which they will be able to 'buy' provision in a variety of approved services both in the education and welfare systems. This measure is highly controversial for a number of reasons. It does nothing to increase the number of publicly funded services; the voucher sum covers only a part-time place in a public sector nursery school or nursery class; and it is worth less than present per capita spending on 4-year-olds in reception classes in primary schools. One inevitable consequence, so it is argued, is a further lowering of standards for 4-year-olds. An added source of contention are the government plans to introduce 'desirable outcomes' which services receiving vouchers will be obliged to meet. Many see this as a forerunner of a prescribed curriculum for the under 5s (Pound, 1995).

B FORMS OF CHILDCARE AND EDUCATIONAL PROVISION

AT A GLANCE

- Diversity of services and providers, split administrative responsibility (education/welfare); growth in private, non-subsidized sector.
- Nursery schools for 3–5-year-olds part of the (non-compulsory) education system, but places available for only just over one quarter of 3 and 4-year-olds.
- Parent-run playgroups widespread – partly because of the lack of places in the public sector.

Table 19.1 illustrates key features of services for preschool-age and school-age children. The main forms of provision are then described in more detail.

Nursery school/nursery class

Nursery schools and nursery classes, mainly for 3 and 4-year-olds (in Northern Ireland for 2 and 3-year-olds), are provided by local education authorities. Provision is non-statutory, i.e. is made at the discretion of the particular local authority, but within the public sector. There are considerable regional differences in the availability of provision, and in England and Wales there are places for only about one quarter of this age-group.

Nursery schools are separate institutions with their own headteacher, whereas nursery classes are attached to primary schools under the supervision of the primary headteacher. Both forms of provision are open for around six

Table 19.1 Childcare and education services for children aged 0–14 years

Form of provision	Age of children/coverage rate	Opening hours	Administrative responsibility
Nursery school, nursery class	3–4 years (some 2-year-olds) (26%*)	$2^{1}/_{2}$–3 hours per day	Ministry of Education/local education authorities
Reception class/primary school	3–4 years (21%*); 5 years (100%)	9.00 a.m. – 3.00 p.m.; supervised mid-day break	Ministry of Education/local education authorities
Combined nursery centre/community nursery	0–5 years (no information available)	8.00 a.m. – 5.00 p.m.	Education and welfare authorities
Local authority day nursery	0–5 years (*c.* 1% in public sector; *c.* 1% in private sector**)	Full-time and part-time places	Ministry of Health/local welfare authorities
Family centre	Children and adults (no information available)	Full-day opening hours, flexible hours of attendance	Local welfare authorities
Playgroup	2–4 years (*c.* 40% of 3 and 4-year-olds**)	For each child: on average 3 hours on 3 days per week	Private initiatives, some with public funding
Care and recreation services for school-age children: • children's clubs • play centres • leisure centres • holiday schemes	5–15 years (*c.* 3% of 5–10-year-olds (estimate)*) (no official information available)	Before and after regular school hours/during school holidays	Local welfare authorities
Family daycare	No figures available	Individually arranged	Local welfare authorities

Notes:
*Figures for 1993, European Commission Network on Childcare, 1996.
** Figures for 1992 (1986 for playgroups), cited in Moss, 1994.

hours per day, but the average length of attendance for most children in England and Wales (88 per cent) is three hours per day. In Scotland, by contrast, most places are on a full-day basis. Both nursery schools and nursery classes are open during term time only. Attendance is free of charge.

Nursery provision is staffed by qualified teachers (see Section C), assisted by trained nursery nurses. This means that there are two qualified members of staff in each group of 20–25 children.

The aims of provision are educational, with an emphasis on holistic concepts of learning and development. The main objective is to further children's social and intellectual development. Play is seen as an important vehicle for learning. There is no prescribed curriculum.

Local authority day nurseries

Local authority day nurseries are public sector provision for children aged 0–5 years, many of whom are referred by health and social workers as being 'in need' or 'at risk'. They cater for only 1 per cent of children under 5. They offer full-time and part-time places. At least half the staff have to be qualified in a related field (nursery nursing, early years education, health visiting, social work, children's nursing).

The specific intake of day nurseries and the large number of children living in stressful situations present the staff with a very challenging task. Day nurseries have been criticized in the past for focusing on care and compensatory aspects and not enough on an appropriate educational input for the children. The Children Act 1989 requires that all daycare provision should offer experiences compatible in quality with those in nursery schools or nursery classes. Recently there has been a move towards a more balanced approach, including closer co-operation with parents.

Combined nursery centres

Combined nursery centres are jointly funded and managed both by education and by social service authorities and staffed by trained teachers and nursery nurses. They were established for the first time in the 1970s, mostly in regions then designated as educational priority areas. The objective was to create a more integrated and flexible form of service aimed at a broader intake of children than the day nurseries with their admission criteria based on children 'at risk'. They are open on a full-day basis, generally from 8.00 a.m. to 5.00 p.m., right through the year. There are comparatively few centres of this kind. However, no national statistics are available on the exact number. About 40 centres are registered with the National Association of Nursery Centres, a professional organization for workers in this kind of provision.

Family centres

This kind of provision has been established predominantly in urban areas. Most family centres offer a combination of activities for adults *and* children, and most are open-door institutions. Some see themselves as a form of compensatory provision for disadvantaged families (these centres are mostly funded by the local social services department). Others consider themselves to be a meeting place for *all* families in the area, and may develop a specific programme focus according to local needs. Some family centres also provide after-school and holiday care for older children.

The Soho Family Centre in London, for example, is attended by over 300 families from 36 different nationalities. It runs a playgroup for 3 and 4-year-olds; a baby and toddler group; a group for lone-parent families; rooms for drop-in visits; advisory services; a toy library; a health clinic; Tai Chi and needlework courses. The Soho Centre also co-ordinates family daycare in the area, providing a flexible system for about 20 children. The daycarers, themselves from varying cultural backgrounds, meet up regularly in the centre, sometimes with the children in their care, sometimes without them in order to exchange experiences and take part in discussions and seminars on child development and educational topics.

Playgroups

Playgroups are parent-managed groups in the voluntary sector. Because of the lack of publicly funded provision they play a significant part in the system as a whole. Some have extended their opening hours during the last few years, but in most cases children may attend for up to 10 hours per week only, spread over two or three days. They are closed during school holidays. This means that for working mothers they are not a satisfactory form of provision. A research study conducted at the end of the 1980s (Lloyd et al., 1989) found that most playgroups were attended by children from middle-class families where the mother was not in the labour force. Only about one quarter of playgroups receive government funding, and this covers less than half the running costs. Parents pay a small fee per session. Playgroups are staffed by volunteers who *may* have a background in teaching or childcare, but there are no binding requirements concerning training. Playgroups are organized nationally under the Pre-School Learning Alliance (formerly: Pre-School Playgroups Association).

Care and recreation services for school children

Primary schools in the UK are usually open from 9.00 a.m. to 3.30 p.m. Provision in terms of care and recreation services for children outside these times has been traditionally very sparse. A government initiative in this area from 1993 to 1996 led to a significant increase in the number of places and it is estimated that there are now some 3,000 centres across the country. However, according to calculations made by the main (private) organization in this area – Kids' Clubs Network – 25,000 centres would be needed in order to meet the demand for such places. Providers are parent groups, companies, church organizations, charities and local authorities. There are no regulations concerning the qualifications of staff and no guidelines on programme content. Centres with children under the age of 8 years come under the Children Act 1989, which means that the local authorities are responsible for registering and inspecting out-of-school provision for children within this age bracket.

Family daycare

Family daycarers ('childminders') normally provide for children up to 8 years of age on a self-employed basis. They negotiate on an individual basis with parents about their conditions of work. Under the requirements of the Children Act they must be registered with the local authority and inspected for quality dimensions such as safety, space, facilities and educational stimulation. Local authorities offer courses and support services for family daycarers at their own discretion. Training for this kind of work has recently been included in the system of National Vocational Qualifications (see Section C). The National Childminding Association is an effective pressure group which is helping to raise the general status of family daycarers.

[C] STAFF TRAINING

AT A GLANCE

- Qualified schoolteachers (primary and nursery education) work with 3–5-year-olds in the public sector education system (some in nursery schools, many in school before statutory school age of 5 years).
- Both qualified staff (predominantly nursery nurses) and unqualified personnel work with 0–5-year-olds in the public and private social services sector.
- No statutory regulations on qualification requirements for staff in out-of-school services.

Staff working with children in childcare and education services may range from workers without any formal qualifications at all to qualified teachers with a four-year university-level training with some kind of specialization in early years education. Among the qualified staff there is also an enormous range – from the graduate-level training mentioned above, to the 200-hour optional courses offered for playgroup leaders – a significant fact considering that there are more children in playgroups than in public sector nursery education. According to a UK occupational mapping survey on persons working with children under 7, the majority of children not already in formal schooling are being cared for by workers who are employed on a part-time basis, some as unpaid volunteers; wages are low and turnover rates high, and most of these workers do not hold any formally recognized qualifications related to their job role (Working with Under Sevens Project 1990, reported in Curtis and Hevey, 1992). The same survey identified some 85 distinct job roles of persons involved in work with young children and their families. The Children Act 1989, although for the first time empowering authorities to provide training for those engaged in childcare, does not *require* them to do so. No particular qualifications are set down, nor is a specification made of the minimum amount of training and support necessary to enable workers to achieve acceptable standards of care (Curtis and Hevey, 1992, p. 202).

This overall situation will presumably change following the introduction in 1992 of National Vocational Qualifications – a multilevel system of awards which recognizes and assesses skills gained through work. But the application of this system to the field of childcare and education is made difficult by factors like the small-scale size of the organizations in the field, the traditional autonomy and responsibility of childcare workers, and the expense of establishing a system of qualified, off-site assessors. The NVQ system has been criticized as likely to entrench the split between 'care' and 'education' (Calder, 1995).

The various training schemes are outlined in Table 19.2. The training of selected professional groups is then described in more detail.

Table 19.2 Staff in childcare and education services

Professional title	Initial training/professional qualification	Fields of work
England and Wales *Teacher* (nursery and primary education)	*Entry requirements:* • 12 years' schooling • General Certificate of Education, A-level in 2 subjects *or* equivalent • General Certificate of Secondary Education in 3 further subjects including English, mathematics and science subject • interview *Training:* 4 years at university or college of higher education *Award:* Bachelor of Education (BEd)/Bachelor of Arts (Education) (BA) with qualified teacher status (QTS) *or* *Training:* 1 year postgraduate study on completion of a university degree *or* a recognized equivalent *Award:* Postgradute Certificate in Education – PGCE (Primary) Since 1993 it is possible to complete the postgraduate training route as a part-time course of study through the Open University (distance learning). Training is primarily school based under the supervision of a designated mentor. In 1988 two further routes into the teaching profession were introduced: *1) Articled Teacher Scheme* *Entry requirements:* • university degree • assessment by university and employer	Nursery school, as class teacher or headteacher Nursery class for 3 and 4-year-olds attached to primary school, as class teacher Reception class, first year of primary school for 5-year-olds, attended by many 4-year-olds Combined nursery centre All primary school classes up to the age of 11 or 12 years

Table 19.2   continued

Professional title	Initial training/professional qualification	Fields of work
	Training: 2 years primarily 'on the job': 80% work placement and 20% tutorials *Award:* Postgraduate Certificate in Education – PGCE (Primary) *2) Licensed Teacher Scheme* *Entry requirements:* • minimum age 24 years • 2 years' higher education • assessment by employer *Training:* 2 years' school based following brief induction course *Award:* Non-graduate qualified teacher status (on recommendation of local authority)	
Scotland *Teacher* (preschool and primary education)	*Entry requirements:* • school leaving certificate in various subjects, including English and mathematics • interview *Training:* 4 years at university *Award:* Bachelor of Education (BEd) with teaching qualification (TQ) *or* *Training:* 1 year at university on completion of a degree *Award:* Postgraduate Certificate in Education – PGCE Both training schemes are followed by a two-year probationary period in order to acquire recognition through the General Teaching Council for Scotland (GTCS) Neither the Articled Teacher Scheme nor the Licensed Teacher Scheme (England and Wales) are recognized by the GTCS *Further awards:* Diploma for Professional Studies in Education (DipSE) – 1-year postgraduate course; Diploma in Early Years Education – 2-year postgraduate course	See England and Wales In Scotland 4-year-olds are admitted to primary school only under exceptional circumstances

Table 19.2 continued

Professional title	Initial training/professional qualification	Fields of work
Northern Ireland *Teacher* (primary and secondary education)	*Entry requirements:* See England and Wales *Training:* 4 years at a college of education *Award:* Bachelor of Education (BEd) and recognized teacher status *or* *Training:* 4 years at university *Award:* BA (Education) with recognized teacher status *or* *Training:* 1 year at a college of education on completion of a university degree	Qualified staff may work in primary and secondary schools with children aged 3–18 years
England and Wales *Nursery nurse/nursery worker*	*Entry requirements:* Completion of compulsory schooling (at age 16) *Training:* 2 years at a college of further education. Part-time training route possible (up to 5 years) with Accreditation of Prior Experience and Learning (APEL) *Award:* Awards are granted by various bodies: • CACHE (Council for Awards in Children's Care and Education, previously National Nursery Examination Board): NNEB Diploma in Nursery Nursing; NNEB Preliminary Diploma in Nursery Nursing; Certificate in Child Care and Education • BTEC (Business and Techology Education Council): National Diploma in Caring Services (nursery nursing) A National Vocational Qualifications system was introduced in 1992, including qualifications in childcare, Levels 2 or 3. The NNEB diploma is estimated to be equivalent to NVQ level 3. A new vocational qualification (GNVQ) for 16–18-year-olds in schools has been introduced, including options in childcare. *Further awards:* Pre-1994: for qualified nursery nurses: Diploma in Postqualifying Studies (DPQS) Post-1994: Advanced Diploma in Child Care and Education (6 modules of 60 hours)	Nursery school/nursery class, as auxiliary worker Reception class, primary school, as auxiliary worker Day nursery, as group leader Workplace nursery, as group leader Family centre, as group leader Private households, as nanny Children's ward in hospitals

Table 19.2 continued

Professional title	Initial training/professional qualification	Fields of work
Scotland *Nurserynurse/ nursery worker*	See England and Wales In Scotland SCOTVEC is the awarding body for SVQs (Scottish Vocational Qualifications)	See England and Wales
Northern Ireland *Childcare worker*	*Entry requirements:* • minimum age 21 years • work experience in a recognized service and *either* • 5 GCSEs, O-level *or* • equivalent qualification *or* • appropriate experiences and proficiency *Training (since 1989):* 1-year part-time (300 hours): 50% at university, 50% in work placement *Award:* Certificate in Preschool Child Development and Practice *Supplementary course:* 1-year part-time, 300 hours; 50% at university, 50% in work placement *Award:* Diploma in Preschool Child Development and Practice	Centres and other services for children under 4 years of age (statutory school entry age in Northern Ireland)
Nursery nurse/nursery assistant	See England and Wales	See England and Wales
England and Wales *Youth and community worker*	*Entry requirements:* • minimum age 21 years, for some schemes 23 years • relevant work experience *Training:* Various schemes, e.g. • 2 years full time, with certificate or diploma award • 3 years part time with certificate or diploma award • 3 or 4 years full time with degree award • 1 year postgraduate course (part time) • apprenticeship schemes	Youth club, youth centre, out-of-school club, playcentre, adventure playground, holiday playscheme
Scotland *Youth and community worker*	See England and Wales	See England and Wales
Northern Ireland	No training schemes	

Table 19.2 continued

Professional title	Initial training/professional qualification	Fields of work
England and Wales *Playgroup leader*	*Entry requirements:* No formal qualifications	Playgroups
	Training (optional): 200 hours (since 1993)	
	Award: Diploma in Playgroup Practice (course content comparable with knowledge and understanding expected of NVQ Level 2 or Level 3 candidates)	
Scotland	See England and Wales	Playgroups
Northern Ireland	See England and Wales	Playgroups

Teacher (nursery and primary education)

Initial training

Provision under the responsibility of the education authorities (e.g. nursery schools, nursery classes, reception classes) is staffed with qualified teachers trained to work with the 3–11 age-range, i.e. for nursery and primary schooling.

There are two main training routes, and a number of newer, shorter forms. The most common routes are

• a four-year degree course at university level; and
• a one-year postgraduate course on completion of a university degree.

Since 1988 a number of other, more school-based forms of training have been introduced (see Table 19.2 for details). A government circular in 1993 outlined further ways of reducing course length (e.g. a three-year instead of a four-year degree course). Additional criteria to be met by 1996 include increasing the National Curriculum subject content of training, and strengthening the role of schools in the training process: the minimum time to be spent in schools will increase from 20 to 32 weeks in four-year courses, from 15 to 24 weeks in three-year courses and from 15 to 18 weeks in primary postgraduate courses (Department for Education, 1993). The specific structure and content of courses have traditionally been a matter for individual higher education institutions. However, in the case of teacher education, the Education Reform Act 1988 gives the government new powers to influence the training curriculum – a development which has been duly criticized in professional circles. Two organizations established in the 1990s are playing a significant role in the implementation of government policy. These are the Teacher Training Agency (TTA) and the inspection organization

Ofsted (Office for Standards in Education). Both are so-called 'quangos' – quasi-autonomous, non-governmental organizations.

This orientation towards the needs of compulsory education means that a specific focus on the early years before compulsory schooling is in danger of being 'squeezed out' of teacher education. (This is not the case in Scotland, where the amount of time spent on nursery education was extended in 1984.)

In-service training, postgraduate studies

In-service training for teachers is offered by the school authorities, school management organizations or is workplace based and organized by the headteacher. Universities and professional associations also offer a range of conferences and seminars. All teachers employed on a full-time basis are granted five days per year for professional development. Teachers with a 'good honours degree' (the first two grade levels) may study for a higher degree (MA, MEd, MPhil, PhD).

Nursery nurse/nursery worker

Information on entry requirements, course length and fields of work for nursery nurses is summarized in Table 19.2. Training usually takes place at colleges of further education, vocational colleges below tertiary level. Courses train candidates for the 0–8 age-range. The course content of the nursery nurse training scheme validated by CACHE (see below) comprises 20 modules. Recommended weighting is as follows (number of hours in brackets):

- Observation and evaluation (60).
- Practical work with children (60).
- Introductory module (15).
- Equality of opportunity (15).
- Foundations of care (50).
- Physical development and care (50).
- Social and emotional development (50).
- Health education/first aid (50).
- Play (20).
- Cognitive and linguistic development (50).
- Children's behaviour patterns (30).
- Nutrition (30).
- Babies 0–1 years (50).
- Health education 2 (30).
- Child protection (30).
- Professional role/professional issues (50).
- Childcare and education in the UK (15).
- Handicapped children and their families (15).
- Co-operation with parents (30).

- Social and legal framework (30).
- Curriculum for the 3–8-year-olds (50).
- Complementary areas of study (140).
- Personal and professional counselling through a tutor (140).

In 1994 a new organization for the validation and award of qualifications in childcare and education was established: CACHE (Council for Awards in Children's Care and Education). CACHE is an awarding body for qualifications below tertiary level. The traditional organization responsible for examining and regulating training schemes for nursery nurses – the National Nursery Examination Board (NNEB) – is now under CACHE. Because of the high 'market value' of the NNEB awards, its name has been retained in award titles.

Another awarding body for childcare qualifications is the Business and Technology Education Council (BTEC). Besides commercial awards, it also validates the National Diploma in Caring Services (nursery nursing).

Nursery workers employed by local authorities have approximately four weeks' annual holiday and have access to the usual social service benefits.

Staff in care and recreation facilities for school-age children

There are no formal training stipulations for this field of work. Some staff are qualified youth and community workers (see Table 19.2). In a study of current provision, Petrie (1994) found that most workers were women without formal qualifications and appropriate experience for the complex work task. Some local authorities offer courses for work in this kind of provision. Staff in holiday playschemes usually attend courses between five hours and a few days which focus on health and safety issues. In recent years, courses of study for 'playwork' (defined by the National Centre for Playwork Education as 'work through developmentally appropriate play with children aged 5–15 years') have been established, such as the Diploma in Playwork at Thurrock College in Essex. This is a two-year full-time course of study which counts as a module towards a university degree in education and community studies. Course content includes: developmental theories; children's rights; principles of playwork; management; children with special needs; counselling; theories of play; self management; options; and work placements. It is also possible to obtain an NVQ qualification in playwork (at Levels 2, 3 or 4).

REFERENCES AND SOURCES

Ball, C. (1994) *Start Right. The Importance of Early Learning.* RSA, London.
Blackstone, T. (1971) *A Fair Start.* Allen Lane, London.
Blenkin, G. M. and Yue, N. Y. L. (1994) Profiling early years practitioners: some first impressions from a national survey, *Early Years*, Vol. 15, no. 1, pp. 13–22.
Calder, P. (1995) New Vocational Qualifications in Child Care and Education in the

UK, *Children and Society*, Vol. 9, no. 1, pp. 36–53.

Cohen, B. and Fraser, N. (1994) *Childcare in a Modern Welfare System. Towards a New National Policy*. Institute for Public Policy Research, London.

Curtis, A. and Hevey, D. (1992) Training to work in the early years, in G. Pugh (ed.) *Contemporary Issues in the Early Years. Working Collaboratively for Children*. Paul Chapman in association with the National Children's Bureau, London.

David, T. (1990) *Under Five – Under-Educated?* Open University Press, Milton Keynes.

Department for Education (1993) *The Initial Training of Primary School Teachers: New Criteria for Courses, Circular 14/93*. DfE, London.

Department of Education and Science (1990) *Starting with Quality: Report of the Committee of Inquiry into the Educational Experiences Offered to Three- and Four-Year-Olds* (Rumbold Report). HMSO, London.

Early Years Curriculum Group (1989) *Early Childhood Education. The Early Years Curriculum and the National Curriculum*. Trentham Books, Stoke-on-Trent.

Lloyd, E., Melhuish, E., Moss, P. and Owen, C. (1989) A review of research on playgroups, *Early Child Development and Care*, Vol. 43, pp. 77–99.

Melhuish, E. (1991) Research on day care for young children in the United Kingdom, in E. Melhuish and P. Moss (eds.) *Day Care for Young Children. International Perspectives*. Tavistock/Routledge, London and New York.

Moss, P. (1994) The Early Childhood League in Europe: problems and possibilities in cross-national comparisons of levels of provision, *European Early Childhood Education Research Journal*, Vol. 2, no. 2, pp. 5–17.

Moss, P. and Penn, H. (1996) *Transforming Nursery Education*. Paul Chapman, London.

National Children's Bureau (1993) *The Future of Training in the Early Years. A Discussion Paper*. National Children's Bureau, London.

National Commission on Education (1993) *Learning to Succeed. A Radical Look at Education Today and a Strategy for the Future*. Report of the Paul Hamlyn Foundation National Commission on Education. Heinemann, London.

Oldman, D. (1991) *Childhood as a Social Phenomenon. National Report Scotland. EUROSOCIAL Reports*, Vol. 36. European Centre for Social Welfare Policy and Research, Vienna.

Penn, H. (1995) The relationship of private daycare and nursery education in the UK, *European Early Childhood Education Research Journal*, Vol. 3, no. 2, pp. 29–41.

Penn, H. and Riley, K. A. (1992) *Managing Services for the Under Fives*. Longman, Harlow.

Petrie, P. (1994) *Play and Care Out of School*. HMSO, London.

Pound, L. (1995) Educational consultancy/inspection in the UK. Paper given at the Conference on Educational Consultancy, Berlin, 11–13 October.

Pugh, G. (1988) *Services for Under Fives. Developing a Co-ordinated Approach*. National Children's Bureau, London.

Van der Eyken, W. (1983) *Day Nurseries in Action. A Report from the Child Health Research Unit*. University of Bristol, Bristol.

Woodham-Smith, P. (1952) The origin of the kindergarten, in E. Lawrence (ed.) *Friedrich Froebel and English Education*. Routledge & Kegan Paul, London.

PART III APPENDICES

and Job Profiles – EU Member State Greece), Universität Kreta.

IRELAND

McKenna, Anne (1994) *Personnel in Early Childhood and Out-of-School Provision. Training and Job Profiles. A Survey in EU Countries: Ireland*, European Commission Network on Childcare, Dublin.

THE NETHERLANDS

Janssen-Vos, Frea and Pot, Liesbeth (1994) *Early Childhood Provisions in The Netherlands. Personnel in Early Childhood and Out-of-School Provision*, Algemeen Pedagogisch Studiecentrum, Utrecht; European Commission Network on Childcare, Castricum.

SPAIN

Palacios, Jesús, Rincón, Enrique, de Prada, María Jesús and de Francisco, María José (1995), *Educación Infantil en España. Algunos Rasgos Característicos (Early Childhood Education in Spain – Some Salient Features)*, Ministerio de Educación y Ciencia, Madrid.

Sainz de Vicuña, Paloma (1994) *La Formación de Educadores Infantiles Antes y Después de la LOGSE (Staff Training Before and After the 1990 Education Reform Act)*, Instituto de Formación Profesional, Madrid.

Balaguer, Irene and Molina, Lurdes (1995) *La Formación de Maesros Especialistas en Educación Infantil en España (The Training of Early Childhood Teachers in Spain)*, Instituto Municipal de Educación and Universidad Autonoma, Barcelona.

Lobo Aleu, Elena (1995) *Formación Permanente de Educadores en España (In-Service Training of Childcare Staff in Spain)*, Escuela de Educadores, Madrid.

II

Interview partners and information sources

We should like to thank our interview partners and others who have supported us with information and advice for this project.

AUSTRIA

Bundesbildungsanstalt für Kindergartenpädagogik, Wien
Dr Heidemarie Nalis
Bundesverband Österreichischer Elterninitiativen, Wien
Dr Maria Menz
Bundesministerium für Jugend und Familie, Sektion Jugend, Wien
Martina Staffe
Bundesministerium für Unterricht und Kulturelle Angelegenheiten, Wien
Maria Dippelreiter
Magistrat der Stadt Wien, Amt für Jugend und Familie, Wien
Dr Christa Raffelsberger
Niederösterreichisches Hilfswerk, 'Familie Aktiv'
Andrea Ristl
Universität Klagenfurt
Prof. Dr Gerald Knapp

BELGIUM

Unité Européenne EURYDICE, Brüssel
Arlette Delhaxhe
Katholike Universiteit Leuven, Faculteit der Psychologische en Pedagogische Wetenschappen, Leuven
Prof. Dr Ferre Laevers
Universiteit Gent, Vormingscentrum voor de Begeleiding van het Jonge Kind
Prof. Dr Jan Peeters
Institut de la Ville de Bruxelles, Section Puéricultrice
Gilberte Clymans
Université de Liège, Service de methodologie générale
Gentile Manni
Institut Supérieur Pédagogique, Namur
Marianne Vanesse

Université Libre de Bruxelles, Ecole de Santé Publique, Brüssel
Perrine Humblet (also: European Commission Network on Childcare)
Inspectrice de l'école maternelle
Nicole Zyra
Unterrichtsministerium der Deutschsprachigen Gemeinschaft, Pädagogische Arbeits-
gruppe
Alfons Bodarve

DENMARK

Menighedernes Daginstitutioner, Copenhagen
Birgit Boelskov
Aarhus Universitet, Psykologisk Institut, Risskov
Hans Weltzer
Aarhus Socialpaedagogiske Seminarium, Aarhus
Peter Friese
Judysk Paedagog-seminarium, Aarhus
Jytte Juul Jensen (also: European Commission Network on Childcare)
Sozialministeriet (Ministry of Social Welfare), Copenhagen
Signe Hemmingsen
Undervisningsministeriet (Ministry of Education), Copenhagen
Per Mollerup
BUPL, Copenhagen
Stig Lund
Frøbelseminariet, Kopenhagen
Henny Hammershøj
The Danish National Institute for Educational Research, Copenhagen
Dr Sven Thyssen, Vagn Rabøl Hansen, Ole Robinhagen
Danmarks Laererhøjskole (Royal Danish School of Educational Studies), Copenhagen
Karin Vilien
Familieinstitutionen Grøften, Greve Strand/Kopenhagen
Søs Klaris-Jensen
Kolding Paedagogseminarium, Kolding
Jørgen Boelskov
Aarhus Social Services Department
Susan Weltzer

FINLAND

Central Union for Child Welfare, Helsinki (Lastensuojelun Keskusliitto)
Pirjo Honkavaara, Mauri Upanne
Ministry for Social Welfare and Health (Sosiaali-ja terveysministeriö)
Kari Ilmonen
Protestant Church in Finland, Centre for Education (Kirkon kasvatusasiain)
Anna-Liisa Kuoppa
University of Helsinki, Department of Teacher Education (Helsingin yliopisto)
Prof. Dr Juhani Hytönen
Association for Kindergarten Nurses (Koulutusasiain sihteeri)
Tuula Pitkänen

University of Tampere, Kindergarten Teacher Training (Tampereen yliopisto, lasten-tarhanopettajan kouluuts)
Dr Kirsti Karila
The Finnish Kindergarten Teachers' Association (Lastentarhanopettajaliitto)
Ritva Semi
OMEP-Finland
Seppo Sauro

FRANCE

OMEP-France, Paris
Madeleine Goutard
German-French Kindergarten, Paris
Petra Gempek
Institut de l'Enfance et de la Famille, Paris
Martine Félix (also: European Commission Network on Childcare)
Université René Descartes, Unité de Recherche Sociologie de l'Education associé au Centre National de la Recherche Scientifique, Paris
Dr Eric Plaisance
École Normale de Bonneuil, Bonneuil-sur-Marne
Prof. Alain Gavard
Ministère de l'Education Nationale, Paris
Mme Martin, Mme Platteaux
Inspectrice des écoles
Colette Durand
École maternelle d'application, rue Dautancourt, Paris
Marie-Claude Terrasson
École maternelle et primaire, rue d'Alésia, Paris
Marie-Thérèse Gauthier
Association des Puéricultrices, Conflans-St-Honorine
Elisabeth Meyer
C.E.M.E.A., Paris
Jean Pierre Picard
CNFPT, Paris
Paul Benezech

GREECE

University of Crete, Rethymnon
As. Prof. Dr Konstantin Zacharenakis
University of Athens, Department of Pre-school Education
Dr Elsie Doliopoulou, Ass. Prof. Dr Thalia Dragonas
University of Thessaloniki, Department of Pre-school Education
Prof. Christos Frangos, Olga Apanomeritaki
College of Technology and Education, Athens
Ioanna Ravani
Nipiaki Agogi, Filothei (Kindergarten and private training centre)
Anna Raftopoulou

OMEP-Greece
Alkistis Kontoyianni
Ministry of Education and Religion, Primary School Department, Athens
G. Dussis, P. Koulouri
Ministry of Health and Social Welfare, Athens
B. Thanos, F. Tsakiri
Education Department, Heraklion, Crete
G. Smyrnakis

IRELAND

European Commission Network on Childcare, Dublin
Anne T. McKenna
Department of Education, Dublin
John Hunt
Dublin Institute of Technology, School of Social Sciences, Dublin
Kathleen Kennedy
University College Dublin, Department of Psychology, Dublin
Dr Eilis Hennessy
Educational Research Centre, Dublin
Sandra Ryan
Irish Preschool Playgroups, Dublin
Peggy Walker
Irish National Teachers' Organization, Dublin
Deirbhile Nic Craith
Department of Equality and Law Reform, Dublin
Michael Aherne
Mary Immaculate College, Limerick
Wyn Bryan

ITALY

Fachhochschule Rheinland-Pfalz, Mainz
Prof. Otto Filtzinger
Assessorato Formazione Professionale, Lavoro, Scuola, Università Ufficio Prescolastico, Bologna
Dr Patrizia O. Ghedini
Autonomous Province of Bozen, Schulamt für die Deutsche Schule, Inspektorat für die Kindergärten
Dr Walter Innerhofer
Centro Europeo dell'Educazione, Roma
Dr Lucio Pusci Ministero della Pubblica Istruzione
Servizio per la Scuola Materna, Roma
Dr Rubagotti, Dr Forini
Ministero della Pubblica Istruzione, Direzione Generale dell'Istruzione Professionale
Dr Ugo Panetta
Scuola Magistrale Statale, Methodo Montessori, Roma
Dr Roberto di Masi

LUXEMBOURG

European Commission Network on Childcare
Jean Altmann
Ministère de la Famille et de la Solidarité, Luxembourg
Claude Janizzi
Ministère de l'Education Nationale, Luxembourg
Othan Neuens
Institut d'Etudes Educatives et Sociales, Hesperange
Dr Jos Matheis, Herr Prussen, Herr Welschbillig
Institut Supérieur d'Etudes et de Recherches Pédagogiques, Walferdange
Georges Wirtgen
École de l'État pour Paramédicaux, Luxembourg
Danielle Schol

THE NETHERLANDS

Algemeen Pedagogisch Studiecentrum, Utrecht
Frea Janssen-Vos
European Commission Network on Childcare
Liesbeth Pot
Universiteit van Amsterdam, Faculteit der Pedagogische en Onderwijskundige Wetenschappen, Amsterdam
Dr Elly Singer
MBO-College, Afdeling MDGO-Deeltijd, Hertogenbosch
Mw. Drs H. J. van Bennekon
Ministry of Social Affairs, Health and Culture, Rijswijk (Ministerie van Welzijn, Volksgezondheid en Cultuur)
– Directie Jeugdbeleid
Drs L. G. M. Bisschops, Ingrid Hantgen, Anke Vedder
– Directie Vluchtelingen, Minderheden en Asielzoekers
Drs M. E. den Elt
EU-Network for School-Age Children, Veendam
Dr Ria Meijvogel
FNV (Central Trade Union Association), Amsterdam
Brenda de Jong

PORTUGAL

Universidade do Minho, CEFOPE
Prof. Dr João Formosinho (also: Conselho Nacional de Educação, Lisboa)
Universidade do Porto, Faculdade de Psicologia e de Ciências da Educação
Prof. Dr Joaquim Bairrão (also: Instituto de Inovação Educacional)
Escola Superior de Educadores de Infância Maria Ulrich, Lisboa
Dra. Maria João Ataíde
Escola Superior de Educadores de João de Deus, Lisboa
Maria da Luz de Deus Ponces de Carvalho
António de Deus Ramos Ponces de Carvalho
Escola Superior de Educação de Lisboa
Dra. Amália Barrios

Ministério do Emprego e Segurança Social
Direcção Geral da Acção Social, Lisboa
  Dra. Ema Delgado, Dra. Teresa Penha, Maria Rosàrio Teixeira Abreu
Ministério da Educação
  – Departamento da Educação Básica, Lisboa
  Maria Isabel Simoes de Oliveira, Teresa Moita
  – Departamento do Ensino Superior, Lisboa
  Prof. Dr Manuel Ferreira Patrício, Dra. Maria dos Anjos Cohen Caseiro
Universidade do Algarve, Escola Superior de Educação
  Dra. Isabel Cruz
Instituto de Inovação Educacional, Lisboa
  Rosário Morgado

SPAIN

Instituto de Formación Profesional, Madrid
  Paloma Sainz de Vicuña Barroso
Universidad de Sevilla, Psicologia Evolutiva y de la Educación
  Prof. Dr Jésus Palacios
Ministerio de Educación y Ciencia, Dirección General de Renovación Pedagógica, Madrid
  Prof. Dr César Coll Salvador
Ministerio de Educación y Ciencia, Servicio de Educación Infantil, Madrid
  Enrique Rincón Alguacil
Instituto Municipal de Educación de Barcelona
  Irene Balaguer (also: European Commission Network on Childcare)
Universidad Autonoma 'Bellaterra', Departamento Psichopedagogia, Barcelona
  Lurdes Molina
Universität Dortmund, Fachbereich 12, Institut für Sozialpädagogik
  Matthias Schilling
Centro de Estudios de Menor, Madrid
  Ferran Casas Aznar
Centro de Investigación y Documentación Educativa, Madrid
  Mercedes Muños Repiso
Escuela de Educadores, Madrid
  Elena Lobo Aleu
Ministerio de Asuntos Sociales, Subdirección General para la Prevención, Madrid
  Victoria Abril Navarro
Comunidad Autónoma de Madrid, Servicio de Educación Infantil, Madrid
  Amador Sánchez

SWEDEN

Stockholm Institute of Education, Stockholm
  – International Office
  Gunilla Kalderén
  – Department of Child and Youth Studies
  Prof. Bengt-Erik Andersson, Kersti 'Py' Börjeson, Lars Caiman, Jan Dunge

– Department of Recreation and Leisure Education
Bengt Colliander
– Directorate
Dr Dimiter Perniklijski
– Secretariat for Education and Research
Asa Cornelius
Ministry of Health and Social Welfare, Stockholm
Barbara Martin-Korpi
Socialtjänsten (Social Welfare Administration, Research Department)
Dr Inge Johannson
University of Uppsala, Uppsala
– Department of In-Service Education
Berit Halvarsson
– Department of Teacher Education
Marja Kuisma
Lärarförbundet (Swedish Teachers Union), Stockholm
Kristina Wester, Britta Sjöström
Daghem, Hammarbyhöjden, Stockholm
Inger Berg
Bergsunds Skolan, Stockholm
Lena Axedin
Comenius (University newspaper), Stockholm
Rolf Marthon

THE UNITED KINGDOM

University of London, Goldsmiths College, London
Geva Blenkin, Vicky Hurst, Prof. A. V. Kelly
University of London, Institute of Education, Thomas Coram Research Unit, London
Peter Moss, Pat Petrie
University of Warwick, Coventry
Prof. Tricia David (now at Christchurch College, Canterbury)
Worcester College of Higher Education, Worcester
Prof. Dr Christine Pascal, Tony Bertram (also: European Early Childhood Research Association)
National Children's Bureau, London
Ann Robinson, Phil Youdan
Scottish Office, International Relations Branch, Edinburgh
Hope Johnston
Scottish Council for Research in Education, Edinburgh
Janet Powney, Stuart Hall
National Council of Voluntary Child Care Organization, London
Sarah Williams
Council for Awards in Children's Care and Education
Dr Richard C. Dorrance
Department of Health, London
Catherine Baines
European Children's Centre, London
Dr Nicola Madge

Lothian Regional Council, Department of Community Education, Edinburgh
  Isobel Pattie, David Dickson
Moray House, College of Education, Edinburgh
  Gaye McCail
General Teaching Council for Scotland, Edinburgh
  D. I. M. Sutherland
Her Majesty's Inspectorate
  Jean Ensing
Kid's Clubs Network
  Anne Longfield
Department for Education, Bangor
  K.V. Jones
Department of Health and Social Services, Belfast
  T.R. Keenan
Department of Education, Bangor
  W.G. Taylor
National Foundation for Educational Research, Education Policy Information Centre, Slough
  Joanna le Métais
SCOTVEC, Scottish Vocational Education Council, Glasgow
  Ann Boyd

III

General references

The following titles are comparative studies containing data from different European countries. Country-specific references are to be found at the end of each country profile.

Bairrão, J. and Tietze, W. (1993) *Early Childhood Services in the European Community: Recommendations for Progress. A Report Submitted to the Commission of the European Community.* Task Force Human Resources, Education, Training, and Youth, Brussels.

Balaguer, I., Mestres, J. and Penn, H. (1991) *Quality in Services for Young Children: A Discussion Paper.* European Commission Network on Childcare, Brussels.

Cochran, M. (ed.) (1993) *International Handbook of Child Care Policies and Programs.* Greenwood Press, Westport, Conn. and London.

David, T. (ed.) (1993) *Educational Provision for our Youngest Children: European Perspectives.* Paul Chapman, London.

European Commission (1995a) *Pre-school Education in the European Union – Current Thinking and Provision.* Office for Official Publications of the European Communities, Luxembourg.

European Commission (1995b) *Key Data on Education in the European Union.* Office for Official Publications of the European Communities, Luxembourg.

European Commission Network on Childcare (1990) Childcare Workers with Children Under 4 – a seminar report, Commission of the European Communities, Brussels.

European Commission Network on Childcare (1993) Mothers, Fathers and Employment 1985–1991: a discussion paper, Commission of the European Communities, Brussels.

European Commission Network on Childcare (1996) A Review of Services For Young Children in the European Union, 1990–1995, Commission of the European Communities, Brussels.

EURYDICE (1994) Die Bildung im Elementar- und Primarbereich in der Europäischen Union, EURYDICE, das Bildungsinformationsnetz in der Europäischen Union, Brüssel.

Karlsson, M. (1995) Family Day Care in Europe, European Commission Network on Childcare, Commission of the European Communities, Brussels.

Lamb, M. E. and Sternberg, K. J. (eds.) (1992) *Child Care in Context. Cross Cultural Perspectives.* Lawrence Erlbaum, Hilldale.

Melhuish, E. C. and Moss, P. (eds.) (1991) *Day Care for Young Children. International Perspectives.* Tavistock/Routledge, London and New York.

Moss, P. (1988) Childcare and Equality of Opportunity. Report to the European Commission, Commission of the European Communities, Brussels.

Moss, P. (1990) Childcare in the European Communities 1985–1990, Commission of the European Communities, Brussels.

Moss, P. (1994) The Early Childhood League in Europe: problems and possibilities in cross-national comparisons of levels of provision. *Early Childhood Education Research Journal,* Vol. 2, no. 2, pp. 5–17.

Oberhuemer, P. and Ulich, M. (1997) *Kinderbetreuung in Europa – Tageseinrichtungen und pädagogisches Personal.* Beltz, Weinheim and Basel.

Oberhuemer, P. and Ulich, M. (1996) Les personnel de la petite enfance: types de formation et offre d'accueil dans les pays de l'Union Européenne, in M. Deleau, F. Laevers and S. Rayna (eds.) *L'Education Préscolaire: quels objectifs pédagogiques?* Nathan, Paris.

Olmsted, P. P. and Weikart, D. P. (eds.) (1989) *How Nations Serve Young Children. Profiles of Child Care in 14 Countries.* High/Scope, Ypsilanti, Mich.

Pascal, C., Bertram, T. and Heaslip, S. (1991) *Comparative Directory of Initial Training for Early Years Teachers. Compiled for the Association of Teacher Education in Europe (ATEE).* Early Years Working Group/ATEE, Worcester.

Rauschenbach, T., Behler, K. and Knauer, D. (1995) *Die Erzieherin. Ausbildung und Arbeitsmarkt* (with Mitarb. von M. Schilling, M. Feldmann, O. Filtzinger, G. Prein and G. Römer). Juventa, Weinheim and München.

Schiersmann, C. (1995) Bedingungen der Vereinbarkeit von Erwerbstätigkeit und Familienarbeit im europäischen Vergleich – unter besonderer Berücksichtigung von Elternurlaubsregelungen. *Zeitschrift für Frauenforschung,* Vol. 13, nos. 1 & 2, pp. 94–114.

Socialministeriet (Danish Ministry of Social Welfare) (1993a) *Parental Employment and Caring for Children: Policies and Services in EC and Nordic Countries.* Conference Report, Copenhagen.

Socialministeriet (Danish Ministry of Social Welfare) (1993b) *Parental Employment and Caring for Children. Developments and Trends in EC and Nordic Countries.* DMSW, Copenhagen.

Tietze, W. and Paterak, H. (1993) Hilfen für die Betreuung und Erziehung von Kindern im Vorschulalter in den Ländern der Europäischen Union, in W. Tietze and H.-G. Roßbach (eds.) *Erfahrungsfelder in der frühen Kindheit. Bestandsaufnahme, Perspektiven.* Lambertus, Freiburg i.Br.

Index of subjects